The Crimes
Women Commit

The Crimes Women Commit

The Punishments They Receive

Third Edition

Rita J. Simon
and
Heather Ahn-Redding

LEXINGTON BOOKS
Lanham • Boulder • New York • Toronto • Oxford

LEXINGTON BOOKS

Published in the United States of America
by Lexington Books
An imprint of The Rowman & Littlefield Publishing Group, Inc.
4501 Forbes Boulevard, Suite 200, Lanham, Maryland 20706

PO Box 317
Oxford
OX2 9RU, UK

British Library Cataloguing in Publication Information Available

Library of Congress Cataloging-in-Publication Data

Simon, Rita James.
  The crimes women commit, the punishments they receive / Rita J. Simon and Heather
Ahn-Redding.— 3rd ed.
    p. cm.
  Previous ed. by Rita J. Simon and Jean Landis.
  Includes bibliographical references and index.
  ISBN 0-7391-1007-1 — ISBN 0-7391-1008-X
  1. Female offenders—United States. 2. Criminal justice, Administration of—United
States. 3. Women prisoners—United States. I. Heitfield, Heather. II. Title.
HV6046.S54 2004
364.3'74'0973—dc22   2004016988

Printed in the United States of America

⊗™ The paper used in this publication meets the minimum requirements of American
National Standard for Information Sciences—Permanence of Paper for Printed Library
Materials, ANSI/NISO Z39.48-1992.

Contents

Tables

Introduction

Women and Crime, the first incarnation of this book, was published in 1975.[1] When it appeared, it joined only a handful of other studies that focused primarily on women's involvement in criminal activities and on how women were treated by the criminal justice system. Writing more than ten years earlier, Barbara Wooton commented:

> It is perhaps rather curious that no serious attempt has yet been made to explain the remarkable facts of the sex ratio in detected criminality; for the scale of the sex differential far outranks all the other tracts (except that of age in the case of indictable offenses) which have been supposed to distinguish the delinquent from the nondelinquent population. It seems to be one of those facts which escape notice by virtue of its very conspicuousness. It is surely, to say the least, very odd that half the population should be apparently immune to the criminogenic factors which lead to the downfall of so significant a population of the other half. Equally odd is it, too, that although the criminological experience of different countries varies considerably, nevertheless the sex differential remains.[2]

All that has changed. Since *Women and Crime* was released in 1975, a rich and complex literature has been devoted to the issues of gender and crime, with a special focus on women's socioeconomic status and their propensity to commit various types of crimes. Studies and monographs also have been published about women in prison, with a special emphasis on their relationships with their children and their opportunities to avail themselves of vocational training and gainful employment during their stay in prison.

The references at the end of this book provide a reasonably thorough sample of the relevant work that has been published since 1975, and throughout this newly revised edition, we refer to studies that have been published since 1990. But since this is a third edition, its major purpose is to update the sta-

1

tistical data on arrests, convictions, and commitment to prisons provided in the first two editions; to make the necessary changes in the data describing demographic characteristics and socioeconomic status; and to update the information about the conditions in women's prisons. We are, however, aware of the theoretical perspectives that have been developed since 1975, primarily those of a feminist, Marxist, or Marxist-feminist nature. Where appropriate, we acknowledge the differences between those theories and ours and try to present the positions of proponents of those theories.

We take a careful look at the statistics describing women's arrests for different types of offenses, women's rates of conviction by types of offense in the state and federal courts, and women's commitment to state and federal prisons. We analyze both the trends in the criminal justice system over a thirty-five-year period and the changes in the types of criminal activities in which women were involved.

To determine what changes have occurred, we examine indexes of women's status in American society—their educational attainment, marital status, labor force participation, and income, especially the income ratios vis-à-vis men. These demographic and socioeconomic indexes, in conjunction with arrest data, are the major sources we used to assess the validity of the explanation for changes in female crime patterns offered in *Women and Crime* (Simon 1975):

> As women become more liberated from hearth and home and become more involved in full-time jobs, they are more likely to engage in the types of crimes for which their occupations provide them with the greatest opportunities. They are also likely to become partners and entrepreneurs in crime to a greater extent than they have in the past. Traditionally, women in criminal activity have played subservient roles. They have worked under the direction and guidance of men who were their lovers, husbands, or pimps. In most instances, their job was to entice victims, to distract or look out for the police, to carry the loot, or to provide the necessary cover. As a function both of expanded consciousness, as well as occupational opportunities, women's participation, roles, and involvement in crime are expected to change and increase.
>
> But the increase will not be uniform or stable across crimes. Women's participation in financial and white collar offenses (fraud, embezzlement, larceny, and forgery) should increase as their opportunities for employment in higher status occupations expand. Women's participation in crimes of violence, especially homicide and manslaughter, are not expected to increase. The reasoning here is that women's involvement in such acts typically arises out of the frustration, the subservience, and the dependency that have characterized the traditional female role. Case histories of women who kill reveal that one pattern dominates all others. When women can no longer contain their frustrations and their anger, they express themselves by doing away with the cause of their condition, most often

a man, sometimes a child. As women's employment and educational opportunities expand, their feelings of being victimized and exploited will decrease, and their motivation to kill will become muted.[3]

In the two decades from 1953 to 1973, there was an increase in women's criminal activities. The increase in serious (Type I) offenses was due almost entirely to women's greater participation in property offenses, especially larceny. As for the Type II offenses, the greatest increases occurred in embezzlement and fraud and in forgery and counterfeiting. The increases were especially marked for the period from 1967 to 1972. In commenting on those data, Simon (1975) wrote: "Should the average rate of change that occurred between 1967 and 1972 continue, female arrest rates for larceny/theft, embezzlement, and fraud will be commensurate to women's representation in the society, or in other words, roughly equal to male arrest rates."[4] About female arrests for violent crimes, she noted, "The proportion of female arrests for violent crimes has changed hardly at all over the past two decades. Female arrest rates for homicide, for example, [have] been the most stable of all violent offenses."[5]

This book reports arrest statistics up through 2001 and provides the opportunity to examine whether the predicted increases in white-collar property offenses have in fact occurred and whether women's involvement in violent offenses have remained constant or declined.

We will try to determine whether women's participation in the labor force continued to increase and whether the type of jobs they hold shifted from those involving less responsibility, authority, and prestige to those involving more of these qualities. We argue that women in higher-status positions are more likely to have access to other people's money and are therefore in a position to commit embezzlement, fraud, and other white-collar offenses. Women's propensity to commit property offenses is in large measure a function of their greater participation in the labor force and of their mobility from lower- to higher-status white-collar positions.

Concerning women's appearance in court, Simon (1975) wrote:

Two schools of thought prevail on how women defendants are treated at the bar of justice. Most observers feel that women receive preferential treatment, which in operational terms means that they are less likely to be convicted than men for the same type of offense; if convicted, they are less likely to be sentenced; and if sentenced, they are likely to receive milder sentences. The factors that are thought to motivate judges toward leniency vis-à-vis women are chivalry, naivete (for example, judges often say that they cannot help but compare women defendants with other women they know well; namely their mothers and wives whom they cannot imagine behaving in the manner attributed to the defendant), and practicality. Most of the women defendants have young children, and sending them to prison places too much of a burden on the rest of the society.[6]

The other view about how women fare at the bar of justice is that judges are more punitive toward women. They are more likely to throw the book at the female defendant because they believe that there is a greater discrepancy between her behavior and the behavior expected of women than there is between the behavior of the male defendant and the behavior expected of men. In other words, women defendants pay for the judges' belief that it is more in man's nature to commit crimes than it is in woman's. Thus, when a judge is convinced that the woman before him has committed a crime, he is more likely to overact and punish her, not only for the specific offense, but also for transgressing against his expectations of womanly behavior.[7]

Simon relied on two sources of data for evaluating these views: (1) the percentage of women versus the percentage of men found guilty for the same types of offenses, and (2) the punishment women received compared to that given men. She also interviewed thirty criminal trial court judges in Chicago, St. Louis, Milwaukee, and Indianapolis. These judges were questioned about their perceptions of female offenders in their courts, the way they responded to them in the determination of guilt or innocence, and whether they treated women differently than men at the time of sentencing.

On the preferential versus punitive debate, Simon (1975) noted the lack of long-term trend data, commenting that "these data allow us to see only that women as recently as 1972 seem to be receiving some preferential treatment at the bar of Justice" and that "the eyes of Justice are neither blinded nor fully opened, rather they seem to be open just enough to be able to discern the sex of the defendant and to allow that characteristic to influence the decision to some extent."[8] The interviews with the judges supported the statistical data in that most of the judges said that they do not distinguish between defendants on the basis of sex when determining whether a defendant is guilty or innocent but that the defendant's sex does have some effect on their decisions concerning sentencing. Most said that they are more likely to treat women more leniently— that is, they are more inclined to recommend probation rather than imprisonment, and, if they do sentence a woman to prison, it is usually for a shorter time than a man who committed the same offense would have to serve.

In this book, we try to determine whether the increase in women's appearances in courts, as well as the increase in the seriousness of the crimes for which they are charged (we focus primarily on the property offenses), has resulted in a decrease in the differences between the percentages of men and women found guilty and in the sentences handed down to men and women.

Under the general rubric of equal rights, Simon (1975) noted the relative absence of vocational programs and industries in women's as opposed to men's prisons. A 1971 survey of female inmates in two of the three federal prisons found that 85 percent wanted more job training and 80 percent wanted more educational opportunities. Nine out of ten respondents said that they expected to work and support themselves when they were released. Drawing on an article titled "The Sexual Segregation of American Prisons,"[9] which appeared in the *Yale Law Journal*, Simon reported:

> The average number of programs in the men's prisons is 10; in the female institutions the average number is 1.7. Whereas male prisoners have a choice of some fifty different vocational programs, the women's choices are limited to cosmetology (and in some states, convicted felons are forbidden by law to work in the field), clerical training, food services, serving, IBM key punching, and nurses' aides. Some of the men's prisons provide vocational training in programs that are available to women inmates as well; but none of the prisons for women are prepared to train their inmates in programs that are available for men.
>
> The industries available at men's and women's institutions that can provide a source of livelihood for the inmates show much the same picture. In the forty-seven prisons for men, there is an average of 3.2 industries as compared to 1.2 in the fifteen female prisons. There is also hardly any overlap concerning the types of industries in which both male and female inmates may work.[10]

A second theme that is carried over from the first book concerns female inmates as mothers of young children. As in the early 1970s, most women in prison today are mothers of young children. In the early 1970s, none of the women's prisons had any provisions for children, either for babies born to women while they were in prison or for their children when they came to visit. As part of our survey of vocational and academic programs, we asked the wardens about provisions and facilities that are currently available for infants and young children. Their responses appear in chapter 6. Finally, in this edition we include a discussion of women on death row. We report the numbers, the racial characteristics, and the crimes for which they were given the death penalty.

To sum up, this book focuses on updating demographic data, which indicate changes in women's social status and involvement in criminal activities, both in the frequency of their participation and in the types of acts for which they are arrested. We examine court data to see whether there has been any change in judges' treatment of women at either the determination of guilt or sentencing stage. And we look at the changes in the opportunities women have to acquire academic and vocation skills and to earn money by working in prison industries, as well as the provisions and programs available for spending time with their children.

NOTES

1. Simon, Rita J. 1975. *Women and Crime.* Lexington, Mass: Lexington Books.
2. Wooten, Lady Barbara. 1963. *Crime and Criminal Law.* New York: Macmillan: 6–8.
3. Simon. 1975: 1–2.
4. Ibid.: 46.
5. Ibid.: 46.
6. Ibid.: 49.
7. Ibid.: 52.
8. Ibid.: 67.
9. Arditi, R.R., F. Goldberg, Jr., M.M. Hartle, J.H. Peters, and W.R. Phelps. 1973. "The Sexual Segregation of American Prisons: Notes," *Yale Law Journal* 82 (6), 1229–1273.
10. Simon. 1975: 82–83.

Chapter One

Women and Crime in Review

When we look back on the theories of female criminality that until only recently dominated sociological schools of thought, these antiquated descriptions of the criminal woman remind us of the great advances made by the feminist movement. From Cesare Lombroso's 1903 portrayal of female criminals as "biological atavists"[1] with dark masculine features, to Otto Pollack's more recent description of deviant females as "innately deceitful"[2] women who hide their crimes just as they can hide their physiological sexual arousal from men, revisions in sociological perspectives on female criminals have paralleled the progress of women's rights in many domains of society. No longer do we give the same credence to Freud's theory of penis envy, or to W. I. Thomas's comparison of women to plants that are "more motionless or conservative than men."[3] We have also drifted from theories dominating the 1950s and 1960s that emphasized femininity or that associated female criminality with "biological processes, such as lactation, menstruation, and menopause."[4] Pollack-Byrne (1990) argues that traditional criminological theories, such as strain theory and differential association, have almost exclusively been applied to men and do little in the way of explaining and describing female criminality.

A new strain of theories on female criminality emerged during the 1970s, and criminologists such as Simon,[5] Adler,[6] and Steffensmeier[7] began to embrace gender-oriented perspectives that emphasized sociological factors and opportunity rather than the previous notion that female criminality originates from the "inherent nature of women"[8] and other biological attributes.

Four basic themes have dominated sociological discussions of the etiology of contemporary female criminality since the publication of *Women and Crime* in 1975. These themes can be classified as (1) the masculinity thesis, (2) the opportunity thesis, (3) the economic marginalization thesis, and (4) the chivalry thesis. The first two themes often are grouped together under the title "liberation thesis," as both attempt to link changes in female crime with the improved status of women, which is viewed as a consequence of the contemporary women's movement. As we shall see, however, there are fundamental differences in the theoretical propositions of these two approaches. The third theme, economic marginalization, disputes the conclusions of the first two. The chivalry thesis questions whether observed increases in female crime are due to the increasing criminality of women or to an increasing willingness on the part of criminal justice personnel to apprehend, prosecute, and punish female offenders.

This chapter reviews these perspectives and broadly sketches relevant theoretical and empirical issues. We do not, however, attempt to catalog or detail the work of the many criminologists who have dealt with issues of women and crime over the past decade and a half.[9]

THE MASCULINITY THESIS

The masculinity thesis was popularized by Freda Adler's *Sisters in Crime*.[10] This perspective is based on a *subjectivist* orientation that links changes in criminality to changes in subjective attitudes engendered by changes in the substantive nature of sex roles. This perspective predicts a causal nexus between the women's movement, changing social roles of women, the masculinization of female behavior (particularly a hypothetical change from passivity to aggressiveness as women assume male social roles), and changes in patterns of female offending.

Specifically, this thesis claims that as women are liberated and assume traditional male social roles, they begin to assert themselves in typically male ways—that is, they become aggressive, pushy, and hardheaded. Moreover, they learn to use crime as a shortcut to success and financial well-being and are more prone to use violence than in the past. The masculinization thesis predicts that to the extent that women's attitudes and behaviors become masculinized through their liberation and consequential assumption of traditional male social roles, their rates and patterns of criminal offending increasingly will approximate those of men. This change will be most evident in patterns of violent offending, which reflect the increasing aggressiveness of liberated women.

Adler's masculinity thesis is a sociological variant of the masculinity complex that Freud attributed to the "maladjusted woman" who, in reaction to penis envy, rebels against her natural inferiority. While not implying that liberated masculinized women are suffering from a psychological maladjustment, this thesis nevertheless focuses on the criminal potential of women who, in their rebellion against social inferiority, aggressively pursue masculine goals of success and power. While masculine qualities generally are viewed as positive ones for men to exhibit, proponents of the masculinization thesis join their Freudian counterparts in imputing a negative connotation to such characteristics in women.[11] Good girls are still those who maintain their allegiance to traditional social roles, while bad girls are those who act like men.

The masculinization thesis has been criticized from several different angles. Numerous studies have examined the relationship between criminal or delinquent behavior and role perceptions and attitudes, finding that the hypothesized relationship between either masculine traits or profeminist (liberated) attitudes and offending behavior is not supported empirically.[12] As Naffine[13] states, "Efforts to uncover the aggressively competitive nature of criminal women looking for their piece of the action or to find signs of feminism among female offenders have met with remarkably little success."

Perhaps most condemning of this perspective are criticisms based on analyses of actual arrest trends, which indicate that the hypothesized post–women's movement increases in violent and aggressive criminality among women are mythical.[14]

THE OPPORTUNITY THESIS

The opportunity thesis of female criminality originated in the first edition of this book, and its general propositions are espoused in this edition. This thesis argues that women are neither more or less moral than men, nor are they more or less inclined to engage in criminal acts. Rather, it assumes an *objectivist* orientation and argues that opportunities, skills, and social networks historically have contributed to men's propensity to commit crimes, while these same factors have limited women's opportunities. It is women's objective locations within the social structure and particularly within the occupational sphere, as well as in the private, family sphere, that influence the nature of their criminality.

Labor force participation is crucial to this argument. A wide range of property offenses can be committed only by persons who have access to other people's money and goods. Thus, crimes such as larceny, theft, embezzlement, and fraud are likely to be committed by persons who are in the labor force, not by full-time homemakers and mothers. The opportunity thesis also predicts a relationship between the positions that persons occupy in the labor force and their opportunities for committing various types of offenses. Executives, managers, and professionals such as accountants and attorneys have opportunities to embezzle much larger sums than do secretaries, bank tellers, and clerks. Thus, the argument goes as more women enter the labor force and move into positions involving expert knowledge and skills, they will have more opportunities to commit the type of employment-related crimes committed by men. Some women will take advantage of these opportunities, just as some men do.

The opportunity thesis posits that as the employment patterns of men and women become more similar, so too will their patterns of employment-related crimes. To the extent that either the quantitative or qualitative labor force experiences of men and women remain dissimilar, so too should their rates and patterns of offending. Similarly, the rates and patterns of crimes committed by men and women outside the context of legitimate employment should be similar to the extent that the structured conditions of their lives resemble one another. Whether changes in labor force and other life conditions have placed men and women in structured social situations that resemble one another is an empirical question, as is the extent to which male and female criminality has changed.

As for violent acts, the argument advanced in the first edition claims that as women become more economically self-sufficient (a function of their increased education and labor force participation), they will be less likely to play the role of victim. As they become less beholden to men for their economic and social status, they will gain self-esteem and confidence. In turn, such women will be more likely to extricate themselves from situations of verbal and physical abuse before they reach a level of desperation at which only the death of the abusive person can release them from their torment.

Overall, the opportunity thesis claims that as women acquire more education, enter the labor force full-time, and assume positions of greater authority, prestige, and technical skills, they will use the opportunities available to them to commit white-collar property offenses in the same proportions as do their male counterparts. Also as a function of an improved socioeconomic status, they will move away from the role of victim and extricate themselves from situations that are likely to result in violent acts. Like the masculinity thesis, the opportunity thesis predicts that changes in the social status of women, which have resulted at least in part from the contemporary women's movement, will result in changes in the offending patterns of women. Unlike the masculinity thesis, the opportunity thesis predicts reduced rates of violent offending among women and increased rates of employment-related property offenses such as larceny/theft, embezzlement, fraud, and forgery. Just as men who commit such offenses need not be considered aggressive, neither should women who commit them.

What this perspective leaves out are the physical differences between men and women, which the women's movement has not changed. Most women are still at a disadvantage vis-à-vis men in personal, violent types of encounters, especially when the potential victim is awake and in control of his or her capacities. Robbery probably best illustrates the greater natural advantages that men have over women. The trends over time for robbery arrests show that it is one of the serious offenses in which women are least represented.

Women also differ from men in the skills they have acquired for carrying out certain types of offenses, as shown in their underrepresentation in male-dominated associations that involve organized crime, fence operations, and apprenticeship opportunities for skills such as safecracking. As long as women remain closed out of such opportunities, the types of offenses in which they engage will be limited.

Criticisms of the opportunity thesis have proliferated since the publication of the first edition of this book. In addition to the argument of theorists espousing the economic marginalization thesis, which is discussed in the next section, two other arguments remain central to the critique. The first is based on the claim that men and women, given the same structural opportunities, will behave differently. The second argument questions whether the improved status of women and/or an increase in their occupationally related crime rates are empirical realities.

To advance their position, supporters of the first argument begin with the observation that the stresses and strains of poverty and blocked opportunity structures, long hypothesized to cause criminality among lower-class males, have not resulted in similar rates and patterns of offending among lower-class females. This gender-ratio problem, so termed by Daly and Chesney-Lind,[15] has obvious implications for all groups of similarly situated men and women. It logically follows that factors that normally drive men to commit white-collar crimes should not be expected to have a similar effect on women.

Eileen Leonard summarizes this position as follows:

> The argument that increased white-collar employment for women will lead to increased white-collar crime among them assumes that women behave the same as men, given apparently similar situations. Yet, we should know that this is not so. The poverty, the unemployment, and the limited opportunities that supposedly drive men to commit crime, have not had the same effect on women. Perhaps the opportunity for white collar crime will not have the same effect on them either. . . . Given their vastly different historical, social, and economic experiences, women should not be expected to behave like men. Even in apparently similar situations, they will behave differently.[16]

Exactly why this is so remains an unsettled topic of discussion. The rationales that have been advanced to explain why women and men have not behaved, and should not be expected to behave, in similar ways when structurally situated in similar economic situations generally stress differences in female so-cialization and/or social control. In essence, the idea is that women, regardless of where or whether they work, are more subject to internal and informal social controls than are men. From birth, they are oversocialized to be dependent, pas-sive, self-sacrificing, and overcontrolled, restricted to the private sphere of home and family or limited in their freedom to assert themselves independently in the public sphere.[17]

In short, these arguments imply that objective structural conditions are pos-sibly mediated by, or interact with, more fundamental patriarchal gender re-lationships, characterized by male domination at home and in the workplace, to create qualitatively different objective social realities and opportunities as well as different subjective situational definitions. Thus, the appearance of structural parity at any level of social status is just that—an appearance. The subordination of women conditions their reality within race, class, and status groupings, making it different from that of their male counterparts.

Proponents of this view do not deny that opportunity plays a large role in differentials between male and female offending patterns and rates. How-ever, they wish to direct attention to differential processes of socialization and social control, which continue to structure both objective opportunities and subjective perceptions of them. Exception is taken to the notion that in-creased female labor force participation alone, or even the (disputable) exis-tence of equal opportunity for women, indicates any measure of true libera-tion. Instead, the focus is on manifestations of male domination in the home, work, and society that constrain women's activity, both criminal and non-criminal.

The second argument against the assertions of the opportunity thesis, that neither the status of women nor their patterns of criminal offending has changed, is advanced by Steffensmeier.[18] Steffensmeier has been the most persistent and frequently cited opponent of the opportunity thesis and the masculinization thesis as well. While his analysis of arrest trends generally supports the prediction that the offending gap between males and females narrowed in the 1970s for the crimes of larceny and fraud and, to a lesser ex-tent, embezzlement and forgery, his interpretation of the substantive meaning of these trends differs from the one offered by proponents of the opportunity thesis. Rather than viewing these rates as indicative of new opportunities for white-collar and/or employment-related criminal activity, Steffensmeier maintains that they simply reflect traditional sex role expectations, behaviors, and opportunities:

> The available research indicates that most arrests of women for larceny are for shoplifting and arrests for fraud involving passing "bad checks," credit card

fraud, fraudulent theft of services, and small con games. Women are not being arrested for frauds which are occupationally related or which tend to be real white-collar crimes, such as false advertising, product defects and so on. Forgery is also a crime that is consistent with female sex roles and fits into the everyday round of activities in which women engage, especially since the skills and techniques required for forging credit cards, checks, etc., are learned in the normal process of growing up. It is the case that those arrested for forgery tend to be amateurs, or "naive forgers."

Contrary to popular assumptions, the person arrested for embezzlement is usually more a petty thief than a white-collar offender. Most arrests for embezzlement are not persons of high social standing and responsibility who commit a crime in the course of their occupation and which involves large sums of money. Rather the typical embezzler is the trusted clerk, cashier or secretary who takes his or her employer's money and the amount taken is usually small.[19]

In essence, Steffensmeier[20] does not dispute the theoretical assumptions underlying the opportunity thesis, only the empirical assertion that women have been able, as a result of the women's movement, to change their structural location in society and that such a change is related to changes in their commission of occupational crimes. He questions whether women actually have new labor force opportunities that would allow them opportunities qualitatively approaching those available to men. He maintains that the status of women is still lower than that of men and that women are still limited to traditionally female occupations providing opportunities for traditionally female crimes. Moreover, he suggests that access to illegitimate opportunities is even more limited to women than is access to legitimate opportunities. Criminal networks, within both the workplace and the criminal underworld, still discriminate on the basis of gender.[21]

Steffensmeier[22] argues that a different kind of opportunity could be related to increases in larceny/theft (which he attributes to shoplifting). Self-service marketing and credit card sales provide increasing opportunities for petty thefts. These opportunities occur in an economic context that has forced the emancipation of many women, requiring them to support themselves and their families in traditionally female, low-paying jobs. Thus, he attributes increases in female property crime to the convergence of market consumption trends and the worsening economic conditions of women "rather than to women's liberation or changing sex roles."[23]

Steffensmeier's argument is consistent with the economic marginalization thesis. But before turning our attention to that theme, we need to look a bit more closely at the issue of white-collar criminality among women. Few studies have addressed this issue, and thus we know little about it. At present, we have no systematic evidence regarding the qualitative nature of contemporary women's white-collar offending relative to that of contemporary men. Have the men and women who represent the national statistics in the crime categories of larceny, forgery, fraud, and embezzlement been arrested for the same types of crimes, and are the reasons motivating these men and women similar? To date, only two studies[24] have tried to address the qualitative dimensions of this issue, but both are limited in their generalizability.

As Daly[25] points out, Zietz's[26] study provides the most sustained inquiry into the nature of female offenders convicted of embezzlement, fraud, forgery, and theft. The purpose of Zietz's study was to compare her sample of women to the typologies of white-collar/property offenders, developed from studying samples of male offenders, particularly Cressey's *Other People's Money*,[27] in order to determine whether these typologies are applicable to women. In short, she concludes that they are not. She finds that generally women are different in the vocabularies they use to justify their crimes, as well as in their motivations for committing criminal acts. In contrast to studies of men, Zietz found that for women, the violation of financial trust is often tied to an emotional relationship to others and the fulfillment of role expectations within that relationship—that is, the money gained is considered necessary to fulfill a caretaking role or to maintain a love relationship rather than to pay for personal excesses.

One could argue that even if Zietz's findings are generalizable, the differential motivations and justifications of male and female offenders do not obfuscate the reality that women's objective location in the occupational structure determines the opportunities they have to fulfill their perceived responsibilities through the violation of financial trust. If they were not in those occupational positions, they would not have access to the means that those positions provide. In short, their behaviors, in taking advantage of their structural opportunities to fulfill their needs, can be similar to the behaviors of similarly situated men, even if the motivational basis of their needs differs.

Thus, Zietz's study, while important and illuminating in its own right, provides little insight into the Simon-Steffensmeier disagreement, except to suggest that the gender structure of the public sphere of work may not be the only relevant issue.[28] Women's social status relative to men has at least two dimensions, and a change in one does not necessarily mean that there is a change in the other. Differentials in perceived role responsibilities in the private sphere of personal relationships may be just as important in explaining female criminality both within and outside of the workplace.

But what of the nature of white-collar crime? Are the offending behaviors of men and women similar? Daly[29] took the first serious qualitative look at gender differences in white-collar offending. Examining a group of federal offenders incarcerated for embezzlement, fraud, and forgery, she found the following:

1. The female share of corporate (or organizational) crime was low.
2. The female share of occupational crime was negligible for all crimes with the exception of bank embezzlement, in which the female share was close to 50 percent.
3. Generally, the women were more likely than the men to offend alone, outside the context of a crime group.
4. The offenses committed by the women involved less financial gain than those committed by the men.
5. The motives of the men and women differed in that the women cited family responsibilities more often than the men but not as much as Zietz's study suggested.

More interesting were the characteristics of Daly's sample, summarized as follows:

Men's white-collar crimes were both petty and major, but almost all the women's were petty. Although half or more of the employed men were managerial or professional workers, most employed women were clerical workers. Higher proportions of women were black and had no ties to the paid labor force; fewer women had a four-year college degree. The women's socioeconomic profile, coupled with the nature of their crimes, makes one wonder if "white-collar" aptly describes them or their illegalities. . . . [T]hese data suggest that if women's share of white-collar arrests increases, it will stem from (1) increasing numbers of women in highly monitored, money-changing types of clerical, sales, or service jobs, and (2) increasing numbers of poor or unemployed women attempting to defraud state and federal governments or banks by securing loans, credit cards, or benefits to which they are not legally entitled.[30]

In conclusion, Daly[31] supports Steffensmeier's contention that the *Uniform Crime Report (UCR)* crime categories of fraud, forgery, and embezzlement are poor indicators of white-collar offenses, particularly for women. She also suggests a preference for the economic marginalization thesis over the opportunity thesis as an explanation for increasing crime among women.

THE ECONOMIC MARGINALIZATION THESIS

The economic marginalization thesis is perhaps the most pervasive alternative to the opportunity thesis. This thesis posits that "it is the absence, rather

than the availability, of employment opportunity for women [that] seems to
lead to increases in female crime"[32] Proponents of this view take as their point
of departure several related notions:

1. Greater participation in the labor force does not necessarily mean either
   more equality between the sexes or an improved economic situation for
   women.
2. The bulk of female offenders, if employed at all, are concentrated in a
   pink-collar ghetto, and their positions are characterized by poor pay and
   unrewarding, insecure work.
3. Female crime, the bulk of which is petty property crime, constitutes a rational response to poverty and economic insecurity.

(See Crites 1976; Klein and Kress 1976; Smart 1976 and 1979; Chapman
1980; Datesman and Scarpetti 1980; Gora 1982; Box and Hale 1983; Chesney-Lind 1986; Feinman 1986; Miller 1985; Messerschmidt 1986.)

Noting that the majority of female offenders are lower-class women who
have committed non-employment-related crimes rather than middle- and
upper-class professional women who have committed employment-related
crimes, proponents of this theory suggest that feminization of poverty, not
women's liberation, is the social trend most relevant to female criminality.
They argue that in general, the economic pressures on women caused by unemployment, poorly paid employment, and/or inadequate welfare payments,
combined with the increasing numbers of female-headed households sup-
porting dependent children, lead more and more women to seek the benefits
of criminal activity as supplements or alternatives to employment. In other
words, economic necessity is forcing the emancipation of women from more
law-abiding standards of conduct.

In short, advocates of the economic marginalization thesis support Steffensmeier's position and reject the idea that the majority of women have improved their social standing in the economic sphere relative to men. While
these theorists do not deny observable increases in labor force participation
among women, they contend that employment opportunities for women remain restricted, and thus the qualitative reality of the occupational distribution of women, while somewhat transformed over the years, remains substantially different from that of men. Occupational segregation concentrates
women in lower-paying, less secure positions than those occupied by their
male counterparts. The relevant implications of this concentration are neatly
stated by Stallard, Ehrenreich, and Sklar (1983): "For men, poverty is often
the consequence of unemployment, and a job is generally an effective rem-
edy, while female poverty often exists even when a woman works full-tine."[33]

In addition, it is argued that the stresses of female poverty often are exacerbated by the responsibilities of caring for dependent children. The disproportionately greater criminality of minority women, who also are disproportionately the heads of households with dependent children, is typically cited to support this assertion.[34] To the extent that these theorists recognize small increases in employment-related crime, they attribute them to increased numbers of employed women who remain trapped in poverty rather than to increased numbers of upwardly mobile professional women.

Chesney-Lind summarizes the bases upon which theorists espousing the economic marginalization thesis refute the opportunity thesis:

> First, since women have not experienced major gains in the economic world, it seems implausible that any wave of female crime could be correctly laid at its door. . . . Second, studies of characteristics of female offenders showed that they bore no resemblance to the liberated "female crook". . . but were instead minority women drawn from backgrounds of profound poverty who had committed "traditionally female" crimes such as petty theft or prostitution.[35]

Feinman,[36] drawing on extensive experience with female offenders, is even more emphatic:

> Poverty and drugs are the major determinants of women's criminality. . . . [T]here is no evidence that could possibly link the women's movement either to the increase in crimes committed by women or to the nature of women's criminal behavior. They continue to act in traditional ways both in the crimes they commit and in the manner in which they commit them. . . .
>
> The women's movement has neither involved nor benefited the majority of women in the U.S. It has not even brought true equal opportunities for the minority of white middle and upper class women who have been most directly involved with the movement. Therefore, any discussion of the link between women's criminality and the women's movement is unrealistic. It only serves to perpetuate myths; it hinders efforts to learn the real causes of women's criminal behavior and to try to eliminate them.

A question that remains to be answered by the economic marginalization thesis is why women's selective criminal participation has continued to increase as women have moved into higher-status occupations. Female upward mobility into managerial, professional, and technical positions is demonstrated by the census data in chapter 3. The economic marginalization thesis would argue that as women move into more responsible positions, their propensities to commit property offenses will decline. The data show that the reverse has occurred. There is a positive relationship between female upward occupational mobility and higher female property, especially white-collar, arrest rates.

Chapter One

THE CHIVALRY THESIS

The final theme running through much of the women-and-crime literature in the past fifteen years has been the issue of chivalry, or the more lenient treatment of female offenders by criminal justice personnel. In the first edition of this book, Simon[37] speculates that a possible side effect of the women's liberation movement might be the decline of chivalry, or the encouragement of police and court personnel to treat women more like men, which presumably meant to arrest, convict, and sentence them to prison more often. This theme suggests that it has been a change in the official reaction to women's criminal behavior, rather than changes in that behavior itself, that accounts for increased numbers of women in official crime and prison statistics.

Simon[38] suggests that women's call for equality in other realms of social, political, and economic life could invoke an unintended reaction in other realms such as criminal justice processing, creating an "if it's equality they want, it's equality they'll get" mentality among male police officers and court officials. Another expected effect of the women's movement on the reduction of chivalry toward female offenders was predicted to occur as more women entered the ranks of criminal justice practitioners, particularly as police officers. The logic of this argument was that female officers would be less likely to be conned into sympathy for female offenders.

The decline of chivalry as an explanation for increases in official rates of female criminality is based on the assumption that historically, chivalry did indeed operate to suppress official recognition of female criminality. This assumption has been challenged on the ground that any chivalry that might have benefited women has been selective chivalry at best. As Clarice Feinman explains, "Chivalry is reserved for white middle and upper class women, except those who flout culturally expected behavior for ladies."[39]

The extent to which justice norms are based on gender has been the topic of considerable empirical inquiry within the criminological literature over the past decade and a half. With regard to police decision making, some empirical evidence suggests that over time, there has been a decline in chivalrous treatment of females at the stage of arrest.[40] However, the bulk of the research has been limited to contemporary cross-sectional analyses and suggests that where chivalry does exist, generalizations about such treatment must be made with considerable caution.[41] Consistent with Feinman's assertion concerning chivalry are studies suggesting that not all women have been the recipients of lenient treatment by gallant police officers. Rather, only those women whose actions during their encounters with police are consistent with appropriate gender stereotypes have become the beneficiaries of chivalry.

After controlling for legal variables, Visher found that in encounters with police officers, those female suspects who violate typical middle-class standards of traditional characteristics and behaviors (i.e., white, older, and submissive) are not afforded any chivalrous treatment during arrest decisions. In these data, young, black, or hostile women receive no preferential treatment, whereas older, white women who are calm and deferential toward the police are granted leniency.[42]

Whether this observed pattern of police encounters with female offenders has changed over the past decade, during which popular assumptions about both minority and women's equality have stabilized and during which the most significant increases in female (including minority female) representation on the police force have occurred, remains a largely unexplored issue.

In later criminal processing decisions, the evidence regarding the chivalrous treatment of women is historical and mixed. Again, general statements must be viewed with caution. Women's treatment by the courts is reported in greater detail in chapter 5.

Factors other than a supposed decline in chivalry or paternalism on the part of individual police and court personnel must be considered when examining the effects of official reactions to female criminality as an explanation for the increased proportions of women in crime statistics. Changes in systematic factors such as surveillance and enforcement patterns, availability of correctional facilities and sentencing alternatives, and changes in reporting practices are the most obvious considerations. For example, if, as Steffensmeier[43] contends, a large proportion of female larceny offenders have been arrested for shoplifting, increases in the female percentage of larceny arrests could be due to the increasing ability or willingness of retail establishments to pursue arrest and prosecution. Similarly, if, as Simon[44] contends, increases in women's property offenses stem from occupational-related crimes, perhaps these increases could be attributable to a greater emphasis on white-collar crimes in recent years. Today large police departments commonly have special white-collar crime units that specialize in techniques appropriate for investigating such activity. Better investigatory practices may converge with the greater labor force participation of women to account for some of the observed increases in female property offending.

CONCLUSION

Contemporary theorists who have accepted the empirical assertion that there has been a rise in female criminality have attributed this phenomenon to one or a combination of historical social trends: (1) the psychological masculinization of women, (2) the increased labor force participation of women, (3) the feminization of poverty, and (4) less biased or more effective and efficient official responses to female criminality. Of these possible explanations, the masculinization thesis has proved the least satisfactory and has for the most part become an obligatory straw man in theoretical discussions of female criminality. Similarly, most contemporary theorists, regardless of their position on the decline of chivalry, would not assert that official reactions to female criminality have changed so drastically as to account for the bulk of observed changes in female criminality, particularly when measured by arrest statistics.

As stated earlier in this chapter, the opportunity thesis espoused in the first edition of this book also is espoused in this edition. But the fact that this perspective has caused considerable theoretical debate over the past fifteen years requires comment and qualification. While much effort has gone into discrediting the opportunity thesis, close examination reveals that it is still theoretically sound. Even proponents of the economic marginalization thesis do not argue against the notion that opportunities contribute to the nature of criminality. Instead, they dispute the following points:

1. The singularity of opportunity as a causal factor (What about differential stresses and strains and ways of perceiving them?)
2. The qualitative nature of women's opportunities (Is there actually increasing gender equality?)
3. The qualitative nature of women's crime (Is there an increase in women's white-collar offending or only in traditional female offending?)
4. The assumption that labor force equity (even if established empirically) suffices to create either objective or subjective social equality between the sexes (What about the interdependent effects of differential family responsibilities, gender role socialization, and informal social controls?)

If the opportunity thesis is recast, as it has been in this chapter, to focus on its prediction that men and women will behave in like manners when occupying similar positions in the social structure (that is, equally subject to the stresses generated by these positions and equally likely to take advantage of available legitimate and illegitimate opportunities that the positions present), discussions of this thesis can be more fruitful, particularly if we include position in family life as a codeterminant of social location. The first question for research becomes to what extent the social positions of men and women have become more similar, considering both their occupational positions and their family responsibilities. The second question is whether the offending behaviors of men and women have changed in a manner that is consistent with the relative changes in their social status vis-à-vis one another. We address these questions in chapters 3 and 4.

The most important question relative to theorizing about the relationship between social position, gender, and crime is this: Within similar social positions, are the offending behaviors of men and women similar to one another? This question cannot be examined using the existing national data. An analysis of this type would take into consideration what the research reported throughout this chapter suggests—namely, that theories about the "universal woman" neglect race/class differences among women and that the opportunity thesis and the economic marginalization thesis need not be mutually exclusive. Increasing numbers of upwardly mobile women may be committing white-collar crimes in the same proportions as similarly situated men at the same time that increasing numbers of their downwardly mobile sisters are committing the petty thievery, shoplifting, forgeries, and frauds that are available to them in their social positions. Conversely, each group of women may experience limitations on the availability of illegitimate opportunities (in the form of sexist exclusion, greater supervision and less independence, or differential socialization) relative to their male counterparts, but neither group can claim moral superiority.

Though the public's focus on women who are involved in the criminal justice system has typically been surpassed by their male counterparts, and while popular interest in female criminality often emerges only after sensationalized Andrea Yates–like crimes, recent spikes in female arrests and incarceration rates are forcing us to take a critical look at the causes and consequences of female criminality.

NOTES

1. Cited in Lilly, Cullen, and Ball 1995: 175.
2. Ibid.: 178.
3. Ibid.: 175. Also see Klein 1973; Thomas 1907, 1923.
4. Pollack-Byrne 1990: 21.
5. Simon 1975.
6. Adler 1975.
7. Steffensmeier 1978; Steffensmeier 1980a; Steffensmeier 1980b.
8. Lilly, Cullen, and Ball 1995: 174.
9. Readers wishing such a review are directed to Leonard 1982; Mann 1984; Heidensohn 1985.
10. Adler 1975.
11. Deming 1977.
12. Leventhal 1977; Norland and Shover 1978; Cernkovich and Giordano 1979; Thorton and James 1979; Widom 1979; Grasmick, Finley, and Glaser 1984.
13. Naffine 1987: 104.

14. Simon 1975; Steffensmeier 1980a; Steffensmeier 1980b; Steffensmeier and Kramer 1982; Leonard 1982; Box and Hale 1983; Feinman 1976; Weisheit and Mahan 1988.

15. Daly and Chesney-Lind 1988: 143.

16. Leonard 1982: 182.

17. Box 1983; Heidensohn 1985; Hagan, Gillis, and Simpson 1985; Messerschmidt 1986; Hagan, Simpson, and Gillis 1979.

18. Steffensmeier 1980a, 1980b, 1982.

19. Steffensmeier 1982: 124.

20. Steffensmeier 1982.

21. Steffensmeier 1982; Steffensmeier and Terry 1986.

22. Steffensmeier 1980a, 1980b.

23. Steffensmeier 1982: 126.

24. Daly 1989c; Zietz 1981.

25. Daly 1989c.

26. Zietz 1981.

27. Cressey 1953.

28. See Bartel 1979.

29. Daly 1989c.

30. Ibid.: 790.

31. Daly 1989c.

32. Naffine 1987: 98. Proponents of the economic marginalization thesis vary widely in their theoretical orientations, from liberal feminist views concerned with the presence or absence of "discrimination" (Feinman 1986; Datesman and Scarpetti 1980; Chapman 1980) to more radical feminist perspectives concerned with the nature of power relations and their relationship to the gender, race, and class stratification of society (Smart 1976, 1979; Klein and Kress 1976; Messerschmidt 1986). For recent discussions of these different feminist perspectives, see Daly and Chesney-Lind 1988; Simpson 1989b.

33. Stallard, Ehrenreich, and Sklar 1983: 9.

34. Lewis 1981; Hagan 1985.

35. Chesney-Lind 1986: 81.

36. Feinman 1986: 28.

37. Simon 1975.

38. Ibid.

39. Feinman 1986: 28.

40. Krohn, Curry, and Nelson-Kilger 1983.

41. DeFleur 1975; Chesney-Lind 1987; Visher 1983.

42. Visher 1983: 23.

43. Steffensmeier 1982.

44. Simon 1975.

Chapter Two

The Contemporary
Women's Movement

The contemporary women's movement was born in the late 1960s, a decade that saw the rise of a civil rights movement and a student-led antiwar movement. Many of those who participated in both these movements became leaders and organizers of various branches of the women's movement. In part, the experiences of younger women in the politics of the New Left served as the spawning ground for their desire to liberate themselves and their sisters. Women discovered that they were treated as second-class citizens even among men who were radical in many of their political and social beliefs, who believed in equality among the races, who advocated major changes in the occupational structure, and who favored redistribution of income and wealth. Women were expected to serve as bearers and servers and as bed companions to men in radical politics whose attitudes toward women did not differ significantly from those of men with more conservative views and lifestyles.

Women who were active in the civil rights movement were struck especially by the similarities between their relationships with men and the relationships of blacks and whites. Using the language of the civil rights movement, women made analogies between a sex-caste system and a race-caste system; women were at the bottom of one system, and blacks were at the bottom of the other.

The array of women's movements in the sixties, from reform to revolutionary, reflected that of earlier movements in the period immediately preceding the Civil War and extending up through the 1920s. The National Women's Party (NWP), formerly the Congressional Union, was more militant than the National American Woman's Suffrage Association (NAWSA) and its successor, the League of Women Voters. Until the passage of the Nineteenth Amendment, both movements concentrated their efforts on the attainment of suffrage. But after 1920, the NWP devoted itself to the passage of an Equal Rights Amendment. In 1929, one year after suffrage had been attained, Alice Paul, leader of the NWP, minimized the value of the victory by stating, "Women today . . . are still in every way subordinate to men before the law, in the professions, in the church, in industry, and in the home."[1]

Leaders of the NWP rejected attempts to form coalitions with other reform or progressive groups that were working for civil rights, disarmament, or improving the lot of the working people. Arguing in much the same vein as the radical women's movement of the 1970s, they reasoned that any expenditure of energy on issues that were extraneous to women's rights would only impede progress toward their major goal: freeing American women from their present condition of enslavement.

The NAWSA, under its new name, the League of Women Votes (LWV), pursued the opposite course. Its leaders contended that the attainment of suffrage had secured for them their most important and fundamental rights. They joined efforts with other groups for sound government, integrity in public life, and reforms in the economic and social spheres. The LWV went out of its way to avoid being identified as a lobby for only one group. Chafe quotes Dorothy Strauss, an LWV leader, as saying, "We of the League are very much for the rights of women, but we are not feminists primarily, we are citizens."[2]

World War II brought an end both to conflict within the women's movement and to the women's movement per se (as it did to most other social reform movements). Not until two decades after the end of the war was the movement revived. And like the earlier movements, the contemporary women's movement followed on the heels of another social movement aimed at redressing the grievances of blacks and other ethnic minority groups. Whenever Americans became sensitive to the issue of human rights, it seemed, the women's movement acquired new support, and the 1960s was no exception to the rule. The civil rights movement did not cause the revival of feminism, but it did help to create a set of favorable circumstances.[3]

Catherine Stimpson[4] describes the historical ties that bound the black liberation and women's liberation movements together for more than a century. She points out that the antislavery movement preceded the first major women's rights movement, that black male suffrage preceded women's suffrage, and that the civil rights movement of the sixties preceded the contemporary women's liberation movement. Paraphrasing Alva Myrdal, she notes that both blacks and women are highly visible; they cannot hide even if they want to. A patriarchal ideology assigns them different qualities—blacks are tough; women are fragile—but both are judged to be naturally inferior in those respects that carry prestige, power, and advantages in society. Stimpson quotes Thomas Jefferson as follows:

Even if America were a pure democracy, its inhabitants should keep women, slaves, and babies away from its deliberations. The less education women and Blacks get, the better; manual education is the most they can have. The only right they possess is the right which criminals, lunatics, and idiots share, to love their divine subordination with the *paterfamilias* and to obey the paterfamilias himself.[5]

Women found that men with whom they had worked side by side against slavery or for civil rights, peace, or the right to organize in trade unions left them when they sought to gain the same rights for women. The behavior of Henry Stanton vis-à-vis his wife, Elizabeth, and the women's movement of that era is a case in point. The Stantons were both activists in the antislavery movement, but Henry left town when Elizabeth organized the women's rights convention in Seneca Falls in 1848.

Samuel Gompers and his successors, as heads of the American Federation of Labor (AFL), attacked the presence of married women in the workforce and asserted that females should direct their energies toward getting married and raising families.[6] In 1921, the Women's Trade Union League (WTUL) petitioned its executive council to issue federal charters that would permit women to organize in sexually segregated unions. The AFL rejected the petition, and when the women accused the executive council of prejudice, Gompers replied that the AFL discriminated against "any nonassimilable race."[7] During World War II, R. J. Thomas, president of the United Auto Workers, claimed that women accepted the advantages of union membership but not the responsibilities. He predicted that at the end of the war, almost all women would lose their jobs.

The more recent feminists found that they received little interest, attention, or sympathy when they tried to have the discrimination they experienced recognized as a legitimate source of complaint:

Like their ancestors in the antislavery movement, some women in the civil rights movement felt abused. They were given work supportive in nature and negligible in influence; they were relegated to the research library and to the mimeograph machine. . . . Not only did movement men tend to be personally chauvinistic, but many of the movement's ideals—strength, courage, spirit— were those society attributes to masculinity. Women may have those characteristics but never more than men.[8]

And Stokely Carmichael, one of the leaders of the civil rights movement, remarked: "The only position for women in SNCC [Student Nonviolent Coordinating Committee] is prone."[9]

In tracing the founding of the contemporary women's movement, Freeman cites an incident that she claims precipitated the formation of the Chicago group, the first independent women's group in the country:

> At the August 1967 convention of the National Conference for New Politics, a women's caucus had met for days only to be told by the chair that its resolution wasn't significant enough to merit a floor discussion. Only by threatening to tie up the convention with procedural motions, did the women succeed in having their statement tacked on to the end of the agenda. But in the end, their resolution was never discussed. The chair refused to recognize any of the many women standing by the microphones. Instead he recognized someone from the floor to speak on the "forgotten American, the American Indian." Five women rushed to the podium and demanded an explanation. The Chairman responded by patting one of them on the head (literally) and saying, "Cool down, little girl. We have more important things to talk about than women's problems."[10]

Another incident that illustrates the lack of empathy that men in the radical politics of the sixties had for women's rights occurred at the University of Washington. A Students for a Democratic Society (SDS) organizer was explaining to a large meeting how white college youths established rapport with the poor whites with whom they were working. He said that sometimes, after analyzing societal ills, the men shared leisure time by "balling a chick together." He pointed out that such activities did much to enhance the political consciousness of the poor white youths. A woman in the audience asked, "And what did it do for the consciousness of the chick?" After the meeting, a handful of enraged women formed Seattle's first women's group.[11]

Women's liberation groups continue to see connections between their status in American society and the status of blacks. In comparing the ideology of the women's movement with that of black civil rights advocates, Stimpson observes, "[The black movement] teaches that the oppressed must become conscious of their oppression, of the debasing folly of their lives, before change can come. Change, if it does come, will overthrow both a class, a social group, and a caste—a social group held in contempt."[12]

Stimpson goes on to make perhaps the strongest statement of the contemporary women's movement on the similarities between themselves and blacks:

1. Women, like black slaves, belong to a master. They are property and whatever credit they gain redounds to him.
2. Women, like black slaves, have a personal relationship to the men who are their masters.
3. Women, like blacks, get their identity and status from white men.

4. Women, like blacks, play an idiot role in the theatre of the white man's fantasies. Though inferior and dumb, they are happy, especially when they can join a mixed group where they can mingle with The Man.

5. Women, like blacks, buttress the white man's ego. Needing such support, the white man fears its loss; fearing such loss, he fears women and blacks.

6. Women, like blacks, sustain the white man: "They wipe his ass and breast feed him when he is little, they school him in his youthful years, do his clerical work and raise him and his replacements later, and all through his life in the factories, on the migrant farms, in the restaurants, hospitals, offices, and homes, they sew for him, stoop for him, cook for him, clean for him, sweep, run errands, haul away his garbage, and nurse him when his frail body falters."

7. Women, like blacks, are badly educated. In school they internalize a sense of being inferior, shoddy, and intellectually crippled. In general, the cultural apparatus—the profession of history, for example—ignores them.

8. Women, like blacks, see a Tom image of themselves in the mass media.

9. Striving women, like bourgeois blacks, become imitative, ingratiating, and materialistic when they try to make it in the white man's world.

10. Women, like blacks, suffer from the absence of any serious study on the possibility of real "temperamental and cognitive differences" between the races and sexes.[13]

Since the end of the 1960s, many variations of the initial women's movement have emerged. These movements and ideologies range from reformist to revolutionary. The National Organization for Women (NOW) is probably the most conservative. Maintaining the civil rights analogy, it is the National Association for the Advancement of Colored People (NAACP) of the women's movement. Founded in 1966 by Betty Friedan, it has concentrated most of its efforts on legal and economic problems. Its membership is, on the average, older than that of the more radical women's groups, but like the more radical groups, it is composed primarily of white, well-educated professional women.

Between the end of the sixties and the early part of the seventies, a variety of women who became disenchanted with, or were thrown out of, New Left or civil rights movements organized Female Liberation First (FLF), Women's International Terrorist Conspiracy from Hell (WITCH), Red Stockings, and the Feminists. The characteristics that distinguish the moderate groups from the more radical ones are the almost exclusive emphasis that the former place on job equality and passage of the Equal Rights Amendment; the strategy of working for change within the system through lobbying, court action, and education; and the willingness to accept men as members. The radical groups consider the entire system corrupt. Their targets are as much the institutions of marriage, the family, and motherhood as unequal opportunities in employment and education. Consciousness raising for these women involves educating their sisters to the belief that every aspect of their relationship with men is exploitive. The "Red Stocking Manifesto" expresses those sentiments:

> Women are an oppressed class. Our oppression is total, affecting every facet of our lives. We are exploited as sex objects, domestic servants, and cheap labor. We are considered inferior beings, whose only purpose is to enhance men's lives. Our humanity is denied. Our prescribed behavior is enforced by the threat of physical violence.
>
> Because we have lived so intimately with our oppressors in isolation from each other, we have been kept from seeing our personal suffering as a political condition. This creates the illusion that a woman's relationship with her man is a matter of interplay between two unique personalities and can be worked out individually. In reality, every such relationship is a class relationship; the conflicts between individual men and women are political conflicts that can only be solved collectively.
>
> We identify the agents of our oppressors as men. Male supremacy is the oldest, most basic form of domination. All other forms of exploitation and oppression (racism, capitalism, imperialism, etc.) are extensions of male supremacy: men dominate women; a few men dominate the rest.
>
> We identify with all women. We define our best interest as that of the poorest, most brutally exploited women. We repudiate all economic, racial, education, or status privileges that divide us from other women.[14]

Some women's groups espouse homosexual relationships as a desirable alternative to heterosexual ones. The Feminists, for example, argue that the basic assumption of most women's groups that women's lives will always be intertwined with men's ignores an important option: Women might consider living separately from men and accepting homosexual relations as an alternative to heterosexual relationships.

Abbott and Love write:

> Recognition of the validity of the lesbian lifestyle and acceptance of lesbian activism in women's liberation is crucial to the women's movement's ultimate goal—a new, harmonious, cooperating, nonauthoritarian society in which men and women are free to be themselves. To end the oppression of the lesbian is to admit of a wider range of being and acting under the generic name "woman." It is a cause that must be undertaken by women's liberation if women are truly to free themselves.[15]

For all the ideological differences and tactical variations that exist within the women's movement, the demographic characteristics of the various groups' membership are extraordinarily homogeneous. In the main, the movement is led by, appeals to, and has as the large majority of its members young white women who are college educated and whose families are middle and upper-middle class. After they leave the university, most of these women enter professions. None of the groups within the movement has substantially incorporated into its ranks blue-collar workers, black women, or high school–educated married women. The gulf between these nonmovement women and the authors of the "Red Stocking Manifesto" may be as great as any that those writers envisage between men and women.

It is still too early to tell how likely it is that the women's movement will significantly alter the behaviors, perceptions, beliefs, and lifestyles of women already involved in criminal careers. But given the characteristics of the members of the women's movement, it is unlikely that it has had a significant impact or that it has made much of an impression on women already involved in crime. Indeed, most of those women have yet to hear of consciousness raising or of sisterhood in a political sense. Those who have may well ridicule those sentiments or attack them as the empty mouthings of women whose lives have always been characterized by material comfort, stability, and security.

Kate Millett's observations of how prostitutes behave in court dramatizes the point:

> The scene in court is astonishing: the woman is absolutely flirting throughout the whole proceedings. She does it when she comes in, she does it when she's going out with the cops and clerks. It doesn't break down for a minute. That interchange is very weird to watch and it's something that would take a long time to explain, but you know the woman's security and advantage lies in maintaining the relationship.[16]

There is one avenue, however, through which the women's movement may already be having a significant impact on women in crime. The movement's rhetoric and activities may alter the treatment that women offenders receive at the hands of the police, prosecutors, and other law enforcement personnel. What we have heard from many police officers is "If it's equality these women want, we'll see that they get it."

A BRIEF UPDATE

In the 1990s, the women's movement was dominated by NOW. The issues that consumed most of women's energies were abortion, childcare, comparable worth, and other work-related matters such as sexual harassment and the development of strategies for the appointment and election of women to public office and important government positions. In 2003, NOW remained a key player in the women's movement. In addition to the issues that were at the forefront of the women's movement over the past thirty years, women then turned their attention toward issues involving women in the military, lesbian and gay rights, affirmative action, and the rights of older women. In 1994, the Supreme Court upheld NOW's right to use federal antiracketeering laws against anti-abortion activists who use violent methods to bar women's access to health clinics. In 1995, NOW announced their resolution to support gay and lesbian marriages and to fight legislative actions seeking to outlaw same sex marriages. Today, NOW also recognizes the growing female prison population, the abuse of women prisoners by guards, harsh drug laws affecting women's sentences, and other issues concerning women in prison.

In 1967, NOW had 700 members in fourteen chapters. In 1971, it had between 5,000 and 10,000 members who belonged to 150 chapters. In 1974, there were 40,000 members and 1,000 chapters. In 1977, NOW reported a membership of 60,000; in 1981, it grew to 150,000; and in 1983, it was 175,000. The expanding membership introduced more heterogeneity into the organization. In recent years, much of NOW's growth has come from lower-level white-collar workers and housewives. Yet in 1974, NOW elected Aileen Fernandez, a black woman, as president. Fernandez told her constituents, "Some black sisters are not sure that the feminist movement will meet their current needs."[17] Today's president, Kim Gandy, who was elected in 2001, continues to lead the fight for gender equality and equal rights.

In the 1980s, NOW became the major umbrella organization for women's interests. Two relatively new groups, the National Abortion Rights Action League (NARAL) and the National Political Caucus, also have gained in membership and support. The former is a one-issue organization; the latter aims to attract more women to run for public office. Currently, under the auspices of NOW are NOW State and Chapter Organizations, the NOW Foundation, which deals with education and legal issues, the NOW Political Action Committee, which aims to attract more women to run for federal office, and the NOW Equality PAC, which supports female candidates running for state or local offices.

As the first decade of the twenty-first century opens, the women's movement that began in the 1960s has grown and become more diversified in its membership as well as in the issues it espouses. The fear that the movement might focus all of its energies on one issue, the passage of the Equal Rights Amendment (ERA), did not materialize. While such an amendment is still an important item on the agenda of the contemporary women's movement, members of the movement may have learned some lessons from their predecessors and not allowed the success or failure of one issue to define the movement's reason for being.

In addition, during the 1980s, comparisons of men's and women's views on both women's issues (such as the ERA, abortion, and workplace issues) and on broader public policy questions revealed no significant differences. Men were no less likely to support the ERA or to assume a pro-choice position on abortion, for example, than were women. Analyses of how women and men reported having voted in presidential elections since the 1950s likewise revealed no significant gender differences.[18]

The woman's movement is still alive and appears to be growing in both membership and scope. Groups that two or three decades ago advocated and predicted the demise of the nuclear family and that viewed marriage and motherhood as institutions that are inherently exploitive of women seem to have receded into the background. The sentiments expressed in the "Red Stocking Manifesto" are barely heard or listened to today, as women tend to view themselves less as victims and more as advocates of causes that will benefit them in particular and society in general.

In addition, two women's organizations have emerged in the late 1980s and early 1990s that espouse conservative and libertarian positions. The older and larger group is the Washington-based Independent Women's Forum and the newer, smaller also Washington-based group is the Women's Freedom Network. The former describes itself as a conservative movement with ties to the Republican Party. On a key issue, it is strongly pro-life and anti-abortion. The Women's Freedom Network (WFN) has adapted a mostly libertarian position. Rita Simon is President and Cofounder of WFN.

NOTES

1. Chafe 1972: 115.
2. Ibid.: 115.
3. Chafe 1972: 233.
4. Stimpson 1971b.
5. Ibid, 623.
6. Chafe 1972.
7. Ibid.: 78.
8. Stimpson 1971b: 646.
9. Freeman 1975: 450.
10. Freeman 1973: 800-801.
11. Ibid.: 801.
12. Stimpson 1971b: 648.

13. Ibid.: 649.
14. Epstein and Goode 1973: 178.
15. Abbott and Love 1971: 621.
16. Millett 1973: 157.
17. The National Organization for Women 1974.
18. Simon and Landis 1989.

Chapter Three

American Women: Their Demographic and Status Characteristics

In this chapter, we examine census and other demographic data in order to up-date trends concerning marriage and divorce, fertility, education, income, and labor force participation among American women. We then assess how these factors are likely to influence women's participation in crime.

One thing we look at is whether increased participation in the labor force provides women with more opportunities for committing certain types of crimes. As those opportunities increase, women's participation in larceny, fraud, embezzlement, and other property and white-collar crime also should increase. As women enter the labor force in greater proportions, however, and as they acquire more skills through educational and occupation training, and as they receive more generous financial compensation, their sense of frustration, feelings of being victimized, and sense of powerlessness should diminish. According to Ward et al.,[1] Reckless and Kay,[2] and others who have studied women who have committed crimes of violence, it is these emotions that stimulate women to violence. The full set of expectations, then, is that women's participation in property and white-collar offenses should increase and their participation in crimes of violence should decrease as they gain greater entry into the work force and are rewarded for their contributions.

DEMOGRAPHIC TRENDS

In 2002, the U.S. Census Bureau[3] estimated there were 144 million women and 138 million men living in the United States, indicating that women out-numbered men by approximately 6 million. Among those who were 18 to 24 years old, there were 100.1 men for every 100 women. Of the 55- to 64-year-olds, the number of men per 100 women dropped to 91.6, and among those who were 85 or older, the ratio decreased even further to 46.3 men for every 100 women.

The percentages of unmarried women in specific age categories from 1950 to 1998 are shown in table 3.1. For all age categories and both races, there was an increase in the percentage of never-married women from 18.5 to 24.7 percent. The percent of women never married who were ages 25 to 29 nearly tripled, increasing from 13.3 percent in 1950 to 38.6 percent in 1998. While 18.5 percent of the white women and 5.2 percent of black women were never married in 1950, 1998 saw 21.9 percent of white women and 41.5 percent of black women unmarried. Among white women 35 years or older, the percentage of those who never married declined continuously from 1950 to 1994, when it reached 6.8 percent, and then dropped to 5 percent by 1998. But among black women 35 years or older, the percentage never married nearly tripled during the same time period, increasing from 5.2 percent in 1950 to 18.4 percent in 1998. While the percentage of white women between 30 and 34 years old who were unmarried slightly more than doubled from 1950 to 1998, the number of black women within the same age category increased fivefold, from 8.9 in 1950 to 47.2 in 1998. Overall, men also experienced an increase in the percentage never married, ranging from 24.9 percent in 1950 to 31.2 percent in 1998. The trend for white males during that time period decreased continuously from 8.9 percent in 1950 to 5.8 percent in 1983, but then increased to 9.5 percent in 1998, whereas the percentage of black males 35 years or older increased from 4.9 percent 1950 to 21.4 percent in 1998.

Table 3.2 shows that between 1980 and 2000, the percentage of persons who had been divorced increased nearly 50 percent. In 1980, 7.1 percent of women and 5.2 percent of men were divorced. By 2000, 10.8 percent of women and 8.8 percent of men were divorced. Though fewer white women were divorced in 2000, they showed a higher increase than did black women since 1980. Both white and black women were more likely to have been divorced than were white and black men.

As of 2000, there were nearly 105 million households in the United States, 68.8 percent of which were family households.[4] This indicates a decline in the percent of households that are family households since 1980, when there were some 80 million households, of which 73.3 percent were families. Of the 72 million family households in 2000, 17.6 were headed by a woman, a 3 percent increase since 1980, and 48.2 percent had children under the age of 18. The data in table 3.3 show that in 2002, 34 percent of the women in these female-headed households had been divorced and 41.7 had never married. These percentages represent large increases since 1960, where only 23.7 percent of the women had been divorced and 4.3 percent

Table 3.1. Percentage of Americans Who Never Married: 1950–1998

Age (years)	Women							Men						
	1950	1960	1970	1980	1983	1994	1998	1950	1960	1970	1980	1983	1994	1998
All Races														
15–19 years	82.9	83.9	88.1	91.2	93.4	94.9	96.4	96.7	96.1	95.9	97.2	98.1	98.4	98.3
20–24 years	32.2	28.4	36.3	51.2	55.5	66	70.3	59	53.1	55.5	68.2	73.2	81	83.4
25–29 years	13.3	10.5	12.2	21.6	24.8	35.3	38.6	23.8	20.8	19.6	32.1	38.2	50.3	51
30–34 years	9.3	6.9	7.4	10.6	13	19.9	21.6	13.2	11.9	10.7	14.9	19.6	29.7	29.5
35+	8.2	7.2	6.5	5.7	5.2	6.8	5	8.8	7.8	7.1	6.3	6.1	9.8	10.6
Total[b]	18.5	17.3	20.6	22.9	22.9	23.7	24.7	24.9	23.2	26.4	29.7	30	31.2	31.2
White														
15–19 years	83.5	83.9	88	90.7	92.8	94.14	95.8	96.8	96.1	95.9	97.2	97.9	98.3	98.4
20–24 years	32.4	27.4	35.1	48.6	52.2	63	67	59.5	52.6	54.9	66.9	71.1	79.4	81.6
25–29 years	13.1	9.8	10.8	19.2	21.8	30.5	34.3	23.6	20	18.7	30.5	35.5	47.5	47.7
30–34 years	9.3	6.6	6.7	9.1	10.9	16.2	19	13.1	11.3	10	13.8	18.3	26.5	26.8
35+	8.5	7.4	6.4	5.3	4.8	5.8	6.3	8.9	7.6	6.8	5.8	5.8	8.7	9.5
Total	18.5	17	19.7	21.2	21.1	21	21.9	24.7	22.6	25.6	28	28.4	28.9	29.1
Black[a]														
15–19 years	78.9	83.8	88.6	95.1	96.9	98.4	98.6	95.6	96.2	95.5	99.6	99.6	98.8	98
20–24 years	31.2	35.4	43.6	67.5	75.3	80.9	85.1	54.7	57.1	58.4	85.2	85.2	88.1	91.9
25–29 years	14.1	15.7	21.3	37	42.6	60.7	59.4	25.2	27.6	25.4	56.6	56.6	66	64.4
30–34 years	8.9	9.6	12.8	21.5	27.2	42.7	47.2	14.4	17.2	16.1	29.3	29.3	51.4	43.2
35+	5.2	6.1	7.1	8.4	9	16	18.4	4.9	9.5	9.5	8.8	8.8	20.2	21.4
Total	18.8	20	26.2	34.1	36	40.3	41.5	26.6	28.3	32.9	40.6	42.4	47.1	46

Sources: Bianchi and Spain 1986: 12, table 1.1. Data are from the U.S. Bureau of Census, Census of Population: 1950, vol. 2, pt. 1, U.S. summary, table 104; Census of Population: 1960, vol. 1, pt. 1, U.S. Summary, table 176; Census of Population: 1970, vol. 1, U.S. Summary, table 203; Census of Population: 1980, vol. 1, chap. D, U.S. Summary, table 264. "Marital Status and Living Arrangements March 1983." Current Population series p-20, no. 389, table 1; "Marital Status and Living Arrangements March 1998 (update)," (P20–514), pg. 1, table 1; "Marital Status and Living Arrangements March 1994." (P20–484), pg. 1, table 1; Census of Population: 1998, "Unpublished Tables—Marital Status and Living Arrangements: March 1998 (update)," table 1, pg. 1; Census of Population, "Marital Status and Living Arrangements March 1994," p 20–484, table 1, pg. 1.

Web Sources: http://www.census.gov/prod/1/pop/p20-484.pdf
http://www.census.gov/population/www/socdemo/ms-la.html
http://www.census.gov/prod/99pubs/p20-514u.pdf
Data for 1983 are from the Current Population Survey and are not strictly comparable to census data from earlier years.

Note:
[a] Data for 1950 and 1960 are for non-whites.
[b] Total from 1994 and 1998 includes ages 15 and older.

Table 3.2.   Percentage of Divorce among Black and White Women and Men:
1980–2000

	Women				Men			
	1980	1990	1995	2000	1980	1990	1995	2000
All races								
Total ever married	52.8	56.7	58.9	60.4	51.8	55.8	57.7	59.6
(in millions)								
Percent divorced	7.1	9.3	10.3	10.8	5.2	7.2	8	8.8
White								
Total ever married								
(in millions)	47.1	49.9	51.3	52.2	46.7	49.5	50.6	51.8
Percent divorced	6.8	9	10.1	10.7	5	7.2	8.1	8.8
Black								
Total ever married	4.5	4.8	4.9	5.1	4.1	4.5	4.6	5
(in millions)								
Percent divorced	9.5	12	12.5	12.8	7	8.8	8.5	10.3

Source: *Statistical Abstract of the U.S.*, table 49, pg. 47 (2002).
Web source: http://www.census.gov/prod/2002pubs/01statab/pop.pdf
Note: Data includes persons 18 years and older.

never married. Further, the percent of these households with women who
are married with an absent spouse decreased from 46.3 percent in 1960 to
20 percent in 2002.

In summary, the demographic data tell us that from 1960 to 1980, the
percent of women with children in female-headed households who had
been divorced increased from 23.7 percent to 41.8 percent, but has since
dropped to 34 percent in 2002. The percentage of all white and black
women who were divorced increased by less than one percent between
1995 and 2000, as did the percentage of white males. Black males experienced a 1.8 percent increase in the number divorced between 1995 and
2000. Between 1950 and 1998, there was an increase in the number of
women who never married, although black men and women experienced a
much larger increase than did white men and women. Among the family
households in 2000, 17.6 were headed by women, most of whom had been
divorced or had never married. Forty-eight percent of those households
contained children.

Women in the Labor Force

Between 1940 and 1980, the percentage of all women in the labor force increased from 27.4 percent to 51.5 percent. Since then, the percentage has increased to 60.1 percent. Table 3.4 indicates that the biggest increase in labor
force participation since 1980 occurred among married women, from 49.9 to

Table 3.3. Children under 18 Years Living with Mother Only, by Marital Status of Mother: 1960 to 2002

Marital Status	Number (thousands)						Percent Distribution						1960–2002 Change	
	1960	1970	1980	1990	2000	2002	1960	1970	1980	1990	2000	2002	Number	Percent
Divorced	1,210	2,296	4,766	5,118	5,655	5,593	23.70	30.80	41.8	36.9	35	34	4,383	362.2
Married, Spouse Absent	2,363	3,234	3,610	3,416	3,224	3,287	46.30	43.40	31.7	24.6	20	20	924	391
Widowed	1,311	1,395	1,286	975	692	720	25.70	18.7	11.3	7	4.3	4.4	−591	−45.1
Never Married	221	527	1,745	4,365	6,591	6,872	4.30	7.1	15.3	31.5	40.8	41.7	6,651	30.1
Total	5,105	7,452	11,406	13,874	16,162	16,472	100	100	100	100	100	100	11,367	222.7

Source: Data are from the U.S. Bureau of the Census, Current Population Survey Reports, "Children Under 18 Years Living With Mother Only, by Marital Status of Mother: 1960 to Present," Table CH-5, pg. 1–2.

Web source: www.census.gov/population/socdemo/hh-fam/tabCH-5.pdf.

Table 3.4. Females in the Labor Force as a Percentage of All Females by Marital Status: 1940–2001

Year	Total	Single	Married	Widowed/ Divorced/ Separated
1940	27.4	48.1	16.7	32
1944	35	58.6	25.6	35.7
1947	29.8	51.2	21.4	36.4
1950	31.4	50.5	24.8	36
1955	33.5	46.4	29.4	36
1956	34.2	46.4	30.2	36.9
1957	34.8	46.8	30.8	37.9
1958	35	45.4	31.4	37.9
1959	35.2	43.4	32.3	38
1960	34.8	44.1	31.7	37.1
1961	36.8	44.4	34	39
1962	35.7	41.7	33.7	36.6
1963	36.1	41	34.6	35.8
1964	36.5	40.9	34.4	36.1
1965	36.7	40.5	35.7	35.7
1966	37.3	40.8	35.4	36.4
1967	39.7	50.7	37.8	35.9
1968	40.7	51.3	38.3	35.8
1969	41.6	51.2	39.6	35.8
1970	42.6	53	41.4	36.2
1971	42.5	52.8	41.4	35.7
1972	43.7	55	42.2	37.2
1973	44.2	55.9	42.8	36.7
1974	45.3	57.4	43.8	37.8
1975	46	57	45.1	37.7
1976	46.8	59.2	45.8	37.3
1977	48	59.2	47.2	39
1978	49.2	60.7	48.1	39.9
1979	50.8	62.9	49.9	40
1980	51.1	61.5	50.7	41
1981	52	62.3	51.7	41.9
1982	52.1	62.2	51.8	42.1
1983	52.3	62.6	52.3	41.2
1984	53.2	63.1	53.3	42.1
1985	54.5	65.2	54.7	42.8
1986	54.7	65.3	55	43.1
1987	55.4	65.1	56.1	42.9
1988	56.6	67.7	56.7	46.2
1989	57.4	68	57.8	47
1990	57.5	66.7	58.4	47.2
1991	57.4	66.2	58.5	46.8

Table 3.4.   (*continued*)

Year	Total	Single	Married	Widowed/ Divorced/ Separated
1992	57.8	66.2	59.3	47.1
1993	57.9	66.2	59.4	47.2
1994	58.8	66.7	60.7	47.5
1995	58.9	66.8	61	47.4
1996	59.3	67.1	61.2	48.1
1997	59.8	67.9	61.6	48.6
1998	59.8	68.5	61.2	48.8
1999	60	68.7	61.2	49.1
2000	60.2	69	61.3	49.4
2001	60.1	68.2	61.4	49.5

Sources: U.S. Bureau of the Census, *Statistical Abstract of the U.S.* (Washington, D.C.: U.S. Government Printing Office, 1988), pg. 374, Table 62.3; *Statistical Abstract of the U.S.*, Table 569, pg. 372 (2003).

61.4 percent, in contrast to women in the single and widowed/divorced/separated categories.

Among the married women, there were big increases in labor force participation among those with young children (table 3.5). In 1990, 58.9 percent of mothers with children under the age of six were in the labor force full-time as opposed to 10.8 percent in 1948. The number inc reased to 63.7 percent in 1998 and to 62.5 percent in 2001.

In the first edition of this book, Simon reported that women's participation in the labor force was based on a sex role definition that "has women performing in service-like roles and in jobs that involve less initiative and responsibility than those occupied by men."[5] In comparing labor force participation across the four broad categories (white-collar, blue-collar, service, and farm), she noted that from 1948 through 1972, the proportion of women in the white-collar category increased from 49.3 to 61.1 percent and the proportion of women in service positions increased from 20.5 to 22.3 percent. In 1971, 34 percent of the women within the white-collar category held clerical positions, compared to 7 percent of the men, and 14.5 percent of the men held managerial positions, as opposed to 4.9 percent of the women (Simon 1975: 24, table 3.4).

Looking at the data in table 3.6, we see that 36.5 percent of employed women in 2000 held managerial, professional, and technical positions, compared to 33.3 percent in 1995 and 28.2 percent in 1990. More specifically, 17.1 percent of women in 2000 held jobs categorized as executive,

Table 3.5. Labor Force Participation Rates of Married Women with Children: 1948–2001[a]

Year	No Children under 18	Children 6–17; None under 6	Children Under 6	Total
1948	28.4	26	10.8	22
1949	28.7	27.3	11	22.5
1950	30.3	28.3	11.9	23.8
1951	31	30.3	14	25.2
1952	30.9	31.1	13.9	25.3
1953	31.2	32.2	15.5	26.3
1954	31.6	33.2	14.9	26.6
1955	32.7	34.7	16.2	27.7
1956	35.3	36.4	15.9	29
1957	35.6	36.6	17	29.6
1958	35.4	37.6	18.2	30.2
1959	35.2	39.8	18.7	30.9
1960[b]	34.7	39	18.6	30.5
1961	37.3	41.7	20	32.7
1962	36.1	41.8	21.3	32.7
1963	37.3	41.5	22.5	33.7
1964	37.8	43	22.7	34.4
1965	38.3	42.7	23.3	34.7
1966	38.4	43.7	24.2	35.4
1967	38.9	45	26.5	36.8
1968	40.1	46.9	27.6	38.3
1969	41	48.6	28.5	39.6
1970	42.2	49.2	30.3	40.8
1971	42.1	49.4	29.6	40.8
1972	42.7	50.2	31.1	41.5
1973	42.8	20.1	32.7	42.2
1974	43	51.2	34.4	43
1975	43.9	52.4	36.6	44.4
1976	43.8	53.7	37.4	45
1977	44.9	55.6	39.3	46.6
1978	44.7	57.2	41.6	47.6
1979	46.7	59.1	43.2	49.4
1980	46	61.7	45.1	50.1
1981	46.3	62.5	47.8	51
1982	46.2	63.2	48.7	51.2
1983	46.6	63.8	49.9	51.8
1984	47.2	65.4	51.8	52.8
1985	48.2	67.8	53.4	54.2
1986	48.2	68.4	53.8	54.6
1987	48.4	70.6	56.8	55.8
1988	65	72.5	57.1	65
1989	65.6	73.4	57.4	65.6
1990	66.3	73.6	58.9	66.3
1991	66.8	73.6	59.9	66.8

Table 3.5. (*continued*)

Year	No Children under 18	Children 6–17; None under 6	Children Under 6	Total
1992	67.8	75.4	59.9	67.8
1993	67.5	74.9	59.6	67.5
1994	69	76	61.7	69
1995	70.2	76.2	63.5	70.2
1996	70	76.7	62.7	70
1997	71.1	77.6	63.6	71.1
1998	70.6	76.8	63.7	70.6
1999	54.4	77.1	61.8	61.6
2000	54.7	77.2	62.8	62
2001	54.8	77.7	62.5	62.1

Sources: U.S. Bureau of the Census, *Historical Statistics of the United States: Colonial Times to 1970*, Bicentennial Edition (Washington, D.C.: U.S. Government Printing Office, 1975), series D63-84, Table D63-74; U.S. Bureau of the Census, *Statistical Abstract of the U.S.* (Washington, D.C.: U.S. Government Printing Office, 1988), pg. 374, table 624; *Statistical Abstract of the U.S.*: Table 577, pg. 373 (2001); Table 578, pg. 373 (2001); Table 570, pg. 373 (2002); Table 571, pg. 373 (2002). Small 2000, "Female Crime in the United States, 1963–1998: An Update," *Gender Issues*, Table 2, pg. 7

Web sources: http://www.census.gov/prod/2003pubs/02statab/labor.pdf
    http://www.census.gov/prod/2002pubs/01statab/labor.pdf
    http://www.census.gov/prod/2001pubs/statab/sec13.pdf

Notes: Data from 1999 to 2001 include persons 16 years and older.
[a] Married women in the labor force as percent of married women in the population.
[b] First year for which figures include Alaska and Hawaii.

administrative, and managerial, while 19.5 percent worked in professional specialty careers. Among technical, sales, and administrative support positions, we have seen a decline in percent that are women. In 1990, about 45 percent of employed women held these positions, whereas in 2001 the percent decreased to 39.9. In 2001, 25.1 percent held administrative support (including clerical) jobs, a large decrease since 31.1 percent in 1990. In summary, the data in table 3.6 show that women have moved upward from service and administrative positions to managerial, professional, and technical positions.

Education

The percentage of bachelor's, master's, and doctorate degrees conferred upon women has more than doubled since 1950 and 2000, and today 57 percent of these degrees are received by women. During that time, the percentage of bachelor's degrees that were conferred upon women increased from 23.9 percent to 57.2 percent (table 3.7). In 1950, only 29.3 percent of master's degrees

Table 3.6. Occupational Distribution by Sex: 1990–2001[a]

	Distribution by Employment							
	Men				Women			
	1990	1995	2000	2001	1990	1995	2000	2001
Managerial, professional, and technical	25.33	26.72	28.21	29.08	29.18	33.13	35.70	36.53
Executive, administrative, managerial	12.89	14.00	14.47	14.93	13.13	15.25	16.56	17.05
Professional specialty	11.84	12.71	13.74	14.15	16.05	17.88	19.14	19.49
Technical, sales, and administrative support	19.52	19.32	19.24	19.19	44.95	42.05	39.92	39.87
Tech and related support	3.55	3.30	3.34	3.34	4.07	3.96	4.05	4.31
Sales	9.47	9.76	9.92	10.01	9.81	10.15	10.43	10.47
Administrative support, including clerical	6.50	6.26	5.98	5.84	31.07	27.95	25.44	25.08
Service	9.32	9.33	9.39	9.53	12.63	12.71	13.14	13.31
Private household	0.02	0.03	0.04	0.03	0.84	0.85	0.80	0.78
Protective service	3.09	3.30	3.15	3.19	0.60	0.70	0.78	0.88
Other service	6.17	6.00	6.21	6.32	11.19	11.16	11.56	11.65
Precision Production	20.70	19.61	19.68	19.70	2.48	2.51	2.49	2.32
Operators, fabricators, and laborers	23.13	22.51	21.03	20.22	10.27	9.10	8.19	7.46
Machine operators, assemblers, inspectors	9.27	8.93	7.53	7.07	7.94	6.72	5.49	4.85
Transportation and material moving	7.57	7.56	7.50	7.42	0.63	0.69	0.84	0.82
Handlers, equipment cleaners, helpers, and laborers	6.29	6.02	6.00	5.73	1.70	1.69	1.86	1.79
Farming, forestry, and fishing	2.63	2.52	2.44	2.27	0.48	0.50	0.55	0.51

Sources: U.S. Bureau of the Census, *Statistical Abstract of the U.S.* (Washington, D.C.: U.S. Government Printing Office, 1988), pg. 403, Table 613 (2003).
[a] Employed persons aged 16 and over.

were earned by women, but by 2001, women were receiving 58 percent of the degrees conferred. Women still lag behind at the doctoral level, however. Over 40 percent of the recipients of doctorate degrees were women in the mid-1990s, which is a big increase from the 9 percent of the 1950s but is clearly less than women's representation in the population.

Table 3.8 shows that while there were big increases in the percentage of women who were awarded professional degrees, men still dominated. Of three major professions (medicine, dentistry, and law), women have made the biggest inroads in medicine and law. In 1980, the percentage of professional degrees awarded to women in medicine, dentistry, and law were 23.4, 13.3, and 30.2, respectively. In 2000, these percentages rose to 42.7, 40.1, and 45.9, respectively.

In an earlier edition, Simon reported that in 1969, "a much smaller proportion of the women in the professional and managerial categories, as opposed to the men, had completed at least four years of college."[6] Sixty-one percent of the men in the professional categories had at least four years of college, compared to 12 percent of the women in the same occupational categories. In their second edition, Simon and Landis (1991), report that the occupational status and years of schooling for men and women showed much greater similarity in 1987 than in 1969. Table 3.9 depicts the scenario today. The gap between men and women with four years of college in the highest-ranking occupational categories since 1969 has decreased significantly. In 1969, 60.9 percent of those with category 1 jobs were men with four years of college, whereas women with the same amount of education held only 11.7 percent of the jobs. Today, the difference is only 6.3 percent, with 66.7 percent of the men and 60.4 percent of the women in these occupations having college training (the 2001 figure does not include postgraduate training).

Overall, the occupational status and years of schooling for men and women show much greater similarity in 2001 than in the 1980s and 1960s. As in 1987, the biggest difference between men and women in 2001 occurred in categories 2 (technical, sales, and administration) and 3 (service), where there are about twice as many college-trained men than women.

Income

Table 3.10 examines the factors that many people view as the most important indicator of women's equality in society: the ratio of women to men's earnings. This table compares men and women's incomes among blacks and whites. Looking first at the ratio of white men versus white women as opposed to black men versus black women, we see that the trends are in the

Table 3.7.   Number of Earned Degrees Conferred upon Women: 1950–2000

	Bachelor's[a]		Master's		
	Total Number	Percent Women	Total Number	Percent Women	Total Number
1950	434	23.9	58	29.3	6.6
1955	288	36.1	58	32.8	8.8
1960	395	35.1	75	32.0	9.8
1965	539	40.6	112	32.1	16.5
1970	833	41.5	209	39.7	29.9
1974	1,009	42.5	278	43.2	33.9
1975	988	43.5	294	44.9	34.1
1976	988	43.6	313	46.3	34.1
1977	993	44.4	318	46.9	33.3
1978	998	45.4	313	47.9	32.2
1979	1,000	46.6	302	50.0	32.8
1980[b]	999	47.3	298	49.3	32.6
1981[b]	1,007	48.0	296	50.3	32.9
1982[b]	1,025	48.6	296	50.7	32.7
1983[b]	1,042	49.1	290	50.0	32.8
1984[b]	1,049	49.0	285	49.5	33.3
1985[b]	1,055	49.4	286	50.0	32.9
1986	988	50.8	289	50.2	34.0
1987	991	51.5	289	51.2	34.0
1988	995	52.1	299	51.5	35.0
1989	1,018	52.6	310	51.9	36.0
1990	1,052	53.2	325	52.6	38.0
1991	1,094	53.9	337	53.7	40.0
1992	1,137	54.2	353	54.1	41.0
1993	1,165	54.2	369	54.2	42.0
1994	1,169	54.5	387	54.5	44.0
1995	1,160	54.7	398	55.0	45.0
1996[c]	1,164	55.2	406	55.9	45.0
1997[c]	1,173	55.6	419	56.8	46.0
1998[c]	1,184	56.1	430	57.2	46.0
1999[c]	1,201	56.8	440	57.7	44.0
2000[c]	1,238	57.2	457	58.0	45.0

Sources: Adapted from U.S. Bureau of the Census, *Statistical Abstract of the U.S.* (Washington, D.C.: U.S. Government Printing Office, 1998), p. 149, Table 254; p.175, Table 276 (2003). Data from U.S. Department of Education, Center for Education Statistics, *Digest of Education Statistics*, annual.

Notes: Numbers are in thousands. Except as noted, data include Puerto Rico. Beginning in 1960, data include Alaska and Hawaii.

[a] Includes first professional degrees.
[b] Data for fifty states and Washington, D.C.
[c] Data beginning in 1996 reflect the new classification of institutions.

Table 3.8. Percentage of Professional Degrees Conferred upon Women: 1960–2000

Year	Medicine Total	% Female	Dentistry Total	% Female	Law Total	% Female
1960	7,032	5.5	3,247	0.8	9,240	2.5
1964	7,342	5.9	3,196	0.44	11,024	3.11
1965	7,347	6.5	3,135	0.73	12,000	3.37
1966	7,720	6.7	3,264	1.07	13,687	3.78
1967	7,767	7.4	3,375	1.07	15,339	4.0
1968	7,987	7.9	3,448	1.54	17,169	4.12
1969	8,082	7.7	3,437	1.09	17,723	4.26
1970	8,314	8.4	3,718	0.9	14,916	5.4
1971	8,919	9.1	3,745	1.12	17,966	4.05
1972	8,250	9.0	3,860	1.04	21,760	6.89
1973	10,307	9.0	4,047	1.36	27,205	7.97
1974	11,356	11.12	4,440	1.91	29,326	11.39
1975	12,447	13.1	4,773	3.1	29,296	15.1
1976	13,426	16.19	5,425	4.39	32,293	19.22
1977	13,461	19.09	5,138	7.28	34,101	22.45
1978	14,279	21.5	5,189	10.9	34,402	26.0
1979	14,786	23.0	5,434	11.8	35,206	28.5
1980	14,902	23.4	5,258	13.3	35,647	30.2
1981	15,505	24.7	5,460	14.4	36,331	32.4
1982	15,814	25.0	5,282	15.4	35,991	33.4
1983	15,484	26.7	5,585	17.1	36,853	36.4
1984	15,813	28.2	5,353	19.6	37,012	36.8
1985	16,041	30.4	5,339	20.7	37,491	38.5
1986	15,938	30.8	5,046	22.6	35,844	39.0
1987	15,620	32.4	4,741	24.0	36,172	40.2
1988	15,358	33.1	4,477	26.3	35,397	40.5
1989	15,460	33.3	4,265	26.8	35,634	40.9
1990	15,075	34.2	4,100	30.9	36,485	42.2
1991	15,043	36.0	3,699	32.1	37,945	43.0
1992	15,243	35.7	3,593	32.3	38,848	42.7
1993	15,531	37.7	3,605	33.9	40,302	42.5
1994	15,368	37.9	3,787	38.5	40,044	43.0
1995	15,537	38.8	3,897	36.4	39,349	42.6
1996	15,341	40.9	3,697	35.8	39,828	43.5
1997	15,571	41.4	3,784	36.9	40,079	43.7
1998	15,424	41.6	4,032	38.2	39,331	44.4
1999	15,562	42.5	4,144	35.5	39,167	44.8
2000	15,286	42.7	4,250	40.1	38,152	45.9

Sources: 1960: U.S. Bureau of the Census, *Statistical Abstract of the U.S.* (Washington, D.C.: U.S. Government Printing Office, 1998), pg. 151, Table 256; pg. 178, Table 281 (2003), Table 289 (2000). Data from U.S. Department of Education, Center for Education Statistics, *Digest of Education Statistics* annual.

Web source: http://www.census.gov/prod/2003pubs/02statab/educ.pdf

Table 3.9.   Educational Achievement for Males and Females over 25 Years of Age by Occupational Category: 1969–2001[a]

1969

	Males						Females					
	1	2	3	4	5	6	1	2	3	4	5	6
High school												
< 4 years	5.9	22.4	29.4	23.6	51.8	62.1	37.4	26.9	20	38.7	52	68.7
≥ 4 years	16.2	32.1	41.9	35	38	31.7	39.5	42.5	59.5	46.9	38.1	28.5
College												
1–2 years	12.8	15.8	15.4	17.8	7	4.4	9.3	14	14.7	9.4	6.5	2.1
3 years	4.3	3.9	3	4.3	1	0.6	2.2	2.6	1.7	1.5	0.9	0.3
≥ 4 years	60.9	25.7	10.3	19.3	1.2	1.1	11.7	13.9	4.2	3.5	2.5	0.5
Total	100	100	100	100	100	100	100	100	100	100	100	100

2001

	Males					Females				
	1	2	3	4	5	1	2	3	4	5
High school										
< 4 years	1.7	4	17	16.2	22	1.3	4.8	21.1	17.6	25.9
≥ 4 years	11.2	25.6	38	45.7	49.8	13	38.1	44.2	43.5	51.7
College										
1–3 years	20.2	34.7	31.6	30.8	22.5	25.3	39.5	27.3	28.3	17.9
≥ 4 years	66.7	35.6	13.5	7.3	5.7	60.4	17.7	7.4	10.5	4.5
Total	100	100	100	100	100	100	100	100	100	100

Sources: Adapted from the 1970 U.S. Bureau of Census of Population (U.S. Dept. of Commerce, 1973), Subject Reports; U.S. Bureau of Census, *Statistical Abstract of the U.S.* (Washington, D.C.: U.S. Government Printing Office, 1988), p. 379, Table 629; *Statistical Abstract of the U.S.*, pg. 385, Table 590 (2002).

[a] Occupational categories in 1969: 1 = professional and technical; 2 = managerial and administration; 3 = clerical and kindred workers; 4 = sales; 5 = craftsmen and foremen; 6 = operatives. Occupational categories in 2001: 1 = managerial and professional; 2 = technical, sales, and administration; 3 = service; 4 = precision production; 5 = operators and fabricators.

opposite direction. Among blacks, male and female incomes move closer together. In 1955, black females earned slightly more than half of what black males earned. During the 1970s, black women began earning closer to 75 percent of what black men earned. Among whites, the earnings gap between men and women widened. In 1955, white women earned two-thirds of what white men earned. In the mid-sixties and up through 1980, they earned less than 60 percent of what white men earned. In 2000, white women's earnings were only 55 percent of those of white men, whereas black women earned 74 percent of what black men earned.

Among women, the gap between blacks and whites has virtually disappeared. In 1955, black women earned about half of what white women earned. By 2000, their earnings increased to 99 percent of what white women were earning.

Controlling for occupational categories does not reveal major gains by women between 1956 and 2000 (table 3.11). Executive, administrative, and managerial women workers continued to earn about two-thirds of what men did in 2000. This is only a two-percentage-point gain since 1956. Among sales personnel, the differential was greater. Women only earned 39 percent of what men earned; this figure increased to 52 percent in 1979 but has since dropped to 39 percent. Female operatives in 1956 earned 62 percent of men's earnings, and by 2000, this figure had increased by only two percentage points.

CONCLUSION

Since the most recent edition of this book in 1991, we have seen a dramatic change in the percent of black women and men who are 35 or older who have never married and of the percent of black men who are divorced. Since 1990, we have also seen a 10 percent increase in the percent of women with children who never married, and since 1999, an 11 percent decrease in the labor force participation rates of those married with no children under age 18. Seven percent more women are working in managerial, professional, and technical positions since 1990.

Women are continuing to earn advanced degrees and are gradually filling the ranks of the medical, dental, and legal professions. Since 1990, the difference between black and white women's earnings has essentially been eliminated. The gap between white women's and white men's earnings has also continued to decrease since 1990.

The picture of the current status of the American woman that emerges from these statistics is that changes have occurred in some areas, but not in others.

Chapter Three

Table 3.10.   Ratio of Median Annual Income of White and Black Women and Men: 1955–2000

	BF/WM	BF/BM	BF/WF	WF/WM	WF/BM	BM/WM
1955	0.34	0.55	0.51	0.65	1.07	0.61
1956	0.35	0.59	0.56	0.63	1.06	0.6
1957	0.37	0.61	0.58	0.64	1.04	0.61
1958	0.39	0.58	0.59	0.63	1.0	0.63
1959	0.41	0.67	0.64	0.61	1.05	0.58
1960	0.41	0.62	0.68	0.61	0.92	0.66
1961	0.39	0.61	0.66	0.59	0.93	0.63
1962	0.36	0.61	0.61	0.6	1.0	0.6
1963	0.37	0.57	0.62	0.59	0.92	0.64
1964	0.41	0.63	0.69	0.59	0.91	0.66
1965	0.39	0.63	0.68	0.58	0.92	0.63
1966	0.41	0.65	0.71	0.58	0.92	0.63
1967	0.43	0.65	0.75	0.57	0.86	0.67
1968	0.43	0.63	0.74	0.58	0.85	0.69
1969	0.47	0.7	0.82	0.58	0.85	0.68
1970	0.49	0.7	0.84	0.59	0.83	0.7
1971	0.52	0.74	0.9	0.58	0.82	0.71
1972	0.49	0.7	0.87	0.57	0.81	0.69
1973	0.49	0.69	0.87	0.56	0.8	0.7
1974	0.55	0.73	0.94	0.58	0.78	0.75
1975	0.57	0.75	0.98	0.58	0.8	0.77
1976	0.55	0.75	0.94	0.59	0.8	0.73
1977	0.55	0.77	0.95	0.58	0.8	0.72
1978	0.56	0.7	0.94	0.59	0.75	0.79
1979	0.55	0.73	0.93	0.59	0.78	0.75
1980	0.56	0.74	0.94	0.59	0.79	0.75
1981	0.55	0.74	0.92	0.6	0.8	0.74
1982	0.57	0.75	0.91	0.62	0.83	0.75
1990	0.39	0.64	0.81	0.49	0.8	0.61
1995	0.46	0.68	0.89	0.52	0.77	0.67
1999	0.52	0.72	0.96	0.54	0.75	0.72
2000	0.54	0.74	0.99	0.55	0.75	0.73

Source: U.S. Census Bureau, *Statistical Abstract of the U.S.*, pg. 438, Table 665.

Since the 1950s and 1960s, and especially in the past twenty years, more women are delaying marriage, more are getting divorced, more are heads of households, and more are in the labor force full-time. The positions that women occupy in the labor force demonstrate upward mobility from clerical and sales positions to managerial, professional, and technical positions. However, there has been little change in the income ratios of men and women for the same job classifications.

Table 3.11. Median Annual Income (in dollars) by Type of Employment and by Sex and Ratio of Female Earnings to Male Earnings: 1956–2000

	Professional and Technical			Managers and Officials			Clerical			Sales Workers			Operatives		
	Male	Female	R	Male	Female	R	Male	Female	R	Male	Female	R	Male	Female	R
1956	7,484	4,672	0.62	7,638	4,512	0.59	5,617	4,026	0.72	6,406	2,675	0.42	5,421	3,369	0.62
1957	7,410	4,713	0.64	7,558	4,812	0.64	5,646	4,066	0.72	6,362	2,831	0.44	5,439	3,230	0.59
1958	7,777	4,950	0.64	7,679	4,503	0.59	5,778	4,045	0.70	6,366	2,786	0.44	5,325	3,278	0.62
1959	8,161	5,236	0.64	8,251	4,697	0.57	6,125	4,171	0.68	6,621	2,794	0.42	5,501	3,482	0.63
1960	8,367	5,125	0.61	7,818	4,132	0.53	6,222	4,204	0.68	6,870	2,809	0.41	5,876	3,492	0.59
1961	8,685	5,670	0.65	8,114	3,967	0.49	6,228	4,325	0.69	7,002	2,781	0.40	5,989	3,432	0.57
1962	8,764	5,566	0.64	7,943	4,306	0.54	6,455	4,400	0.68	7,159	2,998	0.42	6,135	3,629	0.59
1963	9,073	5,658	0.62	8,337	4,282	0.51	6,662	4,469	0.67	7,426	2,758	0.37	6,297	3,539	0.56
1964	9,577	5,753	0.60	8,483	4,170	0.49	6,930	4,540	0.66	7,755	3,052	0.39	6,394	3,640	0.57
1965	9,330	6,082	0.65	8,708	4,635	0.53	6,927	4,658	0.67	7,970	3,232	0.41	6,378	3,610	0.57
1966	9,868	6,195	0.63	9,461	4,794	0.51	7,013	4,626	0.66	8,097	3,287	0.41	6,577	3,631	0.55
1967	10,193	6,590	0.65	9,691	5,182	0.53	7,037	4,688	0.67	8,080	3,380	0.42	6,576	3,783	0.58
1968	10,542	6,610	0.63	9,794	5,101	0.52	7,324	4,778	0.65	8,292	3,388	0.41	6,773	3,956	0.58
1969	11,151	6,935	0.62	10,453	5,549	0.53	7,537	4,898	0.65	8,762	3,519	0.40	6,950	4,082	0.59
1979	21,310	13,701	0.64	21,835	11,705	0.54	16,503	9,855	0.60	17,084	8,880	0.52	14,921	8,562	0.57
1980	23,026	15,285	0.66	23,558	12,936	0.55	18,247	10,997	0.60	19,910	9,748	0.49	15,702	9,440	0.60
1981	25,653	16,508	0.64	25,425	14,820	0.58	18,938	11,755	0.62	22,331	11,238	0.50	16,948	10,301	0.61

	Executive, Administrative, and Managerial			Professional Specialty			Technical and Related Support			Administrative Support			Sales			Operatives[a]		
	Male	Female	R	Male	Female	R	Male	Female	R	Male	Female	R	Male	Female	R	Male	Female	R
1985	33,530	20,565	0.61	32,814	21,781	0.66	26,266	18,177	0.69	22,997	15,157	0.66	25,445	12,682	0.50	20,786	12,232	0.59
1986	34,962	21,432	0.61	35,143	23,076	0.66	27,880	19,236	0.69	22,718	15,509	0.68	26,803	12,956	0.48	20,551	12,324	0.60
1999	51,274	31,912	0.62	50,366	31,339	0.62	38,025	25,274	0.66	24,892	19,337	0.78	31,355	11,428	0.36	25,617	15,066	0.59
2000	52,283	33,527	0.64	51,280	32,428	0.63	41,018	27,423	0.67	25,896	20,267	0.78	31,828	12,303	0.39	26,174	16,721	0.64

Sources: 1956–1969: Adapted from Abbot L. Feris, Indicators of Trends in the Status of American Women (New York: Russell Sage Foundation, 1971); 1979–1981 and 1985–96: U.S. Bureau of the Census, Statistical Abstract of the U.S. (Washington, D.C.: U.S. Government Printing Office, 1980), Table 679; 1981, Table 670; 1982, Table 715; 1986, Table 681, 1987, Table 653; 2003, Table 614.

[a] For 1999 and 2000 data, operatives refers to machine operators, assemblers, and inspectors.

NOTES

1. Ward et al. 1968.
2. Reckless and Kay 1967.
3. U.S. Census Bureau 2003.
4. U.S. Census Bureau Statistical Abstract of the U.S. 2002.
5. Simon 1975: 22.
6. Ibid.: 28.

Chapter Four

Arrest Statistics

With this chapter, we begin our examination of crime data, looking first at the statistics concerning the proportion of women as opposed to men who have been arrested for different types of crimes over the past twenty-five years.

Longitudinal, national data about the number of women involved in crimes and the types of crimes with which they are charged have been available since 1930, when the Federal Bureau of Investigation (FBI) published its first *Uniform Crime Report (UCR)*. This annual report, currently based on data obtained from approximately ten thousand law enforcement agencies across the country, describes the number of arrests in a given year, the offenses for which suspects were arrested, and the age, sex, and racial backgrounds of those arrested. Arrest rates and trends are shown by cities, suburbs, and rural areas, as well as for the United States as a whole.

The FBI divides specific crimes for which arrest data are available into two categories. Type I offenses include the following:

- Criminal homicide, including murder and nonnegligent manslaughter and manslaughter by negligence
- Forcible rape
- Robbery
- Aggravated assault
- Burglary
- Larceny
- Auto theft
- Arson (as of 1979)

Type I offenses are used to establish an index in the Uniform Crime Reporting Program (hereafter referred to as the Crime Index) to measure the trend and distribution of crime in the United States. These particular offenses were selected because "they represent the most common local crime problem. They are all serious crimes either by their nature or due to the volume in which they occur."[1]

Type II offenses include the following:

- Other assaults
- Forgery and counterfeiting
- Fraud
- Embezzlement
- Stolen property (buying, receiving, or possessing)
- Vandalism
- Weapons (carrying, possessing, and so on)
- Prostitution and commercialized vice
- Sex offenses (except forcible rape, prostitution, and commercialized vice)
- Narcotic drug law violations
- Gambling
- Offenses against the family and children
- Driving under the influence
- Liquor law violations
- Drunkenness
- Disorderly conduct
- Vagrancy
- All other offenses

This chapter deals primarily with Type I offenses, as they are the most serious and common. Rape is not included because it is almost exclusively a male offense.[2] We do comment on some Type II offenses, usually because there has been a change in the arrest pattern for women or the arrest rates for women have been consistently high.

As this chapter unfolds, it may appear that we are using arrest statistics as proxies for crime rates without regard for the hazards of doing so. We are aware of the dangers of using the terms *arrest* and *crimes committed* interchangeably and know that arrest statistics may not be the most reliable source of data for determining actual crime rates. Unfortunately, no other data provide information about the characteristics of the suspect as well as the offense.[3] Another problem with the data is that the number of agencies reporting to the *UCR* varies from year to year, sometimes drastically. Between 1963 and 1967, the number of reporting agencies ranged from a low of 3,977 in 1964 to a high of 12,811 in 1981. These differences, however, are only of concern when considering the raw numbers reported. They need not affect the validity of proportional trends within and between gender groupings.

Criminologists usually prefer to use statistics computed on the basis of crimes known to the police for determining crime rates, but unfortunately those statistics do not identify the suspect in any way. We use arrest data to describe female crime patterns and to compare male and female arrests for different types of offenses because they are the only data that distinguish between men and women and that are available on a long-term basis. We also recognize that the proportions of arrests vary considerably from one type of offense to another. For example, the Federal Bureau of Investigation[4] reports that the proportion of all Crime Index offenses that were cleared in 2000 was 20.5 percent, but violent crimes were much more likely to be cleared by arrest than property crimes—47.5 percent versus 16.7 percent. A further breakdown of the Type I offenses that were cleared by arrest reveal the following pattern: murder, 63.1 percent; forcible rape, 46.9 percent; aggravated assault, 56.9 percent; robbery, 25 percent; burglary, 13.4 percent; larceny thefts, 18.2 percent; motor vehicle theft, 14.1 percent; and arson, 16 percent. Arrest rates are obviously more accurate proxies for behavior in violent crimes than they are for behavior in property crimes, and the more serious the crime, the more accurate the proxy.

With these qualifications and precautions in mind, we turn to the arrest data and report first the proportion of women who were arrested for all types of crimes as well as for those crimes included in the Crime Index from 1963 to 1998 (table 4.1). This table also describes the overall rate of change in the proportion of women arrested in both categories for the following time periods: 1963–2001 and 1980–2001.

Table 4.1 shows that in 2001, 22.5 percent of the persons arrested were women. The rate of change over the thirty-eight-year period was 0.97. In 1963, 1 out of 8.6 persons arrested for a serious crime was a woman. In 2001, the proportion had dropped to 1 out of 4.1. The overall rate of increase was 1.28 for the entire period. The overall increase in the proportion of women arrested for serious crimes was greater than the overall increase in the proportion of women arrested for all crimes. Note also that over the entire period, the percentage of women arrested for serious crimes was greater than the percentage of women arrested for all offenses.

Table 4.2 reports the proportions of female and male arrests for serious crimes as a percentage of total male and female arrests for all crimes. In 1963, 1 out of 6.3 women arrested were arrested for a serious crime, as opposed to slightly less than 1 out of 6.5 men arrested. In 2001, a higher proportion of women than men were arrested for serious offenses (1 out of 4.8 for women versus 1 out of 6 for men). Note that the percentage of females

Table 4.1. Female Arrests for All Crimes and for Serious Crimes: 1963–2001

Year	U.S. Total Arrests for All Crimes	Percent Female	U.S. Total Arrests for Serious Crimes	Percent Female
1963	4,510,835	11.4	695,222	11.7
1964	4,685,080	11.7	780,501	12.6
1965	5,031,393	11.9	834,296	13.4
1966	5,016,407	12.2	871,962	13.9
1967	5,518,420	12.5	996,800	14.1
1968	5,616,839	12.9	1,047,220	14.2
1969	5,862,246	13.7	1,111,674	15.7
1970	6,570,473	14.4	1,273,783	16.7
1971	6,966,822	15.0	1,397,304	17.2
1972	7,013,194	15.1	1,417,115	18.0
1973	6,499,864	15.3	1,372,220	18.7
1974	6,179,406	16.1	1,474,427	19.0
1975	8,013,645	15.7	1,901,811	19.5
1976	7,912,348	15.7	1,787,106	19.8
1977	9,029,335	16.0	1,986,043	20.1
1978	9,775,087	15.8	2,169,262	19.9
1979	9,506,347	15.7	2,163,302	19.5
1980	9,703,181	15.8	2,198,077	18.8
1981	10,293,575	16.1	2,293,754	19.1
1982	10,062,343	16.3	2,152,480	19.7
1983	10,289,609	16.6	2,151,120	20.1
1984	8,921,708	16.7	1,834,348	20.8
1985	10,289,609	17.4	2,124,671	21.4
1986	10,392,177	17.4	2,167,071	21.1
1987	10,795,869	17.7	2,266,467	21.6
1988	10,149,896	17.8	2,122,673	21.3
1989	11,261,295	18.1	2,345,498	21.1
1990	11,250,083	18.4	2,328,221	21.9
1991	10,743,755	18.7	2,277,306	22.0
1992	11,893,153	19.0	2,480,524	22.1
1993	11,765,764	19.5	2,422,839	22.7
1994	11,877,188	20.0	2,384,244	23.4
1995	11,416,346	20.4	2,239,934	23.9
1996	11,093,211	20.6	2,054,605	24.5
1997	10,544,624	21.6	1,910,953	25.5
1998	10,544,624	21.8	1,774,103	25.6
1999	14,355,600	22.0	2,320,900	26.0
2000	13,980,297	22.2	2,246,054	26.4
2001	13,699,254	22.5	2,245,597	26.7

Overall rate of change:

1963–2001		0.97		1.28
1970–2001		0.56		0.58
1980–2001		0.42		0.42

Sources: 1963–1987 Data: Adapted from *Uniform Crime Report* (Washington, D.C.: U.S. Department of Justice, Federal Bureau of Investigation, annual; 1963–1987). Total Arrests, Distribution by Sex. 1988–1998 Data: Small 2000. "Female Crime in the United States, 1963–1998: An Update." *Gender Issues*, Summer, pg. 80; 1999–2001 Data: *Uniform Crime Report*, Table 29 (1999); Table 29, pg. 216 (2000); Table 29, pg. 232–233 (2001); Table 42, pg. 251 (2001).

Table 4.2. Males and Females Arrested for Serious Crimes as a Percentage of Their Respective Sex Cohorts Arrested for All Crimes: 1963–1987

	Total Females Arrested (all crimes)	Females Arrested for Serious Crimes as Percent of All Females Arrested	Total Males Arrested (all crimes)	Males Arrested for Serious Crimes as Percent of All Males Arrested	Difference between Females and Males Arrested for Serious Crimes (percent)
1963	513,851	15.8	3,996,984	15.3	0.5
1964	546,981	18.0	4,138,099	16.5	1.5
1965	599,768	18.7	4,431,625	16.3	2.4
1966	609,768	19.8	4,406,639	17.0	2.8
1967	688,502	20.4	4,829,918	17.7	2.7
1968	725,496	20.5	4,891,343	18.4	2.1
1969	804,046	21.7	5,058,200	18.5	3.2
1970	946,897	22.8	5,623,576	18.8	4.0
1971	1,043,770	23.1	2,923,052	19.5	3.6
1972	1,057,411	24.1	5,955,783	19.5	4.6
1973	997,580	25.8	5,502,284	20.3	5.5
1974	994,296	28.2	5,185,110	23.0	5.2
1975	1,262,100	29.4	6,751,545	22.7	6.7
1976	1,240,439	28.6	6,671,909	21.5	7.1
1977	1,448,073	27.5	7,581,262	20.9	6.6
1978	1,547,859	27.9	8,227,228	21.1	6.8
1979	1,494,930	28.2	8,011,417	21.7	6.5
1980	1,532,934	27.0	8,170,247	21.8	5.2
1981	1,660,167	26.4	8,633,408	21.5	4.9
1982	1,637,180	25.9	8,425,163	20.5	5.4
1983	1,705,486	25.4	8,581,823	20.0	5.4
1984	1,489,100	25.6	7,432,608	19.6	6.0
1985	1,790,504	25.3	8,499,105	19.7	5.6
1986	1,805,849	25.3	8,586,328	19.9	5.4
1987	1,914,941	25.6	8,881,528	20.0	5.6
1988	1,809,268	25.0	8,340,628	20.0	5.0
1989	2,037,163	24.3	9,224,132	20.1	4.2
1990	2,068,153	24.7	9,181,930	19.8	4.9
1991	2,014,071	24.9	8,729,684	20.3	4.6
1992	2,259,344	24.3	9,633,809	20.0	4.3
1993	2,290,420	24.0	9,475,344	19.8	4.2
1994	2,372,426	23.5	9,504,762	19.2	4.3
1995	2,332,213	22.9	9,084,133	19.6	3.3
1996	2,289,919	22.0	8,803,292	17.6	4.4
1997	2,282,754	21.3	8,261,870	17.2	4.1
1998	2,245,890	20.2	8,049,239	16.4	3.8
1999	1,997,270	19.8	7,143,931	15.6	4.2
2000	2,020,780	19.6	7,096,187	15.5	4.1
2001	2,100,750	19.8	7,224,203	15.8	4.0

(continued)

Table 4.2.   Males and Females Arrested for Serious Crimes as a Percentage of Their
Respective Sex Cohorts Arrested for All Crimes: 1963–1987 (*continued*)

Total Females Arrested (all crimes)	Females Arrested for Serious Crimes as Percent of All Females Arrested	Total Males Arrested (all crimes)	Males Arrested for Serious Crimes as Percent of All Males Arrested	Difference between Females and Males Arrested for Serious Crimes (percent)
Overall Rate of Change:				
1963–2001	25.3		0.0	
1970–2001	–0.13		–0.16	
1980–2001	–0.27		–0.28	

Sources: 1963–1987 Data: Adapted from *Uniform Crime Report* (Washington, D.C.: U.S. Department of
Justice, Federal Bureau of Investigation, annual; 1963–1987). Total Arrests, Distribution by Sex.
1988–1998 Data: Small 2000. "Female Crime in the United States, 1963–1998: An Update."
Gender Issues, Summer, pg. 81; 1999–2001 Data: *Uniform Crime Report*, Percent Distribution,
Table 42, pg. 229 (1999); Table 42, pg. 233 (2000); Table 42, pg. 251 (2001).

and males arrested for serious offenses peaked in the late 1970s, then declined such that the 2001 figures are lower than they have been since 1967.

Table 4.3 describes the proportion of women arrested for all serious (Type
I) crimes and for all Type I violent and property offenses. This table disputes
a popular myth that women have been committing crimes of violence at a
much higher rate in recent years than in the more distant past. In fact, the increase in the proportion of female arrests for serious crimes may be explained
almost fully by the fact that women seem to be committing more *property* offenses than they did in the past. Indeed, the percentage of women arrested for
crimes of violence does not show a marked change. Between 1963 and 2001,
the percentage fluctuated from a low of 10.3 percent in 1963 to a high of 17.3
percent in 2001. But the picture for property offenses is markedly different.
In 1963, 12 percent of the arrests were women. In 2001, 30 percent of the persons arrested for a serious property crime were women.

Of women arrested for serious crimes in 1963, 15.8 percent were arrested
for violent crimes and the other 84.2 percent were arrested for property
crimes (see table 4.4). Of the men arrested for serious crimes that same year,
18.2 percent were arrested for violent crimes and 81.8 percent for property
crimes. By 1976, the percentage of female arrests for serious crimes that were
violent offenses decreased to 10 percent, but then rose to 18.1 percent in
2001. Table 4.5 provides more details about the types of serious property and
violent offenses for which women were arrested. Note that women accounted
for more than one-third of all arrests for larceny in 2001. Also note that this
proportion did not change much from the proportion in the early 1970s. The

Table 4.3. Percentage of Females Arrested for All Serious (Type I) Crimes and for All Type I Violent and Property Crimes: 1963–2001

	Total Arrested for Serious Crimes	Percent Female	Total Arrested for Violent Crimes[a]	Percent Female	Total Arrested for Property Crimes[b]	Percent Female
1963	695,222	11.7	124,821	10.3	570,401	12.0
1964	780,501	12.6	137,576	10.4	642,925	13.0
1965	834,296	13.4	151,180	10.2	683,116	14.1
1966	871,962	13.9	167,780	10.1	704,182	14.8
1967	996,800	14.1	191,807	9.8	804,993	15.1
1968	1,047,220	14.2	201,813	9.5	845,407	15.4
1969	1,111,674	15.7	216,194	9.6	892,283	17.1
1970	1,273,783	16.9	241,905	9.6	1,028,858	18.7
1971	1,397,304	17.2	273,209	10.0	1,121,327	19.0
1972	1,417,115	18.0	199,221	10.0	1,114,908	20.2
1973	1,372,220	18.7	290,382	10.2	1,078,842	21.1
1974	1,474,427	19.0	294,617	10.2	1,177,584	21.2
1975	1,901,811	19.5	370,453	10.3	1,528,317	21.7
1976	1,787,106	19.8	338,849	10.5	1,445,607	22.1
1977	1,986,043	20.1	386,806	10.4	1,596,304	22.4
1978	2,169,262	19.9	446,122	10.2	1,723,140	22.4
1979	2,163,302	19.5	434,778	10.2	1,728,524	21.8
1980	2,198,077	18.8	446,373	10.0	1,757,704	21.0
1981	2,293,754	19.1	464,826	10.1	1,828,928	21.4
1982	2,152,480	19.7	443,860	10.4	1,708,620	22.1
1983	2,151,120	20.1	443,686	10.8	1,707,434	22.5
1984	1,834,348	20.8	382,246	10.7	1,452,102	23.4
1985	2,124,671	21.4	431,332	10.9	1,693,339	24.0
1986	2,167,071	21.1	465,391	10.9	1,701,680	23.9
1987	2,266,467	21.6	473,030	11.1	1,793,437	24.4
1988	2,122,673	21.3	460,642	11.4	1,662,031	24.0
1989	2,345,498	21.1	537,084	11.4	1,808,414	24.0
1990	2,328,221	21.9	562,481	11.3	1,965,740	25.3
1991	2,277,306	22.0	556,669	11.6	1,720,637	25.4
1992	2,480,524	22.1	641,250	12.5	1,839,274	25.5
1993	2,422,839	22.7	648,416	13.1	1,774,423	26.2
1994	2,384,244	23.4	644,983	14.0	1,739,261	26.9
1995	2,239,934	23.9	619,230	14.9	1,620,704	27.3
1996	2,054,605	24.5	548,146	15.1	1,506,459	27.9
1997	1,910,953	25.5	501,353	16.2	1,409,600	28.8
1998	1,774,103	25.6	481,278	16.8	1,292,825	28.9
1999	1,512,073	26.1	420,156	17.0	1,091,917	29.6
2000	1,496,370	26.4	415,573	17.4	1,080,797	29.9
2001	1,554,737	26.7	434,391	17.3	1,120,346	30.4

(continued)

Table 4.3.   Percentage of Females Arrested for All Serious (Type I) Crimes and for All Type I Violent and Property Crimes: 1963–2001(continued)

	Total Arrested for Serious Crimes	Percent Female	Total Arrested for Violent Crimes[a]	Percent Female	Total Arrested for Property Crimes[b]	Percent Female
Overall rate of change						
1963–2001	1.28		0.68		1.53	
1970–2001	0.58		0.80		0.63	
1980–2001	0.42		0.73		0.45	

Sources: 1963–1987: Adapted from *Uniform Crime Report* (Washington, D.C.: U.S. Department of Justice, Federal Bureau of Investigation, annual; 1963–1987). Total Arrests, Distribution by Sex. 1988–1998 Data: Small 2000. "Female Crime in the United States, 1963–1998: An Update." *Gender Issues*, Summer, pg. 82; 1999–2001 Data: *Uniform Crime Report*, Percent Distribution, Table 42, pg. 229 (1999); Table 42, pg. 233 (2000); Table 42, pg. 251 (2001).

[a] 1963–1998 data include males and females arrested for criminal homicide, forcible rape, robbery, and aggravated assault.

[b] 1963–1998 data include males and females arrested for burglary, larceny and theft, and auto theft. Beginning in 1979, arson was also included.

big increase in women's arrests for larceny occurred between 1963 and 1973. Female arrests for criminal homicide and aggravated assault remained stable over the full thirty-eight-year period, ranging from 15.5 to 12.5 percent and from 14.0 to 13.3 percent, respectively (see table 4.5). While burglary and auto theft were still dominated by men, in 1998 women's participation showed a marked increase. Burglary, perhaps more than any other offense examined thus far, requires skills that are usually acquired within a criminal subculture. Because women have not been part of such criminal networks, their opportunities for acquiring these skills have been much more limited. Even with increased female participation in burglary and auto theft, women did not account for more than 16 percent of the arrests in either of those crime categories.

In table 4.6, we see the percent of men and women arrested for various serious crimes from 1963 to 2001. We see that the percentage of female arrests for criminal homicide decreased from 0.3 percent to 0.1 percent, whereas the percentage of females arrested for burglary, larceny, and auto theft showed slight increases. For both men and women, the number arrested for aggravated assault increased by 140 percent and 70 percent, respectively. Table 4.7 shows that among Type II offenses, the percentage of female arrests that were for fraud, forgery and counterfeiting, and narcotics also increased between 1963 and 2001.

Table 4.4. Females and Males Arrested for Violent and Property Crimes as a Percentage of All Arrests for Serious Crimes in Their Respective Sex Cohorts: 1963–2001

	Total Females Arrested for Serious Crimes	Percent of Females Arrested for Violent Crimes	Percent of Females Arrested for Property Crimes	Total Males Arrested for Serious Crimes	Percent of Males Arrested for Violent Crimes	Percent of Males Arrested for Property Crimes
1963	81,357	15.8	84.2	613,865	18.2	81.8
1964	98,186	14.6	85.4	682,315	18.1	81.9
1965	111,972	13.7	86.3	722,324	18.8	81.2
1966	120,872	14.0	86.0	751,090	20.1	79.9
1967	140,405	13.4	86.6	856,395	20.2	79.8
1968	149,060	12.8	87.2	898,160	20.3	79.7
1969	174,079	12.0	87.8	937,595	20.8	78.9
1970	215,614	10.8	89.1	1,058,169	20.7	79.1
1971	240,979	11.4	88.5	1,156,325	21.3	78.5
1972	255,205	11.7	88.1	1,161,910	23.2	76.6
1973	257,081	11.5	88.4	1,115,139	23.4	76.4
1974	279,811	10.8	89.1	1,194,616	22.1	77.7
1975	370,711	10.3	89.6	1,531,100	21.7	78.1
1976	354,732	10.0	89.9	1,432,374	21.2	78.6
1977	398,625	10.1	89.8	1,587,418	21.8	78.0
1978	431,809	10.5	89.5	1,737,453	23.1	76.9
1979	421,320	10.5	89.5	1,741,982	22.4	77.6
1980	413,138	10.8	89.2	1,784,939	22.5	77.5
1981	438,913	10.7	89.3	1,854,841	22.5	77.5
1982	423,602	10.9	89.1	1,728,878	23.0	77.0
1983	432,809	11.1	88.9	1,718,311	23.0	77.0
1984	380,633	10.7	89.3	1,453,715	23.5	76.5
1985	453,799	10.3	89.7	1,670,872	23.0	77.0
1986	457,152	11.1	88.9	1,709,919	24.2	75.8
1987	489,809	10.7	89.3	1,776,658	23.7	76.3
1995	534,253	17.3	82.7	1,705,681	30.9	69.1
1996	503,341	16.5	83.5	1,551,264	30.0	70.0
1997	487,342	16.6	83.4	1,423,611	29.5	70.5
1998	454,732	17.8	82.2	1,319,371	30.3	69.7
1999	394,586	18.1	81.9	1,117,487	31.2	68.8
2000	395,443	18.2	81.8	1,100,927	31.2	68.8
2001	415,366	18.1	81.9	1,139,371	31.5	68.5
Overall rate of change						
1963–2001		0.15	−0.03		0.73	−0.16
1970–2001		0.68	−0.08		0.52	−0.13
1980–2001		0.68	−0.08		0.40	−0.12

Sources   1963–1987 Data: Adapted from *Uniform Crime Report* (Washington, D.C.: U.S. Department of Justice, Federal Bureau of Investigation, annual; 1963–1987). Total Arrests, Distribution by Sex. 1995–2001 data: *Uniform Crime Report,* Table 42, pg. 251 (2001); Table 42, pg. 233 (2000); Table 42, pg. 299 (1999); Table 42, pg. 227 (1998); Table 42, pg. 239 (1997); Table 42, pg. 231 (1996); Table 42, pg. 225 (1995).

Table 4.5.   Females Arrested as a Percentage of All Arrests for Type I Offenses: 1963–2001

	Total Arrested for Criminal Homicide	Percent Female	Total Arrested for Robbery	Percent Female	Total Arrested for Aggravated Assault	Percent Female	Total Arrested for Burglary	Percent Female	Total Arrested for Larceny	Percent Female	Total Arrested for Auto Theft	Percent Female	Total Arrested for Arson	Percent Female
1963	8,805	15.5	37,836	4.9	68,719	14.0	170,160	3.3	314,402	19.0	85,839	3.7		
1964	9,097	15.5	9,134	5.3	79,895	13.6	187,000	7.0	358,569	20.3	97,356	4.2		
1965	10,163	15.4	45,872	5.2	84,411	13.5	197,627	3.7	383,726	22.1	101,763	4.2		
1966	10,734	15.3	47,031	5.0	98,406	13.2	199,781	3.9	398,623	23.1	105,778	4.1		
1967	12,167	14.8	59,789	5.2	107,192	12.9	239,461	4.1	447,299	23.9	118,233	4.2		
1968	13,538	14.7	69,115	5.6	106,475	12.4	256,216	4.2	463,928	24.4	125,263	4.9		
1969	14,706	14.1	76,533	6.2	113,724	12.6	255,937	4.4	510,660	26.5	125,686	5.3		
1970	15,856	14.5	87,687	6.1	125,971	12.6	285,418	4.7	616,099	27.9	127,341	5.1		
1971	17,317	15.7	101,728	6.3	140,350	13.3	315,376	4.9	674,997	28.1	130,954	6.0		
1972	18,035	14.8	109,217	6.5	155,581	13.2	314,393	5.2	678,673	29.7	121,842	5.7		
1973	17,395	14.5	101,894	6.8	154,891	13.2	316,272	5.4	644,190	31.5	109,226	6.5		
1974	16,044	14.3	108,481	6.8	154,514	13.4	340,697	5.4	729,661	30.7	120,224	7.0		
1975	19,526	14.9	129,217	7.0	202,217	13.1	449,155	5.4	958,938	31.2	110,708	7.0		
1976	16,763	14.1	110,296	7.1	192,753	13.1	406,821	5.2	928,078	31.2	135,196	7.0		
1977	20,096	14.0	122,514	7.4	221,329	12.8	454,193	6.0	1,006,915	31.8	153,270	8.3		
1978	18,755	14.1	141,481	7.0	257,629	12.7	485,782	6.1	1,084,088	31.7	153,270	8.3		
1979	18,264	13.7	130,753	7.4	256,597	12.4	468,085	6.3	1,098,398	30.3	143,654	8.9		
1980	18,745	12.8	139,476	7.2	258,721	12.4	479,639	6.2	1,123,823	28.9	129,782	8.6		
1981	20,432	12.7	147,396	7.2	266,948	12.6	489,533	6.3	1,197,845	29.1	122,188	8.9		
1982	18,511	13.3	138,118	7.3	258,899	12.9	436,271	6.6	1,146,705	29.4	108,736	9.0		
1983	18,064	13.3	134,018	7.4	261,421	13.5	415,651	6.8	1,169,066	29.5	105,514	8.9		

Year														
1984	13,676	13.3	108,614	7.2	231,620	13.4	334,399	7.4	1,009,743	30.2	93,285	9.2		
1985	15,777	12.4	120,501	7.6	263,120	13.5	381,875	7.4	1,179,066	31.0	115,621	9.3		
1986	16,066	12.3	124,245	7.8	293,952	13.2	375,544	7.9	1,182,099	30.7	128,514	9.5		
1987	16,714	12.5	123,306	8.1	301,734	13.3	374,963	7.9	1,256,552	31.1	146,853	9.7		
1988	16,326	12.2	111,344	8.5	304,490	13.4	31,758	8.4	1,162,752	30.5	153,016	10.1		
1989	17,975	11.9	133,830	8.6	354,735	13.4	356,717	8.7	1,254,220	30.4	182,810	10.2		
1990	18,298	10.4	136,300	8.3	376,917	13.3	341,192	8.8	1,241,236	32.0	168,338	10.0		
1991	18,654	10.3	139,182	8.6	368,486	13.7	328,790	8.9	1,215,303	32.0	161,628	10.0		
1992	19,491	9.7	153,456	8.5	434,918	14.8	359,699	9.2	1,291,984	32.1	171,269	10.8		
1993	20,285	9.4	153,533	8.7	442,075	15.7	338,238	9.9	1,251,277	32.7	168,795	11.8		
1994	18,497	9.9	146,979	9.2	449,716	16.6	319,926	10.4	1,236,311	33.3	166,260	12.4		
1995	16,701	9.5	137,811	9.3	438,157	17.7	292,315	11.1	1,164,371	33.3	149,053	13.1		
1996	14,447	10.3	121,781	9.7	387,571	17.9	264,193	11.3	1,096,488	33.8	132,023	13.6		
1997	12,764	10.3	94,034	9.8	372,422	18.8	245,816	11.9	1,033,901	34.6	116,052	15.0		
1998	12,335	11.2	87,129	10.0	359,892	19.6	233,435	12.5	940,243	34.7	107,003	15.7		
1999	9,727	11.4	73,619	10.1	318,051	19.7	192,570	12.9	794,201	35.5	94,335	15.6	10,811	14.4
2000	8,709	10.6	72,320	10.1	316,630	20.1	189,343	13.3	782,082	35.9	98,697	15.8	10,675	15.1
2001	9,426	12.5	76,667	10.1	329,722	20.1	198,883	13.6	806,093	36.5	102,607	16.4	12,763	15.9
Overall rate of change														
1963–2001	−0.19	1.06		0.44		3.12		0.92		3.43				
1970–2001	−0.14	0.66		0.60		1.89		0.31		2.22				
1980–2001	−0.02	0.4		0.62		1.19		0.26		0.91				

Sources: 1963–1987: Adapted from *Uniform Crime Report* (Washington, D.C.: U.S. Department of Justice, Federal Bureau of Investigation, annual; 1963–1987). Total Arrests, Distribution by Sex.
1988–1998 Data: Small 2000. "Female Crime in the United States, 1963–1998: An Update." *Gender Issues*, Summer, pg. 83; 1999–2001 Data: *Uniform Crime Report*, Percent Distribution, Table 42, pg. 229 (1999); Table 42, pg. 233 (2000); Table 42, pg. 251 (2001).

Table 4.6. Females and Males Arrested for Serious Crimes as a Percentage of Their Total Arrests in Their Respective Sex Cohorts: 1963–2001

	Criminal Homicide[a]		Robbery		Aggravated Assault		Burglary		Larceny/ Theft		Auto Theft	
	Female	Male	Female	Male	Female	Male	Female	Male	Female	Male	Female	Male
1963	0.3	0.2	0.4	0.9	1.9	1.5	1.1	4.1	11.6	6.4	0.6	2.1
1964	0.2	0.2	0.4	0.9	2.0	1.7	1.3	4.4	13.3	6.9	0.8	2.3
1965	0.2	0.2	0.4	1.0	1.9	1.6	1.2	4.3	14.2	6.7	0.7	2.2
1966	0.3	0.2	0.4	1.0	2.1	1.9	1.3	4.4	15.1	7.0	0.7	2.3
1967	0.2	0.3	0.5	1.2	2.0	1.9	1.4	4.8	15.5	7.0	0.7	2.3
1968	0.2	0.3	0.5	1.3	1.8	1.9	1.5	5.0	15.6	7.2	0.9	2.4
1969	0.2	0.3	0.6	1.4	1.8	2.0	1.4	4.8	16.8	7.4	0.8	2.4
1970	0.2	0.2	0.6	1.5	1.7	2.0	1.4	4.8	18.2	7.9	0.7	2.1
1971	0.2	0.2	0.6	1.6	1.8	2.1	1.5	5.1	18.2	8.2	0.7	2.1
1972	0.2	0.2	0.7	1.7	1.9	2.3	1.5	5.0	19.1	8.0	0.7	1.9
1973	0.2	0.2	0.7	1.7	2.1	2.4	1.7	5.4	20.4	8.0	0.7	2.0
1974	0.2	0.2	0.7	1.9	2.1	2.6	1.9	6.2	22.5	9.8	0.7	1.9
1975	0.2	0.2	0.7	1.8	2.1	2.6	1.9	6.3	23.7	9.8	0.7	1.7
1976	0.2	0.2	0.6	1.5	2.0	2.5	1.7	5.8	23.4	9.6	0.6	1.5
1977	0.2	0.2	0.6	1.5	2.0	2.5	1.9	5.6	22.1	9.1	0.8	1.6
1978	0.2	0.2	0.6	1.6	2.1	2.7	1.9	5.5	22.2	9.0	0.8	1.7
1979	0.2	0.2	0.6	1.5	2.1	2.8	2.0	5.5	22.2	9.6	0.9	1.6
1980	0.2	0.2	0.7	1.6	2.1	2.8	1.9	5.5	21.2	9.8	0.7	1.5

Year												
1981	0.2	0.2	0.6	1.6	2.0	2.7	1.8	5.3	21.0	9.8	0.7	1.3
1982	0.2	0.2	0.2	1.5	2.0	2.7	1.8	4.8	20.6	9.6	0.6	1.2
1983	0.1	0.2	0.6	1.4	2.1	2.6	1.7	4.5	20.2	9.6	0.6	1.1
1984	0.1	0.2	0.5	1.4	2.1	2.7	1.7	4.2	20.5	9.5	0.6	1.1
1985	0.1	0.2	0.5	1.3	2.0	2.7	1.6	4.2	20.4	9.6	0.6	1.2
1986	0.1	0.2	0.5	1.3	2.1	3.0	1.6	4.0	20.1	9.5	0.7	1.4
1987	0.1	0.2	0.5	1.3	2.1	2.9	1.6	3.9	20.4	9.7	0.7	1.5
1995	0.1	0.2	0.6	1.4	3.3	4.0	1.4	2.9	16.6	8.6	0.8	1.4
1996	0.1	0.1	0.5	1.2	3.0	3.6	1.3	2.7	16.2	8.2	0.8	1.3
1997	0.1	0.1	0.4	1.0	3.1	3.7	1.3	2.6	15.7	8.2	0.8	1.2
1998	0.1	0.1	0.4	1.0	3.1	3.6	1.3	2.5	14.5	7.6	0.7	1.1
1999	0.1	0.1	0.4	0.9	3.1	3.6	1.2	2.3	14.1	7.2	0.7	1.1
2000	0.0	0.1	0.4	0.9	3.2	3.6	1.2	2.3	13.9	7.1	0.8	1.2
2001	0.1	0.1	0.4	1.0	3.1	3.6	1.3	2.4	14.0	7.1	0.8	1.2
Overall rate of change												
1963–2001	-0.8	-0.4	-0.1	0.1	0.7	1.4	0.2	-0.4	0.2	0.1	0.3	-0.4
1970–2001	-0.7	-0.4	-0.4	-0.4	0.9	0.8	-0.1	-0.5	-0.2	-0.1	0.1	-0.4
1980–2001	-0.7	-0.4	-0.5	-0.4	0.5	0.3	-0.3	-0.6	-0.3	-0.3	0.1	-0.2

Source: 1963–1987 Data: Adapted from *Uniform Crime Report* (Washington, D.C.: U.S. Department of Justice, Federal Bureau of Investigation, annual; 1963–1987). Total Arrests, Distribution by Sex.
1995–2001 data: *Uniform Crime Report*, Table 42, pg. 251 (2001); Table 42, pg. 233 (2000); Table 42, pg. 299 (1999); Table 42, pg. 227 (1998); Table 42, pg. 239 (1997); Table 42, pg. 231 (1996); Table 42, pg. 225 (1995).
[a] Includes murder and nonnegligent homicide from 1995 to 2001.

Table 4.7. Females and Males Arrested for Various Type II Crimes as a Percentage of All Arrests in Their Respective Sex Cohorts: 1963–2001

Year	Embezzlement		Fraud		Forgery and Counterfeiting		Offenses against the Family and Children		Narcotic Drug Laws		Prostitution and Vice	
	Female	Male	Female	Male	Female	Male	Female	Male	Female	Male	Female	Male
1963[a]	0.3	0.2	1.6	0.9	1.0	0.6	1.3	1.0	0.8	0.6	3.9	0.2
1964	0.2	0.1	1.8	0.9	1.0	0.6	1.0	1.3	1.0	0.8	4.0	1.0
1965	0.2	0.1	1.8	0.9	0.9	0.6	0.9	1.3	1.0	0.9	4.4	0.2
1966	0.2	0.1	2.0	0.9	0.9	0.5	0.9	1.1	1.4	1.2	4.5	0.2
1967	0.2	0.1	1.9	0.9	1.0	0.5	0.7	1.1	2.0	1.8	4.5	0.2
1968	0.2	0.1	2.1	0.9	1.0	0.6	0.6	1.0	3.3	2.8	4.6	0.2
1969	0.2	0.1	2.2	1.0	1.0	0.6	0.6	0.9	4.5	3.9	4.6	0.2
1970	0.2	0.1	2.6	1.2	1.1	0.6	0.5	0.9	5.7	5.2	4.1	0.2
1971	0.2	0.1	1.7	1.1	1.1	0.6	0.5	0.9	6.1	5.7	3.9	0.2
1972	0.2	0.1	1.7	1.2	1.0	0.6	0.5	0.8	6.3	6.1	3.1	0.2
1973	0.1	0.1	3.0	1.1	1.1	0.6	0.4	0.7	7.0	7.5	3.4	0.2
1974	0.2	0.1	4.0	1.2	1.1	0.5	0.4	0.6	6.5	7.5	4.1	0.3
1975	0.2	0.1	4.8	1.4	1.3	0.6	0.5	0.7	5.6	6.5	3.0	0.2
1976	0.2	0.1	5.3	1.5	1.3	0.6	0.5	0.8	5.5	6.5	3.3	0.3
1977	0.1	0.1	5.9	1.8	1.4	0.6	0.4	0.6	5.5	6.5	3.8	0.3
1978	0.1	0.1	6.6	1.9	1.4	0.6	0.4	0.6	5.3	6.3	3.9	0.4
1979	0.1	0.1	7.1	2.0	1.5	0.6	0.4	0.6	4.7	5.6	3.8	0.3
1980	0.1	0.1	7.1	1.9	1.5	0.6	0.3	0.5	4.7	5.6	3.9	0.3

Year												
1981	0.1	0.1	6.8	1.9	1.6	0.6	0.3	0.5	4.7	5.9	4.6	0.3
1982	0.1	0.1	6.5	1.9	1.6	0.6	0.3	0.5	4.7	5.8	4.8	0.4
1983	0.1	0.1	6.2	1.8	1.5	0.6	0.3	0.5	5.1	6.2	4.9	0.4
1984	0.2	0.1	5.5	1.6	1.4	0.6	0.3	0.4	5.2	6.5	4.1	0.4
1985	0.2	0.1	6.8	1.9	1.4	0.6	0.3	0.5	5.4	7.1	3.9	0.4
1986	0.2	0.1	6.8	1.9	1.4	0.6	0.4	0.5	5.5	6.9	3.5	0.4
1987	0.2	0.1	6.4	1.8	1.4	0.6	0.4	0.4	6.3	7.8	3.4	0.4
1995	0.2	0.1	5.6	2.1	1.4	0.6	0.9	0.9	8.2	10.5	2.1	0.3
1996	0.2	0.1	5.9	2.2	1.4	0.6	1.0	0.9	8.2	10.7	2.1	0.4
1997	0.3	0.1	5.5	1.8	1.4	0.6	1.1	1.0	8.4	11.0	1.9	0.3
1998	0.3	0.1	5.5	1.8	1.4	0.6	1.0	1.0	8.6	11.4	1.8	0.4
1999	0.3	0.1	4.9	1.8	1.3	0.6	1.0	1.0	8.9	11.6	1.9	0.4
2000	0.3	0.1	4.7	1.7	1.4	0.6	1.0	1.0	9.1	12.1	1.9	0.3
2001	0.3	0.1	4.6	1.6	1.5	0.6	1.0	1.0	9.2	12.4	1.9	0.3
Overall rate of change												
1963–2001[b]	0.00	-0.50	1.88	0.78	0.50	0.00	-0.23	0.00	10.50	19.67	-0.51	0.50
1970–2001	0.50	0.00	1.09	0.60	0.36	0.00	1.00	0.11	0.61	1.38	-0.54	0.50
1980–2001	2.00	0.00	-0.35	-0.16	0.00	0.00	2.33	1.00	0.96	1.21	-0.51	0.00

Source: 1963–1987: Adapted from *Uniform Crime Report* (Washington, D.C.: U.S. Department of Justice, Federal Bureau of Investigation, annual; 1963–1987). Total Arrests, Distribution by Sex.
1995–2001 Data: *Uniform Crime Report*, Percent Distribution, Table 42, pg. 225 (1995); Table 42, pg. 231 (1996); Table 42, pg. 239 (1997); Table 42, pg. 227 (1998); Table 42, pg. 229 (1999); Table 42, pg. 233 (2000); Table 42, pg. 251 (2001).

[a] In 1963, embezzlement and fraud were combined.
[b] For embezzlement and fraud, the rates are for the change from 1964 to 2001.

Table 4.8. Female Arrests for Some Type II Crimes as a Percentage of All People Arrested for Various Crimes: 1963–2001

Year	U.S. Total Arrests for Embezzlement	Percent Female	U.S. Total Arrests for Fraud	Percent Female	U.S. Total Arrests for Forgery and Counterfeiting	Percent Female	U.S. Total Arrests for Offenses against the Family	Percent Female	U.S. Total Arrests for Narcotic Drug Law Violations	Percent Female	U.S. Total Arrests for Prostitution and Vice	Percent Female
1963[a]	0	0	0	0.0	30,610	17.6	58,228	9.1	29,304	14.2	26,124	76.9
1964	8,610	17.3	45,998	19.0	30,637	18.2	57,454	9.3	37,802	1.4	28,190	7.8
1965	7,674	17.0	52,007	20.3	30,617	18.4	60,981	8.8	46,069	13.4	33,987	77.5
1966	6,439	19.2	52,041	21.6	29,277	19.8	55,820	9.9	60,358	13.8	34,376	79.5
1967	6,073	19.2	58,192	23.2	33,462	20.8	56,137	8.9	101,079	13.7	39,744	77.7
1968	5,894	19.6	56,710	24.0	34,497	21.8	51,319	8.8	162,177	15.0	42,338	78.3
1969	6,309	20.8	63,445	26.2	36,727	22.7	50,312	9.2	232,690	15.5	46,410	79.6
1970	8,174	24.6	76,861	27.1	43,833	23.7	56,620	8.9	346,412	15.7	49,344	79.3
1971	7,114	24.9	95,610	28.6	45,340	24.5	56,456	8.6	400,606	16.3	52,916	77.7
1972	6,744	26.3	96,713	29.6	44,313	24.8	52,935	9.3	431,608	15.7	44,744	74.1
1973	5,612	23.7	85,467	31.2	41,975	26.7	42,784	9.2	484,242	14.5	45,308	75.5
1974	5,891	26.3	91,176	32.6	39,741	28.6	34,902	11.9	454,948	14.2	54,409	75.6
1975	9,302	31.1	146,253	34.2	57,803	28.9	53,332	11.7	508,189	13.8	50,229	74.3
1976	8,218	31.0	161,429	36.6	55,791	29.6	58,249	10.7	500,540	13.6	58,648	70.7
1977	6,607	22.7	216,672	35.6	67,984	29.1	53,385	10.3	569,293	13.9	77,115	70.7
1978	7,670	25.1	249,207	36.8	73,269	29.7	54,104	10.2	596,940	13.7	89,365	67.7
1979	7,882	25.3	243,461	40.4	70,977	30.9	53,321	9.9	519,377	13.5	83,088	67.5
1980	7,885	28.5	261,787	41.4	72,643	31.1	49,991	10.6	533,010	13.4	85,815	69.5
1981	8,170	28.5	272,900	41.2	81,429	32.1	51,908	10.5	586,646	13.2	103,134	73.4
1982	7,358	30.3	265,663	40.3	79,951	32.6	45,432	11.6	565,182	13.6	111,029	71.0
1983	7,604	32.4	261,844	40.2	74,508	33.4	46,111	11.1	616,936	14.0	119,262	70.2

Year												
1984	6,290	36.9	203,175	40.4	63,359	33.7	32,877	13.9	562,255	13.9	88,337	69.9
1985	9,799	35.6	286,941	42.6	75,281	33.2	48,699	12.7	702,882	13.8	101,167	69.5
1986	10,500	36.4	284,790	43.3	76,546	33.9	47,327	1.5	691,882	14.5	96,882	65.4
1987	10,639	38.1	280,809	43.5	85,517	34.4	48,002	17.4	811,078	14.9	100,950	64.8
1988	11,699	37.9	260,848	45	73,465	33.9	51,035	17.3	850,034	15.5	78,731	68.4
1989	13,034	38.8	289,996	45.7	80,979	33.8	58,525	17.8	1,075,728	16.3	88,536	69.0
1990	12,055	41.2	279,776	44.2	74,393	34.6	65,992	17.8	869,155	16.8	91,093	64.0
1991	10,602	38.9	292,597	42.9	77,066	35.0	72,527	12.7	781,250	16.5	81,536	65.9
1992	11,707	39.0	346,314	42.1	88,649	34.7	84,328	1.8	920,424	16.4	96,988	65.3
1993	10,916	40.5	335,580	40.6	89,487	34.7	89,157	19.3	968,606	16.2	87,712	64.3
1994	11,614	41.2	330,752	39.4	93,003	35.7	92,133	20.8	1,118,346	16.5	81,887	61.4
1995	11,605	43.6	320,046	41.0	91,991	35.9	104,952	20.2	1,144,228	10.0	72,272	61.1
1996	11,449	44.7	324,776	41.7	88,355	35.4	103,800	22.4	1,128,647	16.7	70,619	60.0
1997	12,269	47.1	274,950	46.1	83,051	38.6	104,997	23.9	1,102,335	17.3	72,385	60.2
1998	12,215	48.8	268,351	45.8	81,254	38.9	99,776	21.7	1,108,788	17.5	68,536	57.8
1999	11,208	49.2	225,934	43.6	69,853	38.4	92,849	22.1	1,007,002	17.6	63,927	60.8
2000	12,577	50.0	213,828	44.9	71,268	39.0	91,297	22.4	1,042,334	17.6	61,383	62.1
2001	13,836	49.6	211,177	45.4	77,692	40.2	93,909	23.1	1,091,240	17.8	58,638	66.6
Overall rate of change												
1963–2001[b]	1.87		1.39		1.28		1.54		0.25		–0.13	
1970–2001	1.02		0.68		0.70		1.60		0.13		–0.16	
1980–2001	0.74		0.10		0.29		1.18		0.33		–0.04	

Source: 1963–1987: Adapted from *Uniform Crime Report* (Washington, D.C.: U.S. Department of Justice, Federal Bureau of Investigation, annual; 1963–1987). Total Arrests, Distribution by Sex. 1988–1998 Data: Small 2000. "Female Crime in the United States, 1963–1998: An Update." *Gender Issues*, Summer, pg. 87. 1999–2001 Data: *Uniform Crime Report*, Percent Distribution, Table 42, pg. 229 (1999); Table 42, pg. 233 (2000); Table 42, pg. 251 (2001).

a In 1963, embezzlement and fraud were combined.
b For embezzlement and fraud, the rates are for the change from 1964 to 2001.

The figures in table 4.8 show that in 2001, almost half of all arrests for embezzlement and fraud were women and 40 percent of those arrested for counterfeiting were women. Unlike larceny, the proportion of female arrests for these property offenses increased sharply over the past thirty-five years. Note that the percentage of women arrested for prostitution and vice decreased from 77 percent in 1963 to 66 percent in 2001. The systematic decline began in the 1980s.

In sum, the arrest data tell us the following things about women's participation in crime: (1) the proportion of female arrests in 2001 was greater than the proportion of arrests one or two decades earlier; (2) the increase in arrests was greater for serious (Type I) offenses than it was for all Type I and Type II offenses combined. The increase in arrests for serious offenses can be attributed largely to women's greater participation in property offenses, especially larceny, embezzlement, fraud, and forgery. In 1963, roughly 1 out of 5 arrests for larceny involved a woman. Since 1974, the proportion has been approximately 1 out of 3. Contrary to mass media implications, the proportion of female arrests for violent crimes has changed hardly at all over the past three and a half decades, as witnessed by stable female arrest rates for homicide, aggravated assault, and robbery.

One word of caution about interpreting the statistics reported in this chapter: These statistics describe arrests, not known or observed behavior at the scene of a crime. From the arrests, we infer participation in the criminal act. But in discussing women and crime, this inference might not hold because of the discretion available to police and the way in which police may exercise that discretion.

Remember Pollak's[5] argument that the differential rate of crime attributed to men and women was due in large measure to chivalry on the part of law enforcement officials. Indeed, Pollak and other authors might claim that the sharp increase in the percentage of women arrested in the 1970s and 1980s was due to the fact that police have become less chivalrous or less paternalistic and that they are treating women as they would male suspects. Thus, perhaps changes in female crime rates result from changes in the attitudes and behavior of police rather than in the propensities of women to engage in more crimes. However, the fact that the rates of female arrests have varied according to the nature of the offense indicates that the hypothesized change in police behavior cannot account for all of the increases. It is doubtful that police would respond more punitively to female property offenders than to women suspected of killing or assaulting their victims.

Our view is that women are committing fraud, embezzlement, and forgery more often because their participation in the labor force provides them with greater opportunities to commit these offenses than they had in the past. The data in chapter 3 show that the number of women in the labor force increased in 1963 from 36 percent to 60 percent in 2001. They also show that the types of jobs women occupied were likely to provide them with the opportunities to commit fraud, embezzlement, and forgery. In 1969, 11.7 percent of the college-educated women were working in professional positions and 13.9 percent in managerial and administrative jobs. In 2000, 60 percent were employed in professional positions and 18 percent in administrative jobs. In the 1960s and 1970s they were not in a position to steal hundreds of thousands of dollars, but they were in a position to pocket smaller amounts.

NOTES

1. Federal Bureau of Investigation 1987.

2. Arrests for rape are included in the total arrests for serious crimes and serious violent crimes.

3. National Crime Survey data, which are based on reported victimizations, do provide this information and are thought to give a more accurate account of criminality. However, they were not available until 1973 and thus do not offer enough of a longitudinal perspective.

4. Federal Bureau of Investigation. 2001. Press Release 2001.

5. Pollack 1950.

Chapter Five

Women in Court

Many changes in our country's sentencing practices have occurred over the past thirty years. Since the 1930s, indeterminate sentencing was the prevailing approach to sentencing and judges were empowered with discretionary authority when determining an appropriate sentence for an offender. Judges could use mitigating factors in their decision-making process, treat each case on an individual basis, and rely upon their seasoned professionalism during sentencing. A woman arrested for drug possession, for example, might have been given probation and community service instead of prison if she had young children and a history free of crime. However, this changed during the 1970s when judicial sentencing practices came under intense fire.

The impetus behind the sentencing reform movement of the 1970s was multifaceted, stemming from both academic and political arenas. Liberals questioned whether judges' "unchecked discretion"[1] was resulting in arbitrary sentences. Racial and gender discrimination was another concern in sentencing practices, as well as judges' individual opinions and attitudes toward certain offenses. Other critics focused on the "fundamentally unjust"[2] practice of assigning harsh maximum sentences (or maximum and minimum sentences) based on the assumption that they would be generously trimmed down by discretionary parole boards. Instead, academics argued, prison sentences should be fixed and consistent across similar offenses and similar defendants. This line of attack was accompanied by skepticism over the existing belief that future community behavior could be effectively forecasted by observed prison behavior. The failure of many prison programs to rehabilitate offenders presented a third challenge to indeterminate sentencing[3] and raised "fundamental questions about the wisdom of maintaining a sentencing policy"[4] that lacked evidence demonstrating its effectiveness. A fourth criticism was issued from the political front, where sentencing was perceived as too lenient. Lawmakers believed that judges and parole boards were too soft on crime and argued that prison terms should be tough and fixed in length.[5] Lastly, conservatives criticized the system for failing to control crime, which led to their reexamination of "punishment, deterrence, and incapacitation as justifications for sentencing."[6]

As a solution to these concerns, states began to hand down like sentences for like crimes rather than to impose sentences based on individual history, needs, and circumstances.[7] By shedding previous philosophies of incapacitation and rehabilitation, the courts hope to reduce the disparities between imposed sentence lengths and time served, and to eliminate any potential racial or gender bias in sentencing practices.[8] In doing so, they initiated a wave of punitive sentencing practices that would ultimately reshape sentencing policies across the country.

By 1994, all states had one or more mandatory sentencing laws.[9] Since their adoption, mandatory minimum laws have increased the proportion of drug offenders who are incarcerated and have extended their sentence lengths. Between 1980 and 1992, the probability of receiving a prison term after a drug arrest increased by 447 percent.[10] Between 1985 and 1995, the number of white drug offenders in state prisons increased by 306 percent, and for blacks the number increased 707 percent.[11]

Mandatory sentencing policies have also contributed to the disproportionate increase in females who are incarcerated for drug offenses. Chesney-Lind notes that mandatory sentences can be avoided in certain instances when "the defendant can provide authorities with information that might be useful in the prosecution of other drug offenders."[12] However, this places women at a disadvantage.

> Because women tend to be working at the lowest levels of the drug hierarchy, they are often unable to negotiate plea reductions successfully. Added to this is the ironic fact that it is not uncommon for women arrested for drug crimes to be reluctant to testify against their boyfriends or husbands.[13]

In 1996, the Bureau of Justice Assistance summarized findings of the National Council on Crime and Delinquency's 1996 National Survey of State Sentencing Structures.[14] The survey found that 36 states and the District of Columbia use indeterminate sentencing, all states have a form on mandatory minimum sentencing, most states still retain the use of discretionary parole, and that all but two states (Hawaii and Utah) still grant inmates good time credits.[15] Further, the federal government and nineteen states had developed sentencing commissions. Seventeen states had developed sentencing guidelines, seven of which were voluntary/advisory and the rest presumptive.[16] By the turn of the century, sentencing guidelines had been designed and put into action in eighteen states.[17]

In 1999, Tonry[18] conveyed the state of our country's current sentencing structure in a paper from the Executive Sessions on Sentencing and Corrections entitled *The Fragmentation of Sentencing and Corrections in America*. Tonry described the ramifications of our country's "experiment with sentencing guidelines,"[19] and outlined numerous sentencing practices that are currently used throughout the country. Presently, sentencing policies vary per state, and though many have experimented with alternative sentencing practices, our country has adopted a harsh, "tough on crime" outlook on sentencing.

Recently, as Donziger[20] notes, women have been disproportionately subjected to some of the harshest and most punitive criminal sentencing policies ever implemented over the past century. The recent trend in draconian laws that were designed to deter and incapacitate criminals or would-be criminals has nearly tripled the number of women incarcerated for drug offenses. Chesney-Lind[21] reports that during the 1990s, the female prison population increased by 110 percent, whereas the male prison population grew by only 77 percent. Furthermore, the current rate at which women are being sentenced to prison exceeds the rate at which they are arrested, suggesting a vast change in our society's response to offenses committed by women. Chesney-Lind suggests that the growth in women's incarceration rates and their sentence lengths within the federal system stems not only from the harsh nature of current sentencing policies, but from federal judges' inability to depart from federal sentencing guidelines and "increased policing of women's behavior while on probation or parole."[22]

A major question in the study of women in crime is whether the courts treat women differently than they do men. Much of the data collected for the 1980s and 1990s is examined from that perspective. There also have been some procedural changes in the treatment of women. For example, statutes such as the indeterminate sentence for women no longer exist. Also, the procedure whereby a woman's minimum sentence was decided by a parole board in a closed session at which she was not represented by counsel (in contrast to the situation of men, whose minimum sentence has always been determined by a judge at an open hearing and in the presence of counsel) has been abandoned.

As suggested in chapter 1, two schools of thought prevail or prevailed until the last decade on how women defendants are treated at the bar of justice. Most observers believed that women received preferential treatment, which in operational terms means that they were less likely than men to be convicted for the same type of offense; if they are convicted, they are less likely to be sentenced; and if they are sentenced, they are likely to receive milder sentences. The factors thought to motivate judges toward leniency are chivalry and naivete. For example, judges often said that they could not help but compare a woman defendant with other women whom they know well—namely, their mothers and wives—and whom they cannot imagine behaving in the manner attributed to the defendant. Practicality also is thought to be a main consideration. Most of the female defendants have young children, and sending the women to prison is thought to place a great burden on the rest of the society.

Paternalism is a particular manifestation of the preferential treatment toward women that many attribute to trial court judges. Nagel and Weitzman[23] assert that paternalistic behavior has favorable as well as unfavorable consequences for women defendants. The favorable consequences are that women are less likely than men to remain in custody during the pretrial period. Once tried, they are less likely to be convicted; if convicted, they are likely to receive milder sentences. The unfavorable consequences are that women are less likely to have an attorney, a preliminary hearing, or a jury trial.

Using data originally collected by Silverstein (1965) in a national survey of the defense of the poor, Nagel and Weitzman[24] compared the treatment that men and women charged with assault and larceny received in the courts. Their results are shown in table 5.1. On the basis of these data, Nagel and Weitzman concluded that paternalism prevails almost equally for both types of offenses, except that women are more likely to be jailed in assault cases than in larceny cases. They attribute the different treatment of men and women in assault cases to the fact that assault is a more manly type of crime and that women who commit it pay the price for their behavior by being treated more like men.

The other view about how women fared at the bar of justice was that judges were more punitive toward women. They were more likely to throw the book at a female defendant because they believed that there was a greater discrepancy between her behavior and the behavior expected of a woman than there was between the behavior of a male defendant and the behavior expected of a man. In other words, women defendants pay for the judges' belief that it is more in a man's nature to commit crimes than it is in a woman's nature. Thus, it was maintained, when a judge was convinced that the woman before him has committed a crime, he was more likely to overreact and punish her not only for the specific offense but also for transgressing against his expectations of womanly behavior.

In the past, the existence of statutes, such as the indeterminate sentence for women and the sanctioning of a procedure whereby only convicted male defendants had their minimum sentence determined by a judge at an open hearing and in the presence of counsel, were cited as evidence of the unfair, punitive treatment accorded women in the court. In an article titled "Discriminatory

Table 5.1. How the Treatment of Female Defendants in Criminal Cases Differs from That of Male Defendants[a]

Case Type and Treatment Stage	Number of Defendants with Available Information		Percent Receiving Treatment		Difference in Percentage Points	Does Paternalism Hypothesis Seem to Be Confirmed?
	Females	Males	Females	Males		
I. Grand Larceny Cases						
A. Being Jailed						
1. Released on bail	63	771	76	50	25	Yes
2. Had less than two months' delay (of those awaiting trial in jail)	10	231	60	67	X	Too few women not released on bail
3. Case dismissed or acquitted	71	841	24	13	11	Yes
4. Received suspended sentence or probation (of those convicted)	47	656	64	43	21	Yes
5. Received less than one year imprisonment (of those imprisoned)	9	241	33	45	X	Too few women
B. Formal Safeguards						
1. Received preliminary hearing	42	606	57	55	2	Difference too small
2. Had or given a lawyer	61	781	90	87	3	Difference too small
3. Received a jury trial (of those tried)	18	283	47	31	X	Too few women

(continued)

Table 5.1. How the Treatment of Female Defendants in Criminal Cases Differs from That of Male Defendants (*continued*)

Case Type and Treatment Stage	Number of Defendants with Available Information		Percent Receiving Treatment		Difference in Percentage Points	Does Paternalism Hypothesis Seem to Be Confirmed?
	Females	*Males*	*Females*	*Males*		
II. Felonious assault cases						
A. Being Jailed						
1. Released on bail	43	615	77	58	19	Yes
2. Had less than two months' delay (of those awaiting trial in jail)	6	152	17	49	X	Too few women released on bail
3. Case dismissed or acquitted	45	638	36	23	13	Yes
4. Received suspended sentence or probation (of those convicted)	25	415	44	36	8	Yes
5. Received less than one year imprisonment (of those imprisoned)	9	172	89	57	X	Too few women imprisoned
B. Formal Safeguards						
1. Received preliminary hearing	31	451	74	73	1	Difference too small
2. Had or given a lawyer	42	620	88	89	1	Difference too small
3. Received a jury trial (of those tried)	24	262	19	45	26	Yes

Source: Adapted from Nagel and Weitzman 1971.

[a] Based on 1,103 grand larceny cases and 843 felonious assault cases from all fifty states for 1962.

Sentencing of Women Offenders," Temen[25] argued for passage of the ERA on the ground that it would make null and void all existing statutes that prescribed longer sentences for female offenders and that permitted only females to receive an indeterminate sentence.[26]

The 1967 opinion of the Superior Court of Pennsylvania on the matter of indeterminate sentences for women[27] is worth noting:

> This court is of the opinion that the legislature reasonably could have concluded that indeterminate sentences should be imposed on women as a class, allowing the time of incarceration to be matched to the necessary treatment in order to provide more effective rehabilitation. Such a conclusion could be based on the physiological and psychological make-up of women, the type of crime committed by women, the relation to the criminal world, their role in society, their unique vocational skills and their reaction as a class to imprisonment, as well as the number and types of women who are sentenced to imprisonment rather than given suspended sentence.

When the Pennsylvania Supreme Court overruled the lower court's decision, it stated, "While legislative classification on the basis of sex alone did not violate the equal protection clause, it [the court] could find no reasonable justification for a statute which imposed longer sentences on women than on men convicted of the same crime."[28] The Pennsylvania legislature responded by enacting a law that in essence provided for another type of indeterminate sentence for women. The law stated that only men would have their minimum sentence determined by the court. This procedure entitled a male offender to have his minimum sentence set by a judge at an open hearing during which representation by counsel was constitutionally mandated. A woman's minimum sentence was decided by a parole board during a closed session at which she had no representation or any procedural rights.

The Supreme Court of Pennsylvania declared the act unconstitutional under the state's equal rights amendment and the equal protection clause of the U.S. Constitution. The court also stated that under the reasoning of *Commonwealth v. Daniel*, gender-based discrimination in parole eligibility was not permissible.[29]

In 1973, Debra Anthony conducted twenty-three interviews with judges in Chicago, St. Louis, Milwaukee, and Indianapolis on their experiences with female offenders. She concluded:

> More than half of the Judges said that they do treat women more leniently and more gently than they do men; that they are more inclined to recommend probation rather than imprisonment; and if they sentence a woman, it is usually for a shorter time than if the crime had been committed by a man. Only a small proportion of the Judges said that they were less likely to convict the women. The

point at which they differentiate in favor of the woman is at the time of passing sentence.[30]

Simon and Sharma's 1979 study of criminal processing in Washington, D.C., found little evidence of gender effects on court decisions to dismiss a case, to adjudicate, or to incarcerate.[31] These findings were supported by Kempinen's[32] study of sentencing decisions in Philadelphia during the 1970s, which found no evidence of gender-based leniency. In a more recent study of criminal processing in Honolulu, Ghali and Chesney-Lind[33] found that arrested females were more likely than arrested males to be prosecuted and that women were more likely than men to enter a guilty plea for less serious offenses. In later decisions, at the district court level (less severe cases), the findings supported those of Simon and Sharma.[34] No evidence of a gender effect on the court's pretrial dismissal, adjudication, or sentencing decisions was found. At the circuit court level (felonies), there was no evidence of a gender effect on the court's adjudication decisions, but there was an effect on sentencing. Controlling for legal and social characteristics, females were more likely than males to receive probation.

In 1988, Angela Musolino interviewed twelve judges in the Washington, D.C., metropolitan area and reported that, with one exception, all of them tended "to treat women more gently than they do men."[35] The reasons cited were the responsibility that the women had for the rearing of young children and the way the judges were taught to view women. In the words of one jurist, "I am more lenient toward women, and I've just not been able to grasp why that is, except I love my mother very much."[36] Another observed, "I don't think there's any rational or objective thought about it, but there's a feeling that incarceration for a woman is far more degrading than for a man, and you'll never see them (women) back because they'll do everything they can to keep from going back."[37] Musolino concluded that chivalry, or the theory of preferential treatment for women, received a lot of support at the sentencing stage but not in the determination of guilt or innocence.

In addition to findings about more or less severe punishments, some data suggest that courts differentially invoke legal and extralegal variables in determining punishments among male and female defendants.[38] For example, Nagel et al.[39] found that offense severity was the most important influence on the sentencing of male offenders but that it was not significant in the sentencing of women. In contrast, being married strongly influenced the probability of a woman's being sentenced to prison but had little effect on the decision to incarcerate a man.[40]

As we might expect, findings of preferential or even differential treatment of female offenders are not without qualifications. As with police arrest decisions, chivalry in the courts is not universal but has been found to be applied selectively within samples of female offenders. For example, in Kruttschnitt's tests of Black's[41] propositions regarding the behavior of law, she found that women who were "more respectable" and economically better off, as well as women who were more economically dependent (and thus subject to more informal social control), received the least severe court sanctions.[42] Similarly, several studies have found that family composition has a significant effect on the sentencing of female offenders.[43] Married women tended to receive less severe punishments than their single sisters, and women with children were less severely punished than their childless counterparts.

Research by Daly[44] suggests that differences in court sanctioning, both within and between gender groupings, are most dependent on the family status of defendants. In a statistical analysis of court outcomes, she found no evidence of gender-based sentencing disparities among "nonfamilied" men and women, both of whom were sentenced more severely than their "familied" counterparts. In interviews with sentencing judges, she discovered that differentials in sentencing of familied men and women hinged not on judicial chivalry or paternalism, but rather on judicial concern for the care of dependent children:

> The judges' responses suggest that there are concentric circles of judicial protection of children and families that radiate from a central focus on the welfare of children. Effective care-giving labor is the first ring, and economic support, the second. Simultaneously, extant gender divisions of labor place women in the first ring, and men in the second. Therefore, the good family women were viewed as more critical for the maintenance of family life, and the social costs of jailing the family women were seen to be greater.[45]

Daly's findings go beyond the conclusions of other studies of judicial decision making by suggesting that chivalry, or even paternalism, is an inappropriate characterization of the motivational basis for gender differences in the dispensation of courtroom justice. Again, we are directed to consider a female offender's status and role vis-à-vis her family life, as it continues to differ from that of her male counterpart, when examining the factors that propel her into, or shield her from, inclusion in official crime statistics. In doing so, we must again be cautious of theorizing about the universal woman. Given what we know about female prison populations—that they disproportionately comprise poor and minority women, the majority of whom are mothers—we must consider carefully the implications of such findings and wonder about the validity with which judges determine the good family woman from the bad one.[46]

The remainder of this chapter focuses on data that describe rates of convictions and types of sentences received by men and women who are accused of having committed the same type of offense.

One source of court data is the Administrative Office of the United States Courts, which, since 1963, has published an annual report that describes how defendants are disposed of in the eighty-nine U.S. district courts. These reports contain statistics that describe the proportion of men and women convicted by category of offense.

The following offense categories are included in these reports:

Class I: Fraud, embezzlement, and obscene mail
Class II: Income tax fraud and other fraud
Class III: Liquor and Internal Revenue Service violations
Class IV: Theft, postal fraud, and forgery
Class V: Assault, homicide, border registration of addicts and narcotics violators, and miscellaneous general offenses
Class VI: Counterfeiting, burglary, interstate transportation of stolen property, violations of the Selective Service Act and other national defense laws, and sex offenses
Class VII: Auto theft
Class VIII: Narcotics violations and robbery

As noted in the first edition of this book, the limitations of these data should be obvious, especially after reading the descriptions of the offense categories upon which the statistics are based. Most defendants in the United States, be they males or females, are tried in state courts because they have broken a state law. Thus, the offenses listed represent only a small proportion of all criminal trials.

But one purpose these federal statistics serve is in the comparison of longitudinal trends—that is, the proportions of females who have been convicted in the federal courts from 1963 through 2000. Table 5.2 describes the number and proportion of female defendants who were convicted each year for all of the offense categories combined. Note that from 1980 on, the percentage of females convicted leveled off to about 17 percent, with no sharp increase or decline in the last twenty years.

Table 5.3 compares the proportion of convictions of women in selective offense categories between 1964 and 2000. The offense for which the highest proportion of women were convicted was embezzlement. In 2000, 14.6 percent of all federal convictions were women (see table 5.2), and from 1980 on, women accounted for 45 percent or more of all embezzlement convictions in the federal courts (see table 5.3). While women were not nearly as visible in other white-collar and property offenses, they made up a greater share of federal offenders convicted of larceny/theft and forgery than they did of those convicted of robbery, assault and homicide, and drug law violations. Consistent with the arrest data, these are the types of offenses most congruent with

Table 5.2.   Number of Males and Females Convicted and Percentage of Females among Convictions in Eighty-nine U.S. District Courts: 1963–2000

Year	Males Convicted	Females Convicted	Percent Female
1963	26,914	2,086	7.0
1964	26,228	2,080	7.1
1965	25,975	1,957	6.8
1966	24,528	1,975	7.2
1967	23,766	1,805	6.7
1968	23,069	2,033	7.9
1969	24,060	2,109	7.9
1970	25,203	2,382	8.5
1971	28,581	2,931	9.1
1972	35,160	3,788	9.7
1973	33,126	3,632	9.9
1974	32,643	3,470	9.6
1979	29,248	3,536	10.8
1980	15,961	3,309	17.2
1981	17,892	3,125	14.9
1982	21,702	3,955	15.4
1983	25,398	4,980	16.4
1984	23,651	4,902	17.2
1985	18,795	3,945	17.3
1986	25,202	4,977	16.5
1987	27,277	5,668	17.2
1993	35,649	6,368	15.2
1994	34,291	6,230	15.4
1995	31,777	5,492	14.7
1996	37,747	7,011	15.7
1997	42,116	7,445	15.0
1998	44,900	8,082	15.3
1999	48,092	8,844	15.5
2000	51,674	8,820	14.6
Overall Rate of Change:			
1963–2000	0.93	3.23	1.09
1970–2000	1.05	2.70	71.80
1980–2000	2.24	1.67	–0.15

Sources: 1963–1987 Data: Adapted from *Federal Offenders in the U.S. District Courts* (Washington, D.C.: Administration Office of the U.S. Courts, 1963–1974; 1976–1987); 1993–2000 Data: *Compendium of Federal Justice Statistics,* Table 3.3, pg. 45, chpt. 3 (1999); Table 3.4, pg. 44, chpt. 3 (1994), Table 3.5, pg. 45, chpt. 3 (1995); Tables 3.5, pgs. 45, chpts. 3 (1996, 1997); Table 4.5, pg. 57, chpt. 4 (1998), Tables 4.5, pgs. 59, chpts. 4 (1999, 2000).

the theory that as more women enter the labor force and assume positions of trust and authority, female crime rates will increase, especially for embezzlement, fraud, forgery, and theft.

The figures in table 5.4 show that among those convicted of felonies in state courts, the percentage who are female has steadily risen since 1992. In

Table 5.3. Percentage of Females among Convictions by Specific Offense Categories in Eighty-nine U.S. District Courts: 1964–2000

	1964		1965		1966		1967		1968		1969	
	Total	% Female	Total	% Female	Total	% Female	Total	% Female	Total	% Female	Total	% Female
Class 1												
Fraud	666	12.4	515	16.7	555	18.9	300	18.7	250	26.4	257	21.8
Embezzlement	1,231	20.7	1,207	19.7	1,148	21	1,220	24.5	1,231	24.6	1,421	26.4
Class IV												
Theft [a]	2,418	10.5	2,256	10.8	2,223	9.7	2,137	8.9	2,282	10.6	2,281	9.8
Forgery [b]	1,517	22.4	2,117	12.9	1,958	23.5	1,642	24.1	1,787	24.5	1,441	25.3
Class V												
Assault and Homicide	333	8.6	214	8.4	254	2.8	914	12.9	953	9.4	354	7.1
Class VIII												
Narcotics	919	10.6	1,116	10	1,052	11.7	914	12.9	953	9.4	1,007	11.9
Robbery	524	3.4	660	2.0	577	5.5	703	2.6	862	3.8	961	4.0

	1970		1971		1972		1973		1974	
	Total	% Female	Total	% Female	Total	% Female	Total	% Female	Total	% Female
Class 1										
Fraud	236	33.1	235	28.1	2,203	10.8	2,596	9.8	2,859	10.0
Embezzlement	1,602	27.3	1,940	26.7	1,681	29.2	1,480	28.5	1,494	27.8
Class IV										
Larceny and Theft	2,488	10.5	3,088	11.8	3,612	13.5	3,574	16.6	3,280	12.9
Forgery and Counterfeiting	1,741	26.3	2,042	27.1	4,429	20.8	3,985	19.4	4,118	20.1
Class V										
Assault and Homicide	390	7.4	364	6.0	712	8.3	741	9.4	580	9.3
Class VIII										
Narcotics	919	10.9	1,158	11.3	5,910	10.8	8,538	8.9	8,246	8.6
Robbery	1,002	3.4	1,359	5.3	5,789	9.8	5,669	9.9	4,833	10.3

	1979		1980		1981		1982		1983	
	Total	% Female	Total	% Female	Total	% Female	Total	% Female	Total	% Female
Class 1										
Fraud	5,149	13	3,667	18.0	3,853	16.5	4,409	19.5	4,991	19.6
Embezzlement	1,652	31.7	1,159	45.5	1,464	44.7	1,878	44.3	1,936	49.0
Class IV										
Larceny and Theft	3,919	16.7	2,360	22.3	2,393	16.8	2,479	20	3,295	20.5
Forgery and Counterfeiting	2,712	21.2	1,633	24.4	1,548	21.5	1,798	23.6	2,348	25.0
Class V										
Assault and Homicide	529	6	388	8.0	455	10.3	449	10.2	522	9.0
Class VIII										
Narcotics	5,067	8.7	3,824	12.7	4,361	11.7	3,563	12.6	4,396	12.3
Robbery	5,149	13.8	3,288	17.7	3,492	13.1	1,367	5.3	1,333	6.0

	1984		1985		1986		1987	
	Total	% Female	Total	% Female	Total	% Female	Total	% Female
Class 1								
Fraud	5,131	20.8	4,081	19.5	5,304	19.1	6,143	19.7
Embezzlement	1,688	49.4	1,366	51.0	1,711	49.0	1,923	48.7
Class IV								
Larceny and Theft	3,140	23.9	2,331	23.6	2,632	23.4	2,496	24
Forgery and Counterfeiting	1,993	26.7	1,590	26.2	1,997	27.0	1,858	28.5
Class V								
Assault and Homicide	472	10.6	377	11.4	385	9.4	452	8.8
Class VIII								
Narcotics	4,837	12.8	4,523	14.4	7,189	14.0	8,640	15.2
Robbery	1,220	6.1	4,523	6.9	994	4.9	988	5.7

(continued)

Table 5.3. Percentage of Females among Convictions by Specific Offense Categories in Eighty-nine U.S. District Courts: 1964–2000 (continued)

	2000[c]	
	Total	% Female
Fraud	6,273	25.6
Embezzlement	940	58.0
Larceny	2,411	35.1
Auto Theft	221	35.1
Forgery and Counterfeiting	1,313	22.4
Assault	471	10.0
Murder	78	7.7
Arson	71	4.2
Drug Trafficking	23,220	13.1
Robbery	1,721	6.6

Sources: Adapted from *Federal Offenders in the U.S. District Courts* (Washington, D.C.: Administration Office of the U.S. Courts, 1964–1974; 1979–1987); *2000 Sourcebook of Federal Sentencing Statistics*, (Washington, D.C.: U.S. Sentencing Commission, 2001), table 5.26, pg. 428.

[a] From 1964 to 1971, this category was labeled "Theft"; in 1972, it was labeled "Larceny"; in 1973, it was labeled "Larceny and theft."
[b] From 1964 to 1971, this category was labeled, "Forgery"; from 1972 on, it was labeled "Forgery and counterfeiting."
[c] Data for 2000 include offenders who were sentenced in U.S. District Courts under the U.S. Sentencing Commission.

Table 5.4. Felony Convictions of Women in State Courts (as percent of total)

	1992		1994		1996		1998		2000	
	Percent Female	Percent Male	Percent Female	Percent Male	Percent Female	Percent Male	Percent Female	Percent Male	Percent Female	Percent Male
All Offenses	13	87	15	85	16	84	17	83	17	83
Violent Offenses	7	93	8	92	8	92	10	90	10	90
Murder	10	90	11	89	9	91	8	92	9	91
Sexual Assault/Rape [a]	2	98	3	97	1	99	3	97	2	98
Robbery	6	94	6	94	7	93	8	92	7	93
Aggravated Assault	10	90	11	89	11	89	14	86	14	86
Other violent	7	93	11	89	10	90	11	89	11	89
Property Offenses	17	83	19	81	23	77	25	75	25	75
Burglary	5	95	7	93	7	93	8	92	8	92
Larceny	19	81	20	80	23	77	24	76	25	75
Fraud	38	62	39	61	41	59	42	58	41	59
Drug Offenses	15	85	17	83	17	83	18	82	17	83
Possession	17	83	19	81	19	81	21	79	19	81
Trafficking	14	86	16	84	16	84	16	84	16	84
Weapon Offenses	4	96	5	95	4	96	6	94	5	95
Other Offenses	10	90	13	87	11	89	12	88	12	88

Sources: Bureau of Justice Statistics, Felony Convictions in State Courts, Table 5 (2000, 1998, 1996, 1994, 1992).

Table 5.5. Adjudication of Most Serious Arrest Charge by Type and as Percent within Defendant's Sex Cohort: 1990–1998

Most Serious Arrest Charge	1990						1992					
	Plea Bargain		Acquittal		Guilty		Plea Bargain		Acquittal		Guilty	
	Male	Female	Male	Female	Male	Female	Male	Female	Male	Female	Male	Female
Murder	26.3	16.7	6.3	16.7	67.5	66.7	22.6	23.1	6.3	16.7	67.5	66.7
Rape	44.0	66.7	2.9	x	53.1	33.3	37.9	x	2.9	x	53.1	33.3
Robbery	40	43.2	0.8	1.2	59.3	55.6	34.1	35.9	0.8	1.2	59.3	55.6
Assault	50.1	58.2	2.0	3.3	48	38.5	44.2	52.9	2.0	3.3	48	38.5
Other violent	30.7	42.1	1.9	x	67.5	57.9	34	39.1	1.9	x	67.5	57.9
Burglary	28.1	33.3	1.1	1.2	70.8	65.4	23.7	26.9	1.1	1.2	70.8	65.4
Theft	30.0	31.7	0.6	0.7	69.4	67.6	28.1	31.4	0.6	0.7	69.4	67.6
Other property	38.3	33.3	1.6	1.9	60.1	64.7	32.3	33.9	1.6	1.9	60.1	64.7
Drug trafficking	21.7	22.8	1.2	0.3	77.2	76.9	20.3	26.8	1.2	0.3	77.2	76.9
Other drug	38.1	45.3	0.7	1.1	61.2	53.6	36.0	38.5	0.7	1.1	61.2	53.6
Weapons	39.3	38.5	1.6	7.7	59.1	53.8	26.5	47.6	1.6	7.7	59.1	53.8
Driving-related	15.5	31.3	0.9	x	83.6	68.8	9.8	47.8	0.9	x	83.6	68.8
Other public-order	31.7	15.4	2.2	x	66.1	84.6	31.6	29.9	2.2	x	66.1	84.6

Most Serious Arrest Charge	1994						1996					
	Plea Bargain		Acquittal		Guilty		Plea Bargain		Acquittal		Guilty	
	Male	Female	Male	Female	Male	Female	Male	Female	Male	Female	Male	Female
Murder	25.0	20.0	4.2	x	70.8	80.0	28.6	x	6.1	x	65.3	100.0
Rape	29.7	50.0	31.1	x	67.2	50.0	37.1	x	0.6	x	62.4	x
Robbery	33.3	44.7	1.1	1.3	65.6	53.9	28.1	24.6	1.1	1.6	70.8	73.8
Assault	41.3	51.7	2.7	2.6	56	45.7	41.8	56.9	2.4	2.3	55.8	40.8

(continued)

Table 5.5. Adjudication of Most Serious Arrest Charge by Type and as Percent within Defendant's Sex Cohort: 1990–1998 (continued)

Most Serious Arrest Charge	1994 Plea Bargain		1994 Acquittal		1994 Guilty		1996 Plea Bargain		1996 Acquittal		1996 Guilty	
	Male	Female	Male	Female	Male	Female	Male	Female	Male	Female	Male	Female
Other violent	28.7	30.2	1.9	1.9	69.4	67.9	32.2	42	1.9	1.4	65.9	56.5
Burglary	21.8	33.7	0.5	2.1	77.7	64.2	21.9	25.3	1.8	x	76.4	74.7
Theft	22.9	22	0.8	0.6	76.3	77.4	29.2	27.4	1.4	0.5	69.4	72.0
Other property	25.5	22.2	0.7	x	73.8	77.8	31.0	24	0.3	x	68.7	76.0
Drug trafficking	18.5	19.2	0.8	0.3	80.7	80.5	20.2	24.6	0.9	0.5	79	74.9
Other drug	29.0	28.9	1.1	0.6	69.9	70.5	30.0	31.8	1.0	0.2	68.9	67.9
Weapons	23.5	50.0	1.6	x	74.9	50.0	23.4	41.2	1.7	x	74.9	58.8
Driving-related	12.2	20.0	0.3	x	87.4	80.0	18.5	25	1.3	x	80.2	75.0
Other public-order	26.8	26.5	0.4	2	72.8	71.4	30.4	32.2	1.2	x	68.4	67.8

1998

Offense	Pleaded Guilty		Dismissed/Acquitted		Found Guilty	
	Male	Female	Male	Female	Male	Female
All felonies	66	66	30	31	5	2
Violent felonies	55	45	38	52	7	3
Property felonies	67	73	28	25	4	2
Drug felonies	70	70	26	28	4	2

Source: National Consortium of State Court Data; Women Offenders, *Bureau of Justice Statistics*.

2000, 17 percent of all felony convictions in state courts were women, a 4 percent increase since 1992. Many of these increases can be seen among those convicted of property offenses. In 1992, women accounted for 17 percent of felony convictions for property offenses; by 2000, this figure rose to 25 percent.

Beginning in 1986, when comprehensive state court data became available via the Bureau of Justice Statistics (BJS) and the Sourcebook of Criminal Justice Statistics, we can compare the percentages of men and women whose cases were dismissed, who were found not guilty and who pleaded or were found guilty of the most serious charge for which they were arrested. Table 5.4 compares the percentage of men and women who were convicted of violent, property, drug, and other offenses from 1992 through 2000. The percentage remained relatively stable over the ten year period. Women were most likely to be convicted of fraud and larceny.

Between 1990 and 1996, men are more likely to be found or plead guilty to the violent charge for which they were arrested than women. In a few of the years women were more likely to be found or plead guilty to property charges other than theft and burglary. But for all the years the differences in outcomes for men and women are small. For example, a difference of 13 percent is the biggest difference for all crimes except the use of weapons but for that offense the number of women charged is very small (i.e., less than twenty for all the years).

Overall, these data support the impressions gained from interviews with judges, who maintain that justice is blind, or almost so, in determining the guilt or innocence of men and women. In chapter 6, we discuss the number of women in state and federal prisons, some of their demographic characteristics and the conditions in the prisons and the opportunities for occupational training and educational enhancement.

NOTES

1. Walker 1993: 115.
2. Morval 1993: 306.
3. Tonry 1999a.
4. Forst 1995: 376.
5. Morris 1993.
6. Walker 1993: 115
7. Tonry 1999b.
8. Ibid.
9. U.S. Dept. of Justice Bureau of Justice Statistics 1998. "1996 National Survey of State Sentencing Structures."

10. Mauer 1999.
11. Mauer 1999: 151–152
12. Chesney-Lind 2002: 89.
13. ibid.: 89.
14. U.S. Bureau of Justice Assistance 1998.
15. ibid.: 4.
16. ibid.: 4–5.
17. Lubitz and Ross 2001: 2.
18. Tonry 1999a.
19. Lubitz and Ross 2001: 1.
20. Donziger 1996.
21. Chesney-Lind 2002.
22. ibid.: 91.
23. Nagel and Weitzman 1971.
24. Ibid.
25. Temen 1973.
26. See, for example, *State v. Heitman*, 105 Kan. 139, 181 p. 630 (1919); *Ex parte Dankerton*, 104 Kan. 481, 179 p. 347 (1919); *Platt v. Commonwealth*, 256 Mass. 539, 152 N.E. 914 (1926); *Ex parte Gosselin*, 141 Me. 412, 44 A. 2d 882 (1945), cert. denied sub nom. Gosselin v. Kelley, 328 U.S. 817 (1946); *Ex parte Brady*, 116 Ohio St. 512, 157 N.E. 69 (1927). These cases upheld discriminatory sentencing acts against constitutional challenges.
27. *Commonwealth v. Daniel*, 210 Pa. Super. 156, 167, 232 A2d 247, 253, (1967).
28. 430 Pa. at 649, 243, A2d. at 403.
29. 458 Pa. 299, 328, A.2d 857.
30. Anthony 1973: 51–52.
31. Simon and Sharma 1979.
32. Kempinen 1983.
33. Ghali and Chesney-Lind 1986.
34. Simon and Sharma 1979.
35. Musolino 1988: 15.
36. ibid.: 16.
37. ibid.: 16.
38. Fenster 1977; Nagel et al. 1982; Kruttschnitt 1984.
39. Nagel et al. 1982.
40. See also Fenster 1977; Farrington and Morris 1983.
41. Black 1976.
42. Kruttschnitt 1980–1981, 1982.
43. Fenster 1977; Nagel et al. 1982; Kruttschnitt 1984; Daly 1987.
44. Daly 1989a, 1989b.
45. Daly 1989b: 19.
46. Indeed, Glick and Neto's (1977) study of female prison populations and Lewis and Bressler's (1981) study of the San Francisco jail populations revealed that "black women inmates were far more likely to be living with and responsible for their children than white inmates" (Lewis 1981: 97).

Chapter Six

Women in Prison

In the 1960s, women in prison were referred to as the forgotten offenders by those who wanted to call attention to their plight and to bring about changes in their situation. Part of the reason for the lack of interest in female inmates is that there were so few of them. In 2000, about 22 out of 100 persons arrested for a serious crime were women. In the same year, about 10 out of 100 persons convicted of a serious crime were women, and 6.6 out of every 100 persons sentenced to a federal or state prison were women. In 2001, 93,031 women and 1,259,481 men were in state and federal prisons. Men are about 15 times more likely than women to be incarcerated in state and federal prison. At the present time, there are 6 federal institutions for women, 84 for men, and 13 jails that house both men and women. There are 51 state institutions for women, 536 for men, and 19 that are coed.

Another reason for the lack of interest in female inmates is that the inmates themselves have called so little attention to their situation. Prison reforms—and, indeed, public and official interest in prisoners—are strongly influenced by the amount of disruption and violence that occur inside prisons. Prisoners are likely to receive attention only if they riot, destroy property, endanger the lives of guards and fellow inmates, and submit a list of demands for reforming the institution. Following such activities, the public demands an investigation, the governor appoints a blue-ribbon fact-finding commission, and prison officials acknowledge that reforms may be needed and are likely to be made. During the 1960s and 1970s, a number of serious prison riots occurred in large federal and state institutions. But throughout this period, the number of women's institutions that engaged in such behavior was practically nil, and the amount of publicity and interest that such institutions received was proportionate to their failure to call attention to themselves. The 1980s showed no deviation from this pattern among female inmates.

A third reason for the lack of interest in women prisoners is that the crimes women commit usually inconvenience society less than the crimes that men commit. The overwhelming majority of women offenders have not been involved in organized crime, in crimes involving high losses of property, or in crimes that endangered large numbers of people.

Since the 1990s, more attention has been drawn toward women's encounters with the criminal justice system. Over the past two decades, the backlash of the wars waged against drugs and crime can be observed in our growing female prison populations and in the draconian sentencing laws that have brought forth this mass incarceration. Women are no longer the "forgotten offenders" of the 1960s, and although they still make up a small proportion of our country's prison population, their situations and needs are eliciting more attention from prison administrators, prisoner's rights organizations, lawmakers, and researchers.

The number of prisons designed to house women has increased rapidly. While only two new women's prisons were built during the 1940s, the 1980s ushered in an additional thirty-four prisons for women.[1] Still, the proportion of female to male prisons remains small, and convicted women are often uprooted from their communities and incarcerated far from their children. In addition, Richie[2] estimates that approximately 75 percent of women in prison have children, many of whom are relinquished into the custody of the foster care system.

WHO ARE THE WOMEN IN PRISONS?

Table 6.1 shows the percentage of women and men who were sentenced to all the federal and state institutions for selected years from 1971 to 2001. Note that over a period of three decades, the percentage of women in federal prisons ranged from 3.7 to 6.9 percent. In state prisons, in which the bulk of prisoners are housed, the percentage of women changed only by 40 percent. These data show that the rate of commitment to prison did not keep up with the rate of female arrests from 1963 to 2001 (that is, an increase in arrests for serious crimes from 11.7 percent in 1963 to 26.7 percent in 2001). In other words, although a higher percent of women were arrested for serious crimes, the rate at which they were sentenced to state prisons remained somewhat stable, while the rate at which they were sentenced to federal prisons increased by 89 percent.

Going back even further to 1925 (table 6.2), we see that between 1925 and 1979, the aggregate female incarceration rate ranged from 6 to 10 per 100,000 female population compared to the male range of 149 to 264 per 100,000 male population. From 1979 to 2001, there was an increase in the

Table 6.1. Females as a Percentage of All Sentenced Prisoners by Type of Institution: 1971–2001

Year	Number of Sentenced Prisoners in State and Federal Prisons [a]	Percent Female [b]	Percent Female in Federal Institutions [c]	Percent Female in State Institutions [d]
1971	198,061	3.2	3.7	4.7
1972	196,183	3.2	3.7	3.1
1973	204,349	3.3	4.1	3.1
1974	229,721	3.5	4.4	6.2
1975	253,816	3.8	4.6	6.4
1976	262,833	3.8	5.4	3.8
1977	300,024	4.10	5.90	3.70
1978	306,602	4.2	6.2	3.9
1979	314,006	4.2	5.9	3.9
1980	329,821	4.1	5.8	4.0
1981	369,930	4.2	5.6	3.9
1982	413,806	4.3	5.5	4.2
1983	436,855	4.4	5.5	4.3
1984	462,002	4.5	5.8	4.4
1985	502,507	4.6	6.0	4.5
1986	544,972	4.9	6.4	4.7
1987	585,084	5.0	6.3	4.8
1988	603,732	5.0	x	x
1989	680,907	5.5	x	x
1990	773,919	5.7	7.6	5.5
1991	789,610	5.5	x	x
1992	846,277	5.5	x	x
1993	932,074	5.8	x	x
1994	1,054,702	6.11	7.51	5.97
1995	1,125,874	6.1	7.38	5.95
1996	1,183,368	6.32	7.3	6.22
1997	1,242,153	6.41	7.35	6.32
1998	1,300,573	6.49	7.47	6.39
1999	1,363,701	6.64	7.33	6.57
2000	1,391,261	6.6	7.05	6.66
2001	1,406,031	6.6	6.99	6.57
Overall rate of change 1971–2001		1.06	0.89	0.4

Sources: U.S. Department of Justice, Prisoners in State and Federal Institutions; Prisoners 1994, 1995, 1996, 1997, 1998, 1999, 2000, 2001 (Washington, D.C.: Bureau of Justice Statistics), annual; Statistical Abstract of the U.S., Table 324, pg. 202 (2003).

Note: Figures include all inmates sentenced for more than one year.

[a] 1971–1979 Data: *Prisoners in State and Federal Institutions.* 1980–1987, 1990, 1994–2001 Data: *Prisoners 2001, 2000, 1999, 1998, 1997, 1996, 1994.* 1988, 1989, 1991–1993: Data on the total number of sentenced prisoners from the *Statistical Abstract of the U.S.*, 2003.

[b, c, d] 1971–1987 Data: *Prisoners in State and Federal Institutions* 1980–1987, 1990, 1994–2001 Data: *Prisoners 2001, 2000, 1999, 1998, 1997, 1996, 1994.* 1988, 1989, 1991–1993: Data on the percent female from the *Statistical Abstract of the U.S.*, 2003.

Table 6.2.   Prisoners in State and Federal Institutions—Aggregate Incarceration Rates: 1925–2001

Year	Males	Rate	Females	Rate
1925[a]	88,231	149	3,438	6
1926	94,287	157	3,704	6
1927	104,983	173	4,363	7
1928	111,836	182	4,554	8
1929	115,876	187	4,620	8
1930	124,785	200	4,668	8
1931	132,638	211	4,444	7
1932	133,573	211	4,424	7
1933	132,520	209	4,290	7
1934	133,769	209	4,547	7
1935	139,278	217	4,902	8
1936	139,990	217	5,048	8
1937	147,375	227	5,366	8
1938	154,826	236	5,459	8
1939	173,143	263	6,675	10
1940[b]	167,345	252	6,361	10
1941	159,228	239	6,211	9
1942	144,167	217	6,217	9
1943	131,054	202	6,166	9
1944	126,350	200	6,106	9
1945	127,609	193	6,040	9
1946	134,075	191	6,004	8
1947	144,739	202	6,343	9
1948	149,739	205	6,238	8
1949	157,663	211	6,086	8
1950	160,309	211	5,814	8
1951	159,610	208	6,070	8
1952	161,994	208	6,239	8
1953	166,909	211	6,670	8
1954	175,907	218	6,994	8
1955	178,655	217	7,125	8
1956	182,190	218	7,375	9
1957	188,113	221	7,301	8
1958	198,208	229	7,435	8
1959	200,469	228	7,636	8
1960	205,265	230	7,688	8
1961	212,268	234	7,881	8
1962	210,823	229	8,007	8
1963	209,538	225	7,745	8
1964	206,632	219	7,704	8
1965	203,327	213	7,568	8
1966	192,703	201	6,951	7
1967	188,661	195	6,235	6
1968	182,102	187	5,812	6
1969	189,413	192	6,594	6
1970	190,794	191	5,635	5
1971[c]	191,732	189	6,329	6
1972	189,823	185	6,269	6

Table 6.2. (*continued*)

Year	Males	Rate	Females	Rate
1973	197,523	191	6,004	6
1974	211,077	202	7,389	7
1975	231,918	220	8,675	8
1976	252,794	238	10,039	9
1977[d]	267,097	249	11,044	10
1977	274,244	255	11,212	10
1978	282,813	261	11,583	10
1979	289,465	264	12,005	10
1980	303,643	274	12,331	11
1981	339,375	303	14,298	12
1982	379,075	335	16,441	14
1983	401,870	352	17,476	14
1984	426,713	370	19,395	16
1985	460,210	394	21,406	17
1986	497,540	426	24,544	20
1987	533,990	453	26,822	22
1988	573,587	482	30,146	24
1989	643,643	535	37,264	29
1990	699,416	564	44,065	31
1991	745,808	595	43,802	33
1992	799,776	631	46,501	35
1993	878,298	685	53,968	40
1994	990,306	739	64,396	45
1995	1,057,810	781	68,477	47
1996	1,107,109	810	74,811	51
1997	1,161,766	840	79,196	53
1998	1,217,592	885	84,427	57
1999	1,222,799	901	90,668	59
2000	1,298,027	915	93,234	59
2001	1,259,481	896	93,031	58

Sources: Bureau of Justice Statistics, *State and Federal Prisoners, 1925–1985* (Washington, D.C.: U.S. Department of Justice, 1986); *Prisoners in 2001, 2000, 1999; Correctional Populations in 1997, 1995, 1993.*

Note: Incarceration rates are the number of prisoners per 100,000 residential population.

[a] Data for 1925 to 1939 include sentenced prisoners in state and federal prisoners and reformatories whether committed for felonies or misdemeanors.
[b] Data for 1940 to 1970 include all adult felons serving sentences in state and federal institutions.
[c] Data for 1971 to 1987 include all adults and youthful offenders sentenced to state or federal correctional institutions whose maximum sentence was more than a year.
[d] Before 1977, only prisoners in the custody of state and federal correctional systems were counted. After 1977, all prisoners under the jurisdiction of state and federal correctional systems were counted. Figures for both custody and jurisdiction are shown for 1977 to facilitate comparisons.

incarceration rates of both men and women, but the increase for women was substantially greater. From 1990 to 2001 alone, the male rate increased from 564 to 896 per 100,000, while the female rate increased from 33 per 100,000 to 58 per 100,000. Since this book's most recent publication in 1991, the female aggregate incarceration rate increased by 76 percent, whereas the male incarceration rate rose 51 percent.

Table 6.3 shows the type of institution to which men and women are committed at the state and federal levels. Between 1990 and 1995, the number of minimum-security institutions designed to house only females increased from 27 to 48, whereas the number of institutions for males at the same security level only increased from 350 to 366. During the same time period, 159 new institutions were built, 33 of which were for female prisoners only. Note that among male-only and female-only prisons in 1990, about 12 times as many men as women were committed to minimum security prisons, whereas in 1995, there were only 9 times as many men as there were women. Looking at maximum-security prisons, there were 22 times more men than women in 1990, but by 1995 this figure had increased to 30.

Table 6.4 compares the offenses for which men and women were sentenced to all state prisons in 1979 and in 2000. In 2000, women represented a smaller percentage of the violent offenders than they did in 1979: 31.3 percent versus 49 percent. Of the violent offenses, murder and robbery were the most frequently cited offenses for both men and women. In 1979, the second highest crime category for which women were incarcerated was robbery, but in 2000 it was assault. Among the property offenders, women were more likely to be

Table 6.3.   State and Federal Confinement Facilities by Sex of Prisoners Housed, Security Level, and Number of Prisoners: 1990 and 1995

	Confinement Facility					
	1990			*1995*		
Security Level	*Males Only*	*Females Only*	*Both Sexes*	*Males Only*	*Females Only*	*Both Sexes*
Minimum	350	27	23	366	48	26
Medium	338	28	37	388	36	34
Maximum	201	16	17	254	20	24
Total	889	71	77	1,008	104	84

	Number of Prisoners					
	1990			*1995*		
Security Level	*Males Only*	*Total Prisoners Females Only*	*Both Sexes*	*Males Only*	*Total Prisoners Females Only*	*Both Sexes*
Minimum	81,962	6,895	4,149	126,926	13,547	9,622
Medium	307,806	11,294	32,800	423,606	26,821	28,039
Maximum	232,777	9,493	11,394	333,290	11,024	19,458
Total	622,545	27,682	48,343	883,822	51,392	57,119

Sources: Bureau of Justice Statistics, *Census of State and Federal Correctional Facilities, 1995,* Table 10, pg. 7; Table 11, pg. 8.

incarcerated for fraud and larceny; men were more likely to be committed for burglary. While the percent of women and men incarcerated for violent and property crimes decreased between 1979 and 2000, the percent of women incarcerated for drug offenses rose from 10.5 to 32.33, and 6.2 to 10.5 percent for men.

Table 6.4.   Offense Distribution of State and Federal Prison Inmates by Sex: 1979 and 2000

	Percent of State Prison Inmates			
	1979		2000	
	Male	Female	Male	Female
Violent Offenses				
Murder [a]	12.2	15.5	13.11	10.73
Manslaughter	3.8	9.8	1.36	2.36
Rape	4.5	0.4	2.69	0.39
Other sexual assault	2.0	0.3	7.27	1.18
Robbery	25.6	13.6	13.57	6.94
Assault	7.7	7.6	9.84	7.46
Other violent	0.3	0.4	2.16	2.23
Total	53.3	49.0	50.00	31.29
Property Offenses				
Burglary	18.6	5.3	9.54	4.71
Larceny	4.5	11.2	3.53	7.59
Motor vehicle theft	1.5	0.5	1.60	0.92
Fraud	3.8	17.3	2.19	9.95
Other property	0.8	0.4	2.53	1.96
Total	29.2	34.7	19.39	25.13
Drug Offenses	6.2	10.5	20.03	32.33

	Percent of Federal Prison Inmates			
	1979		2000	
	Male	Female	Male	Female
All Offenses			92.8	7.2
Violent offenses			96	4
Property offenses			8	17
Fraud			90.1	9.9
Other			91.6	8.4
Drug Offenses				
Public-order offenses			x	x
Regulatory			88.5	11.5
Other			96.8	3.2

Sources: Prisoners in 2001 (Table 17); Bureau of Justice Statistics, Profile of State Prison Prisoners (Washington, D.C.: U.S. Department of Justice, 1986); Bureau of Justice Statistics, Compendium of Federal Justice Statistics, 2000, Table 7.10.

* Figures do not add up to 100 percent because two offense categories ("public-order offenses" and "other offenses") were excluded from the table.

[a] 2000 figure includes non-negligent manslaughter.

Table 6.5 shows the age and education of prisoners of federal and state correctional institutions for 1991 and 1997, as recorded in the Bureau of Justice Statistic's *Survey of State and Federal Prisoners*. Most noticeable were the increases in education levels of all the prisoners in custody. By 1997, approximately 32 percent of all male prisoners and 30 percent of all females in federal custody had some college education, compared to 27 percent of the males and 29 percent of the females in 1991. Data for state prisoners show a similar pattern. These percentages increased from 13.2 percent of males and 16.8 of all females in 1991, to 14.7 percent of males and 18 percent of females in 1997. In 1997, nearly one-fifth of state prisoners and nearly a quarter of all federal prisoners had graduated from high school.

The age distribution of state and federal prisoners has not changed much over the years, although the highest percent of male and female state prisoners no longer falls in the 30-to-34 age range, but instead falls within the 25-to 29-year-olds. Among the federal prisoners, the percentage of male prisoners within the 25-to-29 age range fell slightly during 1991 and 1997, whereas the percentage within the 30-to-34 age range increased. Among the female prisoners in federal institutions, most fell within the 30-to-34 age range.

INSIDE WOMEN'S PRISONS

Among the one and a half million prisoners incarcerated in state and federal prisons today, only 6.6 percent are women. This small percentage, only a 1.6 percent increase since 1980, continues to influence the conditions of their incarcerations in many crucial ways. Chesney-Lind[3] emphasizes that the effect begins from the moment a woman is sentenced. The sentence she receives is likely to be much lengthier than one she might have received twenty years ago. Chesney-Lind states that in 1991, only 28 percent of women were given probation as sentences. In 1984, a female drug offender would serve an average of 27 months. By 1991, the average sentence length had increased to 67 months. Chesney-Lind describes the situation today:

> Women in conflict with the law have become the hidden victims of our nation's imprisonment binge, and as a consequence women's share of the nation's prison population, measured in either absolute or relative terms, has never been higher. All of this has occurred without serious planning, consideration, or debate. Even more alarming, it appears that the incarceration binge is beginning to spread to the juvenile justice system as well, where stark increases in girls' detention have been observed.[4]

Because there are fewer institutions for females than there are for men, a female drug offender is likely to be sent much farther away from her commu-

Table 6.5. Age and Education of Prisoners in Federal and State Correctional Institutions: 1991 and 1997

	(Percents)							
	1991				1997			
	State		Federal		State		Federal	
	Male	Female	Male	Female	Male	Female	Male	Female
Age (years)								
17 or younger	0.6	0.6	0.0	0.0	0.7	0.1	0.0	0.0
18–24	19.8	10.9	8.9	8.6	21.6	16.3	9.1	11.3
25–29	18.8	17.8	18.5	15.6	24.1	26.1	16.2	19.5
30–34	19.0	25.7	18.2	19.8	21.3	24.2	19.5	20.7
35–39	17.3	22.4	15.7	16.5	14.0	16.6	17.5	19.4
40–44	11.8	11.8	14.8	15.5	8.6	8.9	15.5	11.9
45–49	6.2	6.5	9.8	12.5	4.4	4.0	9.4	8.4
50–54	3.6	2.5	6.3	5.7	2.2	2.1	5.9	3.8
55–59	1.5	1.2	4.6	3.1	1.5	0.9	3.8	3.2
60–64	0.7	0.4	17	1.6	1.0	0.4	2.0	1.1
65 or older	0.7	0.3	1.4	1.1	0.8	0.4	1.1	0.7
Education								
8th grade or less	14	13.2	11.7	11.1	14.4	12.1	11.0	12.0
Some high school	25.4	28.3	14.6	13.8	26.7	19.5	12.0	15.3
G.E.D.	29.0	22.4	24.3	26.3	24.7	20.2	22.6	19.6
High school graduate	18.5	19.3	22.9	20.0	19.5	20.2	22.6	23.0
Any college	13.2	16.8	26.5	28.9	14.7	18.0	31.8	30.1

Source: Adapted from Bureau of Justice Statistics, *Survey of State and Federal Prisoners, 1997:* Table 4.2, pg. 49.

nity than is her male counterpart. Women prisoners thus experience greater difficulty in keeping track of their families and their possessions. In a letter the superintendent at the California Institution for Women characterized the situation as follows:

> Almost all the women who come to prison have husbands and children. If a man goes to prison, the wife stays home and he usually has his family to return to and the household is there when he gets out. But women generally don't have family support from the outside. Very few men are going to sit around and take care of the children and be there when she gets back. So—to send a woman to prison means you are virtually going to disrupt her family. She knows that when she gets out she probably won't have a husband waiting for her. It will really mean starting her life over again.

Richie estimates that about 75 percent of women in prison have children and that nearly 1.5 million children have parents who are incarcerated.[5] She estimates that 120,000 of these children have a mother in prison and that 6 to 10 percent of incarcerated women are pregnant.[6] She describes the "obstacles to parenting"[7] that occur when a parent is incarcerated. Often, the separation is unexpected and fast. When children are able to visit their mothers, they encounter transportation difficulties, visitor hour changes, and financial strains. It is also more difficult for a woman to communicate with her lawyer and to gain access to the parole board.

Hagan and Dinovitzer[8] review the literature that differentiates the consequences of incarcerating women as compared to men. About 90 percent of the children of male prisoners live with their mothers, according to the Bureau of Justice Statistics,[9] but only 25 percent of the children of imprisoned women live with their fathers. When fathers are incarcerated, they can often turn to their child's mother for assistance and support. However, when a mother is incarcerated, she often has fewer resources to turn to and in many cases, the father is not around. Often a family member or friend will care for a child whose mother is in prison, but this can be burdensome, financially difficult, and disruptive to that person's normal lifestyle,[10] and emotionally unhealthy for the child. In a national study conducted by Bloom and Steinhart,[11] it was found that over half of the children with incarcerated mothers never saw their mothers.[12] As a result of their separation from children, many women in prison experience isolation, depression, and guilt. Many of these emotions stem from not knowing the locations of their children, from pending divorces, and from the abandonment of their husbands or partners.[13]

In addition to being separated from children and uprooted from their communities, women in prison must cope with the realities of prison life. Pollock-Byrne[14] describes the current conditions of women's prisons. Because there are so few female correctional facilities, women who are low-risk are often incarcerated under the conditions afforded to medium- or maximum-security inmates. The institutional rules are usually similar to those that house male prisoners. In Strickland's study of women's prisons, Pollock-Byrne reports that women are often punished for infractions involving personal hygiene and clothing. Staff members appear concerned with the women's appearances and day-to-day living conditions. Punishments for infractions vary from loss of privileges to added sentence time. However, "fewer women receive serious punishments, such as loss of good time and segregation; this difference is related to the lack of serious infractions in women's facilities."[15]

From recent data provided by the Maryland Division of Corrections, we examined prison infractions within a women's prison for maximum, medium, minimum, and prerelease prisoners, and within a male institution holding prisoners of the same security levels. The women's prison had a population of 1,140 and the men's institution held 1,762 prisoners. Over the course of a year, there were 106 assaults on other prisoners or fights and 10 sexual assaults within the women's institution. Other infractions included alcohol use and possession, escapes or attempted escapes, weapons, and drugs. Within the men's prison, there were 146 assaults on other prisoners or fights and 24 sexual assaults. Other common infractions included assaults on staff members, escapes or attempted escapes, and weapon charges.

PROGRAMS

In *Women and Crime*, Simon[16] noted that one of the major sources of criticism of women's prisons was the quality and variety of the educational and vocational training programs available in those institutions. For example, based on a survey conducted among inmates in two of the three federal prisons for women, the Women's Bureau of the Department of Labor concluded that 85 percent of the inmates wanted more job training and 80 percent wanted more educational opportunities than were available at those institutions.[17] Nine out of 10 of the respondents also said that they expected to work to support themselves when they were released. A majority also expected that they would support others who were dependent on them.

A survey by Arditi et al.[18] showed that the average number of programs in men's prisons was 10, compared to 2.7 in women's prisons. Whereas male prisoners had a choice of some fifty different vocational programs, the women's choices were limited to cosmetology, clerical training, food services, serving, IBM keypunching, and training as nurse's aides. Some of the men's prisons provided vocational training in programs that were available to women inmates as well, but none of the prisons for women were prepared to train their inmates in programs that were available to men.

The industries available at men's and women's institutions showed much of the same picture. In the forty-seven prisons for men, there was an average of 3.2 industries, as compared to 1.2 in the fifteen female prisons. There was also very little overlap concerning the types of industries in which both male and female inmates could work. According to Burkhart,[19] both male and female prisoners were still employed in the personal service of prison administrators. Women prisoners often worked as housemaids and cooks for the families of prison superintendents.

By 1980, a General Accounting Office (GAO) report to Congress denied that gender equality had made headway within prison walls. The title of the report, "Women in Prison: Inequitable Treatment Requires Action," served as an appropriate indicator of its general message. That the type and variety of programs, services, and opportunities for women in prison had not reached parity with those provided to men in prison was attributed to long-standing factors such as the following: (1) the small numbers of women incarcerated, (2) cost, and (3) attitudes among correctional officials who "maintain[ed] a traditional view toward the training programs and other vocational needs of women offenders."[20] In other words, little had changed.

Indeed, gender equality within prisons has been the subject of a considerable amount of state and federal litigation, much of it successful—in edict if not in practice. By 1983, there was active litigation regarding educational programs for women in at least thirteen states, regarding vocational programs in at least twelve states, and regarding prison industries in at least eight states (Ryan 1984).

Since 1975, at least two comprehensive national studies of services, programs, and work opportunities available to female inmates have been conducted—one in 1975[21] and the other in 1983.[22] Summarizing the historical perspective achieved by comparing these two studies, Ryan notes:

> ABE [Adult Basic Education] programs have increased by 23 percent, GED/high school diploma programs have increased by 21 percent and college programs have increased by 19 percent. In 1975, correctional institutions reported offering one to nine vocational programs, with clerical skills, cosmetology, and food services the most common. In 1983, correctional institutions reported offering from one to 13 programs with clerical skills/business education the most common, followed by food services and cosmetology. . . . The study by Glick and Neto (1977) did not report on prison industries. In 1983, it was found that 53 percent of the facilities responding had prison industries, with one to three industries.[23]

In 1984, the Federal Bureau of Prisons became the target of a class-action suit representing the claims of two thousand minimum-security female inmates charging discriminatory treatment in the type and quality of facilities in which they were being housed.[24] Specifically, in contrast to minimum-security male inmates who traditionally are housed in small, relatively open camps, at cushy "Club Feds," or at military installations, minimum-security women have been housed in full-scale prisons offering fewer amenities and freedom, after being subject to much more stringent security conditions. While to date this suit has been successful in pressuring the Bureau of Prisons into opening three minimum-security camps for women, it has not yet resolved claims that the women's camps do not offer comparable educational, employment or recreational opportunities and that the special medical needs of women and those of women with children are not adequately addressed.[25]

To determine the current state of training, programming, and work opportunities provided to incarcerated women, we analyzed the Bureau of Justice Statistic's 1995 *Census of State and Federal Correctional Facilities*.[26] Our selection of institutions included only those whose primary function was categorized as general population confinement. Among the institutions we examined, 826 (85 percent) held men, 86 (9 percent) held females, and 59 (6 percent) housed both men and women. Of the 971 institutions, 243 (25 percent) were classified as maximum-security, 391 (40 percent) were medium-security, 335 (34.5 percent) were minimum-security, and 2 (0.2 percent) were administrative units.

The survey revealed that prisoners in female facilities were more likely to have access to work programs involving prison industries and facility support. A higher percentage of women's prisons also offered educational programs than did male-only or coed prisons. We see in table 6.6 that 77 of female prisons offered vocational programs, as opposed to 70 percent of male facilities, 52 percent offered college courses, 12 percent more than the percent of male facilities, and 80 percent offered employment programs, as opposed to 74 percent of male-only prisons. A greater percentage of female facilities offered psychological programs, drug dependency programs, and life skills and parenting classes than were available to male facilities. The percentage of prisons offering study release, employment, and public works employment opportunities was highest among the coed prisons.

When broken down by security levels, the differences between male and female prisons become clearer. As shown in table 6.7, 19 (22 percent) of the female-only prisons were maximum-security, 33 (38) were medium-security, and 33 (38 percent) were minimum-security. 210 (25 percent) of the male-only prisons were maximum-security, while 332 (40 percent) were medium-security and 283 (34 percent) were minimum-security. Of the 59 prisons that housed both sexes, 14 (24 percent) were classified as maximum-security, 26 (44 percent) were medium-security, and 19 (32 percent) were minimum-security.

Among the maximum-security prisons, a greater percentage of those housing only females provided vocational programs, college courses, study release, employment programs, and drug dependency and parenting classes than did prisons for males only or that housed both genders. For example, 18 percent of maximum-security prisons for men, and 57 percent of those housing both genders offered parenting classes, whereas 95 percent of female maximum-security prisons offered parenting classes. A higher percentage of prisons for men only provided life skills or psychological programs than did prisons for only women.

Table 6.6.   Programs by Sex of Prisoners Housed

	Male-Only Prisons	Percent of Male Prisons	Female-Only Prisons	Percent of Female Prisons	Both Sexes	Percent of Coed Prisons
Work Program						
Prison industries	436	52.78	55	63.95	24	40.68
Facility support	706	85.47	84	97.67	52	88.14
Farming	288	34.87	18	20.93	14	23.73
Public works	473	57.26	40	46.51	37	62.71
Other	71	8.60	9	10.47	6	10.17
Education						
Basic Adult	732	88.62	80	93.02	52	88.14
GED	741	89.71	81	94.19	53	89.83
Special Education	543	65.74	60	69.77	34	57.63
Training						
Vocational	576	69.73	66	76.74	37	62.71
College Courses	333	40.31	45	52.33	25	42.37
Study Release	37	4.48	9	10.47	11	18.64
Employment	608	73.61	69	80.23	55	93.22
Psychological	661	80.02	70	81.40	44	74.58
Drug Dependency	758	91.77	81	94.19	51	86.44
Alcohol Dependency	766	92.74	79	91.86	51	86.44
Life Skills	549	66.46	73	84.88	42	71.19
Parenting	265	32.08	70	81.40	30	50.85

Among the medium-security prisons, a higher percentage of female-only and coed prisons offered basic adult education and special education programs. All of the prisons provided employment programs. A higher percentage of female than male facilities offered psychological, drug and alcohol dependency, life skills, and parenting programs. Of the minimum-security prisons, a greater percentage of female facilities continued to offer educational programs. More women's prisons also offered vocational programs, college courses, study release and employment programs, drug dependency programs, life skills classes, and parenting classes than did male facilities.

We can see that as security levels decrease, female-only prisons offer more work programs in certain areas, fewer basic adult and GED education programs, and fewer special services such as psychological programs. Overall, it appears that a greater number of programs are accessible to medium-security female facilities than to maximum- or minimum-security female prisons.

Table 6.7. Programs by Security Level, Gender of Prisoners, and as a Percent of Prisons within Each Security Level

					Maximum-Security/Closed Custody	
	Total Male	*Percent of Male Prisons*	*Total Female*	*Percent of Female Prisons*	*Total Both Sexes*	*Percent of Prisons for Both Genders*
Work Program						
Prison industries	155	73.81	14	73.68	4	28.57
Facility support	205	97.62	19	100.00	14	100.00
Farming	91	43.33	4	21.05	4	28.57
Public works	84	40.00	9	47.37	9	64.29
Other	14	6.67	1	5.26	1	7.14
Education						
Basic Adult	200	95.24	19	100.00	14	100.00
GED	204	97.14	19	100.00	14	100.00
Special Education	115	54.76	10	52.63	7	50.00
Training						
Vocational	171	81.43	16	84.21	13	92.86
College Courses	98	46.67	12	63.16	6	42.86
Study Release	4	1.90	2	10.53	2	14.29
Employment	126	60.00	13	68.42	11	78.57
Psychological	195	92.86	16	84.21	12	85.71
Drug Dependency	199	94.76	19	100.00	14	100.00
Alcohol Dependency	201	95.71	18	94.74	14	100.00
Life Skills	151	71.90	13	68.42	12	85.71
Parenting	37	17.62	18	94.74	8	57.14

(continued)

Table 6.7. Programs by Security Level, Gender of Prisoners, and as a Percent of Prisons within Each Security Level (*continued*)

		Medium-Security				
	Total Male	Percent of Male Medium Security	Total Female	Percent of Female Medium Security	Total Both Sexes	Percent of Medium Security Prisons for Both Genders
Work Program						
Prison industries	187	56.33	25	75.76	16	61.54
Facility support	328	98.80	33	100.00	26	100.00
Farming	120	36.14	7	21.21	5	19.23
Public works	190	57.23	14	42.42	17	65.38
Other	28	8.43	3	9.09	4	15.38
Education						
Basic Adult	308	92.77	33	100.00	26	100.00
GED	306	92.17	33	100.00	26	100.00
Special Education	145	43.67	17	51.52	8	30.77
Training						
Vocational	266	80.12	30	90.91	20	76.92
College Courses	146	43.98	16	48.48	13	50.00
Study Release	6	1.81	3	9.09	2	7.69
Employment	332	100.00	33	100.00	26	100.00
Psychological	289	87.05	32	96.97	22	84.62
Drug Dependency	305	91.87	32	96.97	20	76.92
Alcohol Dependency	309	93.07	32	96.97	20	76.92
Life Skills	230	69.28	32	96.97	17	65.38
Parenting	122	36.75	27	81.82	15	57.69

Minimum-Security

	Total Male	Percent of Male Minimum Security	Total Female	Percent of Female Minimum Security	Total Both Sexes	Percent of Minimum Security Prisons for Both Genders
Work Program						
Prison industries	94	33.22	16	48.48	4	21.05
Facility support	173	61.13	32	96.97	12	63.16
Farming	77	27.21	7	21.21	5	26.32
Public works	199	70.32	17	51.52	11	57.89
Other	29	10.25	5	15.15	1	5.26
Education						
Basic Adult	224	79.15	28	84.85	12	63.16
GED	231	81.63	29	87.88	13	68.42
Special Education	283	100.00	33	100.00	19	100.00
Training						
Vocational	139	49.12	20	60.61	4	21.05
College Courses	89	31.45	17	51.52	6	31.58
Study Release	27	9.54	4	12.12	7	36.84
Employment	150	53.00	23	69.70	18	94.74
Psychological	177	62.54	22	66.67	10	52.63
Drug Dependency	254	89.75	30	90.91	17	89.47
Alcohol Dependency	256	90.46	29	87.88	17	89.47
Life Skills	168	59.36	28	84.85	13	68.42
Parenting	106	37.46	25	75.76	7	36.84

Women's prisons appear to have made some inroads in providing services to female prisoners, such as parenting classes, drug dependency programs, educational, and vocational programs. However, women housed in coed facilities still lack access to many of the services that are provided to single-sex facilities, such as educational and vocational programs, psychological programs, and drug and alcohol dependency classes.

Another concern that is often overlooked is the rate of HIV among prisoners, especially women. The Bureau of Justice Statistics[27] reported that in 2000, 3.6 of all female state prisoners and 2.2 percent of all male state prisoners were HIV positive. Since 1995, the percent of state prisoners estimated to be HIV positive increased by 0.7 percent for men and 2.1 percent for women.

Anno[28] also describes female prisoners as having a higher rate of sexually transmitted diseases than their male counterparts, and as having more needs for mental health intervention. Many women prisoners have histories of physical and sexual abuse, and 66 percent used drugs prior to their incarceration.[29] These statistics stress the urgent need for health care and medical services for women.

SEXUAL ABUSE OF WOMEN IN PRISON

That many prisoners have been sexually abused by other prisoners and guards should not surprise anyone. Nor should the claims of many incarcerated women who have reported sexual abuse by guards. For many years, women in prison have been subjected to physical and sexual abuse by prison staff, with few legal venues through which to seek emotional, physical, and legal assistance. With the rising population of women in prison, more attention is being directed toward women's claims of sexual abuse in prison, although proving such incidents in court still remains difficult.

In a 1996 report by the Human Rights Watch, it was determined that in eleven prisons over the course of two-and-a-half years,

> . . . male correctional employees have vaginally, anally, and orally raped female prisoners and sexually assaulted and abused them. We found that in the course of committing such gross misconduct, male officers have not only used actual or threatened physical force, but have also used their near total authority to provide or deny goods and privileges to female prisoners to compel them to have sex or, in other cases, to reward them for having done so. In other cases, male officers have violated their most basic professional duty and engaged in sexual contact with female prisoners absent the use or threat of force or any material exchange. In addition to engaging in sexual relations with prisoners, male officers have used mandatory pat-frisks or room searches to grope women's breasts,

buttocks, and vaginal areas and to view them inappropriately while in a state of undress in the housing or bathroom areas. Male correctional officers and staff have also engaged in regular verbal degradation and harassment of female prisoners, thus contributing to a custodial environment in the state prisons for women which is often highly sexualized and excessively hostile.[30]

The report does not state that abuses occur among one particular subgroup of female prisoners, but it notes that women who are mentally ill, lesbian, or those who have angered a guard in some manner are particularly vulnerable.

In 1995, thirty female prisoners from two different prisons filed a lawsuit against the state of Michigan in *Nunn v. State of Michigan*, stating they had been sexually abused by correctional officers and retaliated upon after reporting the abuse. According to the *Michigan Daily*,

> The class-action suit outlines abuses that range from rape and sexual assault to inappropriate visual surveillance and strip searches performed by male prison guards. Furthermore, those women who have leveled such accusations have been the victims of retaliation at the hands of those whom they accuse. Many women interviewed by Human Rights Watch reported being written up for sexual misconduct themselves after reporting abuse; in addition, several inmates said that they had lost "good time" (accrued toward early release), were subjected to punitive segregation and often lost privileges such as visiting rights after speaking out against the abuse that they suffered.[31]

While women are speaking out about the abuses they have faced in prison, and while more legal channels are opening up to hear such cases, retaliation by prison officials remains a reality and may therefore preclude women's attempts to report incidents of abuse.

WOMEN ON DEATH ROW

Between 1900 and 1975, the year when *Women and Crime* was first published, thirty-nine women were executed in the United States. In the eighteen years following its publication, an additional ten women were executed by means of electrocution or lethal injection (Death Penalty Information Center). A racial breakdown of these 49 executions shows that 14 (28.6 percent) of the women were black, 33 (67.3 percent) were Caucasian, and that two (4.08 percent) were designated *other* (see table 6.8). Though men comprise the overwhelming majority of death row prisoners, Streib notes that "the pace of executions of female offenders has picked up significantly during the past five years."[32]

In 1971, the three women on death row made up 0.5 of the death row population, as seen in table 6.9. After the United States Supreme Court reinstated

Table 6.8.   Women Executed by Crime and Race: 1900–2002

	Murder	Robbery/ Murder	Kidnapping/ Murder	Conspiracy to Commit Murder	Spying/ Espionage	Serial Murder	Total
White	21	5	1	4	1	1	33
Black	7	7	x	x	x	x	14
Other	2	x	x	x	x	x	2
Total	30	12	1	4	1	1	49

Sources: Capital Punishment USA, *"American Female Executions 1900–2002," "Executions in the United States, 1608–1987: The ESPY File,"* Espy, M. Watt and John Ortiz Smykla, Principal Investigators, Funded by the National Science Foundation.
www.geocities.com/trctL11/amtem.html

capital punishment in 1976; the first woman executed was in 1984, followed by the second and third female executions in 1998. Of the 44 prisoners executed thus far in 2003, two were women. As of April 1, 2003, the 48 women with death sentences make up 1.36 percent of the total death row population.[33] When we look at the proportion of death sentences that are imposed on women in table 6.10, the figures for 1973 and 2002 are 2.4 and 2.6, respectively. The proportion peaked in 1989, when 4.25 percent of those receiving death sentences were women.

Of the 49 women who have been executed since 1900, the 20 (61.2 percent) who were convicted of *murder* constitute the highest proportion of crimes for which the women were executed. The second largest crime category for which 12 were executed was *robbery/murder*, making up nearly 25 percent of all executions. The third most common crime category was *conspiracy to commit murder,* for which 4 (8.2 percent) women were executed, followed by the remaining crimes of *kidnapping/murder*, *spying/espionage*, and *serial killing,* for each of which 1 (2 percent) woman was executed. Breaking down the crimes by race, we see that of the Caucasian women, 21 (63.6 percent) were executed for *murder*, 5 (10.2 percent) were executed for *robbery/murder*, 4 (12.1) for *conspiracy to commit murder,* and 1 (3.0 percent) for each of the crime categories of *kidnapping/murder, spying/espionage*, and *serial murder.* Of the black women, 7 (50 percent) were executed for *murder* and the other 7 (50 percent) for *robbery/murder.* The remaining 2 (4.1 percent) women for which no racial data was available were both executed for *murder.*

Five methods of execution have been used since 1900: electrocution, gas chamber, hanging, firing squad, and lethal injection.[34] Of the women who have been executed since 1900, 26 (53 percent) were electrocuted, 8 were hanged (16 percent), another 8 died of lethal injection (16 percent), and 7 (14 percent) died in the gas chamber (see table 6.11). Based on available data for forty-seven of the women, the average age at which the women were exe-

Table 6.9. Female Executions as Percent of Total Executions and Females on Death Row as Percent of Total

Year	Total Executions	Female Executions	Female Executions as Percent of Total	Year	Total on Death Row	Total Females on Death Row[b]	Percent Women Women on Death Row
2003	44	2	4.5	2003	3,525[a]	48[a]	1.36[a]
2002	71	2	2.82	2002	3,692	50	1.35
2001	66	3	4.55	2001	3,581	51	1.42
2000	85	0	x	2000	3,601	54	1.50
1999	98	0	x	1999	3,527	51	1.45
1998	68	2	2.94	1998	3,452	48	1.39
1997	74	0	x	1997	3,335	44	1.32
1996	45	0	x	1996	3,219	47	1.46
1995	56	0	x	1995	3,054	48	1.57
1994	31	0	x	1994	2,890	41	1.42
1993	38	0	x	1993	2,716	35	1.29
1992	31	0	x	1992	2,580	34	1.32
1991	14	0	x	1991	2,491	36	1.45
1990	23	0	x	1990	2,356	35	1.49
1989	16	0	x	1989	2,250	31	1.38
1988	11	0	x	1988	2,124	25	1.18
1987	25	0	x	1987	1,984	23	1.16
1986	18	0	x	1986	1,781	20	1.12
1985	18	0	x	1985	1,591	19	1.19
1984	21	1	4.76	1984	1,405	18	1.28
1983	5	0	x	1983	1,209	13	1.08
1982	2	0	x	1982	1,050	14	1.33

(continued)

Table 6.9. (contiued)

Year	Total Executions	Female Executions	Female Executions as Percent of Total
1981	1	0	x
1980	0	0	x
1979	2	0	x
1978	0	0	x
1977	1	0	x
1976	0	0	x
1975	0	0	x
1974	0	0	x
1973	0	0	x
1972	0	0	x
1971	0	0	x
1970	0	0	x
1969	0	0	x
1968	0	0	x
1967	2	0	x
1966	1	0	x
1965	7	0	x
1964	15	0	x
1963	21	0	x
1962	47	1	2.13
1961	42	0	x
1960	56	0	x
1959	49	0	x

Year	Total on Death Row	Total Females on Death Row[b]	Percent Women Women on Death Row
1981	856	11	1.29
1980	691	9	1.30
1979	539	8	1.48
1978	482	5	1.04
1977	423	6	1.42
1976	420	5	1.19
1975	488	8	1.64
1974	244	2	0.82
1973	134	2	1.49
1972	334	4	1.20
1971	642	3	0.47

Year			
1958	49	0	x
1957	65	1	1.54
1956	65	0	x
1955	76	1	1.32
1954	81	2	2.47
1953	62	3	4.84
1952	83	0	x
1951	105	1	x
1950	82	0	x
1949	119	0	x
1948	119	0	x
1947	153	2	1.31
1946	131	2	1.53
1945	117	1	0.85
1944	120	3	2.50
1943	131	2	1.53
1942	147	1	0.68
1941	123	1	x
1940	124	0	x
1939	160	0	x
1938	190	2	1.05
1937	147	1	0.68
1936	195	1	0.51
1935	199	3	1.51
1934	168	1	0.60
1933	160	0	x
1932	140	0	x
1931	153	1	0.65

(continued)

Table 6.9. *(continued)*

Year	Total Executions	Female Executions	Female Executions as Percent of Total	Year	Total on Death Row	Total Females on Death Row[b]	Percent Women Women on Death Row
1930	155	2	1.29				
1929	102	1	0.98				
1928	145	1	0.69				
1922	144	1	0.69				
1912	161	1	0.62				
1909	139	1	0.72				
1905	156	1	0.64				
1903	131	1	0.76				
Total	5,701	49					

Sources: Death Penalty Information Center. Bureau of Justice Statistics: Capital Punishment Statistics: Capital Punishment Statistics, Key Findings, *Executions*; Capital Punishment Statistics, Key Findings, *Executions*; Capital Punishment Statistics, Key Findings, *Executions*; Capital Punishment Statistics, Key Findings, *Executions*; Capital Punishment Statistics; Correctional Populations 1997, *Prisoners under sentence of death*; Capital Punishment 2001, 2000, 1998, 1997, 1996, 1995, 1993, *Bureau of Justice Statistics; Correctional Populations 1997, 1994, 1993*; "Executions in the United States, 1608–1987: The ESPY File," M. Watt Espy and John Ortiz Smykla, Principal Investigators, funded by the National Science Foundation, http://users.bestweb.net/~rg/execution/FEMALES.htm; Bureau of Justice Statistics, Women Offenders; Death Penalty Institute of Oklahoma, "Executions by Year 1930–1975," www.dpio.org/executions/By_Year_1930–1975.htm

a As of April 1, 2003

b Data for 1971 to 1989 from Bureau of Justice Statistics, Women Offenders.

Table 6.10. Women with Death Sentences and as a Percentage of Total Death Sentences Imposed

	Total Death Sentences Imposed	Female Death Sentences Imposed	Female Death Sentences Imposed as Proportion of Total
1973	42	1	2.38
1974	149	1	0.67
1975	298	8	2.68
1976	233	3	1.29
1977	137	1	0.73
1978	185	4	2.16
1979	151	4	2.65
1980	173	2	1.16
1981	224	3	1.34
1982	266	5	1.88
1983	253	4	1.58
1984	285	8	2.81
1985	267	5	1.87
1986	300	3	1.00
1987	289	5	1.73
1988	291	5	1.72
1989	259	11	4.25
1990	253	7	2.77
1991	266	6	2.26
1992	287	10	3.48
1993	288	6	2.08
1994	317	5	1.58
1995	318	7	2.20
1996	319	2	0.63
1997	277	2	0.72
1998	303	7	2.31
1999	282	5	1.77
2000	229	7	3.06
2001	155	2	1.29
2002	155	4	2.58
Total	7,251	143	

Source: Death Penalty Information Center, 2003, Washington, D.C. www.deathpenaltyinfo.org
Note: As of December 31, 2002, only 50 women remained on death row in seventeen states.

cuted was 39.42 years (median = 38). Of the 33 women who were white and the 14 women who were black, the average age at execution was 42 and 31.5 years, respectively.

According to the Death Penalty Information Center (DPIC), 854 men have been executed since 1976 (as of July 2003) and 8,144 (as of June 30, 2003) since 1900.[35] DPIC also notes that female executions and death sentences comprise a small fraction of the total death row population and of those executed.

Whereas women account for approximately 10 percent of arrests for murder, they represent only 1.9 percent of those who receive death sentences, 1.5 percent of those actually on death row, and as of year-end 2002, only 1.2 percent of all executions since 1976.[36] This suggests an attenuation in the percentage of women who are involved in each phase of the death penalty process. In table 6.12, we see that from January 1, 1973, through June 30, 2003, approximately 51 percent of the death sentences imposed on women were reversed, 8.5 percent were commuted, and 7 percent were carried out. Currently, about 33 percent of those who received death sentences are on death row. Of the total population, Caucasian women constituted about 37 percent of the death sentences that were reversed, 1.5 percent of the commutations, 18 percent of those on death row, and about 6 percent who were executed. African Americans made up 11 percent of the death sentences that were reversed, 5 percent that were commuted, 11 percent of those on death row, and less than one percent who were executed.

Within both racial groups, the percent receiving sentence reversals decreased since 1973. The number of commutations received by African Americans decreased from the mid-1970s through the mid-1990s, but then increased from 1994 through 2003, while the number of Caucasian women with commuted sentences decreased. The percent of women who remain on death row has increased within both racial groups since 1973. Between the time periods of 1973 to 1984 and 1994 to 2003, the percent of African American women within their racial group who received death sentences and currently remain on death row increased from 11.11 to 66.66, a 500 percent increase. Similarly, the percent of Caucasian women within their racial cohort who received death sentences and who are now on death row increased from 0 to 72, a 72 percent increase. The percent of women within their racial cohorts who were executed spiked during the time period of 1984 to1993 and then decreased for African Americans.

Though Johnson asserts that "the contrast between men's and women's death rows is sharp,"[37] he has noted a paucity of literature regarding women on death row. As the need for research on female crime rates and women in prison has grown over the past several decades, so too has the need for research on women living on death row, their crimes, their backgrounds, and their executions.

LIFE ON THE ROW

Because there are so few women on death row at any given time, the experience of a woman who is awaiting execution is often very different from those

Table 6.11.   Methods of Execution for Females: 1900 to Present

Method	Total	Percent of Total
Hanging	8	16.32
Electrocution	26	53.06
Gas	7	14.29
Lethal injection	8	16.33
Total	49	100

Source: Death Penalty Information Center

Average Age of Women Executed by Race: 1990–2002

White	41.9
Black	31.4
Total average	39.42
Median	38

Notes: Averages include only those with age data.
Age data is not available for the two women with racial categories of "other."
Source: Capital Punishment USA, *"American Female Executions 1900–2002," "Executions in the United States, 1608–1987: The ESPY File,"* M. Watt Espy and John Ortiz Smykla, Principal Investigators, Funded by the National Science Foundation.

of men, as well as of other women. Johnson (1998) describes the reaction of one reporter, who characterized one state's death row as "cozy and congenial, more like group homes or even private homes than life prisons or death rows,"[38] and another as having an "inviting" and relaxed environment.

Kathleen O'Shea, on the other hand, recounts a very different experience of one woman on Pennsylvania's death row:

We are only permitted three showers in a seven-day period. We are young women with female issues that men do not have. When a woman is on her menstrual cycle, daily hygiene is the most important thing. Three pairs of underpants may be fine for men, but women have hygienic problems which we have no control over. We should be allowed a change of underwear every day.[39]

Another woman on death row in Idaho explains the physical and emotional isolation that women face:

I starve for human touch, but touching is forbidden. It is not done under any circumstances. The women here have gone to the hole over it. Two went for embracing. One had just gotten off the telephone with bad news, was crying, and needed a hug. They both did thirty days in the hole for sexual contact. . . . Another example was two women who were talking and laughing. When one put her hand on the other's arm to tell her to stop what she was saying, you guessed it—to the hole.[40]

Table 6.12. Outcomes of Imposed Sentences on Women: January 1, 1973, through June 30, 2003

Outcome	1973–1983				1984–1993				1994–2003			
	White	Black	Other	Total	White	Black	Other	Total	White	Black	Other	Total
Reversed	21	7	2	30	26	7	3	36	5	2	0	7
Commuted	1	1	1	3	1	4	1	6	0	2	1	3
Now on death row	0	1	0	1	8	6	1	15	18	8	5	31
Executed	2	0	0	2	5	1	0	6	2	0	0	2
Total	24	9	3	36	40	18	5	63	25	12	6	43

Outcomes of Imposed Sentences on Women by Percentage of Total Sentences during Each Time Period: January 1, 1973, through June 30, 2003

Outcome (percent within each time category)	1973–1983				1984–1993				1994–2003			
	White	Black	Other	Total	White	Black	Other	Total	White	Black	Other	Total
Reversed	58.33	19.44	5.56	83.33	41.26	11.11	4.76	57.13	11.63	4.65	0	16.28
Commuted	2.78	2.78	2.78	8.34	1.59	6.35	1.59	9.53	0.0	4.65	2.33	6.98
Now on death row	0	2.78	0	2.78	12.70	9.52	1.59	23.81	41.86	18.60	11.63	72.09
Executed	5.56	0	0	5.56	7.94	1.59	0	9.53	4.65	0	0	4.65
Total	66.70	25.00	8.30	100	63.49	28.57	7.94	100	58.14	27.90	13.96	100

Outcomes of Imposed Sentences on Women by Percent within Each Racial Group

	1973–1983			1984–1993			1994–2003		
	White n=24	Black n=9	Other n=3	White n=40	Black n=18	Other n=5	White n=25	Black n=12	Other n=6
Reversed	87.5	77.78	66.67	65	38.89	60	20	16.67	0
Commuted	4.17	11.11	33.3	2.5	22.22	20	0.0	16.67	16.67

(continued from previous page)

Now on death row	0	11.11	0	33.33	20	72	66.66	83.33
Executed	8.33	0	0	5.56	0	8	0	0
Total	100	100	100	100	100	100	100	100

Outcomes of Imposed Sentences on All Women by Race: January 1, 1973, through June 30, 2003

	Reversed	Percent Reversed	Commuted	Percent Commuted	Now on Death Row	Percent on Death Row	Executed	Percent Executed
White	52	36.62	2	1.41	26	18.31	9	6.34
Black	16	11.27	7	4.93	15	10.56	1	0.70
Other	5	3.52	3	2.11	6	4.23	0	0
Total	73	51.41	12	8.45	47	33.10	10	7.04

Total Outcomes: January 1, 1973, through June 30, 2003

	Total	Percent of Total
Reversed	73	51.41
Commuted	12	8.45
Now on death row	47	33.1
Executed	10	7.04
Total	142	100

Source: Victor L. Streib, 2003. "Death Penalty for Female Offenders January 1, 1973, through June 30, 2003," Appendix A, Female Death sentences Imposed January 1, 1973 through June 30, 2003.
Web source: http://www.law.onu.edu/faculty/streib/femdeath.htm
Note: Sorted by date of sentence.

Despite a growing female death row population, most prison systems are not adequately equipped to house and provide for this generally small subgroup of prisoners.

NOTES

1. Since the nineteenth century, social reformers, clinicians, and law enforcement officers have been concerned about the physical conditions and facilities under which women inmates must live, the types of educational and vocational training programs available to them, the quality and background of the personnel who supervise them, and the social organization within the prisons. The latter topic has attracted particular attention in the past two or three decades with the publication of works such as Giallombardo's *Society of Women* (1966), Ward and Kassebaum's *Women's Prisons* (1965), and Burkhart's *Women in Prison* (1973). These books, especially the first two, place great emphasis on the informal organization that develops among the inmates and types of obligations and responsibilities, especially sexual, that prisoners develop among themselves. But much of this literature on female inmates, while interesting in itself, is not directly relevant to the major issues that this book addresses.

2. Donziger 1996.

3. Richie 2002.

4. Chesney-Lind 2002.

5. Ibid.: 94.

6. Richie 2002: 139.

7. Ibid.: 140.

8. Ibid.: 139.

9. Hagan and Dinovitzer 1999. See Koban 1983; Smith and Elstein 1994; Genty 1995.

10. Bureau of Justice Statistics 1993 (cited in Hagan and Dinovitzer 1999).

11. Hungerford 1993 and Hairston 1995 (cited in Hagan and Dinovitzer 1999).

12. Bloom and Steinhart 1991.

13. Cited in Dodge and Pogrebin 2004.

14. Dodge and Pogrebin 2004.

15. Pollock-Byrne 1990.

16. Ibid.: 99.

17. Simon 1975.

18. Koontz 1971: 7.

19. Arditi et al. 1973.

20. Burkhart 1973.

21. U.S. Comptroller General 1980: 22.

22. Glick and Neto 1977.

23. Ryan 1984.

24. Ibid.: 28.

25. The case *Butler v. Meese* is now *Butler v. Thornburgh*.

26. Kornhauser 1989.

27. U.S. Dept. of Justice Bureau of Justice Statistics 1995. Census of State and Federal Adult Correctional Facilities [Computer file]. Conducted by U.S. Dept. of Commerce, Bureau of the Census. ICPSR ed. Ann Arbor, MI: Interuniversity Consortium for Political and Social Research [producer and distributor], 1998.

28. U.S. Dept. of Justice Bureau of Justice Statistics 2002. "HIV in Prisons, 2000."

29. Anno 2000.

30. Ibid.

31. Human Rights Watch 1996. "All Too Familiar—Sexual Abuse of Women in United States State Prisons," New York: 16.

32. *The Michigan Daily* 1998. "Abuse behind bars: states must end rights violations in its prisons."

33. Streib 2003. Retrieved from an online article: www.law.onu.edu/faculty/streib/femdeath.htm.

34. Death Penalty Information Center 2003. "Death Row Facts: Size of Death Row Population from 1968 to the Present." Washington, D.C.

35. From the Death Penalty Information Center (www.dpic.org).

36. Streib 2003.

37. Death Penalty Information Center; Streib 2003.

38. Johnson 1998: 86.

39. Ibid.

40. Kathleen O'Shea 2000: 58.41. Ibid.: 77.

Epilogue

In the twenty-seven years since the first edition of this book was published, women and crime has become a major intellectual and professional specialty. Within criminology and criminal justice, and among the subfields within sociology, psychology, and economics, research on women who commit crimes has grown into a major area of interest.

In this edition, we have brought up to date the demographic data and the arrest, conviction, and prison statistics reported in the first edition. Overall, the trends are consistent. Women's participation in the labor force has not abated; indeed, a higher percentage of women—including those who are married and have preschool children—than ever before are working full-time. Not only are more women working outside their homes, but they are occupying positions in the labor force that involve more training, responsibility, and authority than they had in the past. Along with women's greater participation in the labor force, promotion to higher-status positions, and increased representation in the professions, there is also a higher percentage of female-headed households in which women are the caretakers of young children.

With these data as background for understanding the position of women in American society, we turned to the female crime statistics and examined trends in these data. The findings were not dramatic, but the pattern we saw forming in the late 1960s and early 1970s has continued. Women's participation in property and white-collar crimes has continued to increase. In 1987, 31 percent of all larceny, 44 percent of all fraud, 34 percent of all forgery, and 38 percent of all embezzlement arrests were of women offenders. In 1998 those figures changed to 35 percent for larceny, 46 percent for fraud, 39 percent for all forgery, and 49 percent for all embezzlement arrests. The percentages of women arrested for robbery (8 percent) and burglary (8 percent) also increased to 10 percent for robbery and 13 percent for burglary. It is also worth noting that the percentage of women arrested for prostitution has declined between 1963 and 2001. In 1963, 77 percent of all arrestees were women and in 2001, 66.6 percent were women. These figures are consistent with women's increasing participation in legitimate occupations in the labor force. Note also that in 1975, women accounted for 10.3 percent of Type I violent offense arrests; in 1987, women accounted for 11.1 percent of those arrests and in 2001 for 17 percent of all arrests for Type I violent offenses.

Thus, the overall pattern of women's participation in criminal activities has not changed dramatically since 1975. The increase observed in the 1980s was for the same types of offenses reported earlier: property and white-collar crimes that women now have greater opportunities and skills to commit. Although there is no evidence that women have been any more involved in organized crime than they were at earlier times, their arrests for Type I violent offenses have increased from 1987 to 2001.

Has there been a difference in the manner in which the courts have responded to female offenders? In 1975, Simon reported the reactions of criminal court judges interviewed in the Midwest and commented, "Most of the judges treat women more leniently than they do men. They are more inclined to recommend probation rather than imprisonment, and if they sentence a woman, it is usually for a shorter time than if the crime had been committed by a man."[1] The profile reported in this edition shows that judges are still inclined to treat women more gently than they do men. They believe today, as they did in 1975, that incarceration for a woman is far more degrading than for a man. They also believe that women are less likely than men to be repeat offenders.

The federal and state judicial statistics reveal a pattern that is consistent with recent arrest data—namely, that there has been an increase in the percentage of women charged with and convicted of property offenses. For example, the percentage of women convicted in federal courts increased by 3.8 percent, from 10.8 percent in 1979 to 14.6 percent in 2000. In 2000, 25.6 percent of the fraud, 58 percent of the embezzlement, 35 percent of the larceny, and 22.4 percent of the forgery convictions were of women. In the state courts, women accounted for 25 percent of the larceny convictions and 41 percent of fraud convictions.

As of 2001 women accounted for 6.6 percent of the prison population: 7 percent in federal institutions, and 6.6 percent in state institutions. In 1971 and in 1987 women accounted for 3.2 and 5.0 percent of the overall prison population. Since 1971 the increase has been greater for federal institutions, going from 3.7 to 7 percent, almost a 100 percent increase. In the state institutions the percent increased from 4.7 to 6.6. There have also been changes in the conditions under which women do time. The vast discrepancies between women's and men's opportunities for vocational training and jobs for pay have diminished. Not only do all women prisons now offer academic classes, but they also offer a broader range of training in vocations that will help provide female inmates with jobs once they are released from prison. Some prisons also have industries that offer women an opportunity to earn money while doing time.

Perhaps even more dramatic than the improvement in the opportunities for vocational training and industry have been the accommodations available for women to spend time with their children. In some women's prisons, children may visit as often as at least once a week and stay for as long as eight hours per visit. Some have weekend programs. At least nineteen of the state and federal institutions responding to our survey also reported the availability of furlough programs whereby mothers may visit their children at home or in halfway houses. Since some 70 percent of female inmates are mothers of young children, these changes are probably most welcome.

In closing, we note again that women are more represented in official crime statistics today than they have been at any time since systemic national data have been available. Their criminal niche seems to be property offenses, especially white-collar offenses. Such criminal activities appear to be most consistent with their skills and opportunities.

NOTE

1. Simon 1975: 109.

Women and Crime the World Over

Nina W. Chernoff and Rita J. Simon[1]

This appendix examines female crime rates in twenty-eight countries over the past thirty-five years. The results show that there has been an overall increase in total crime rates for all of the countries, and that the more economically advanced and industrialized countries have higher crime rates than the less developed nations. All countries also experienced an increase in the percent of all crimes committed by women. The percentages of violent crimes committed by women—specifically homicide and robbery—were consistently low across countries and increased only slightly over time. The percentages of property and financial crimes committed by women—specifically theft and fraud—were consistently higher than the percentages for violent crimes, and have increased substantially over time. In addition, an analysis of the most recent data revealed a positive and significant relationship between women's overall crime rates and the countries' economic development. In those countries in which women occupy a higher status, as measured by formal years of schooling and representation in the labor force, we found some positive and significant correlations with the arrest rates for theft and fraud. There were also some strong negative relationships between female arrest rates for homicide and their status in society.

In this appendix on women and crime the world over we continue a tradition that began some twenty-five years ago when Rita J. Simon wrote *Women and Crime*. The 1975 volume included an appendix that compared female arrest rates in major offense categories for twenty-five countries in 1963, 1968, and 1970. In essence, Simon compared the proportion of female arrest rates for different types of crimes across societies that differed in their economic development, their political ideology, and their religious and social values. In that appendix she raised and answered these questions:

1. Has female visibility in crime increased?
2. Has it increased for certain types of offenses?
3. Has it increased in different types of societies?

For example, she questioned:[2]

> ... are women more likely to be arrested for property and white-collar offenses in the technologically and economically more advanced societies of Western Europe in which presumably they comprise a larger portion of the commercial labor force than they are in the more traditional societies of Africa and Asia? And are women in the latter societies more likely to be apprehended for crimes of violence, the targets of which are usually relatives or persons to whom they feel bound?

Briefly, the results showed that over the three time periods the countries that had the highest overall crime rates for men and women were more economically and technologically advanced. The countries that had the highest female arrest rates for property offenses were primarily those in which a large proportion of the women were employed outside the homes in commercial occupations. There was no relationship between countries that had high female arrest rates for violent offenses and those that had high female arrest rates for property offenses.

Simon next reported on these issues in 1991, in *The Crimes Women Commit: The Punishments They Receive*, the first revised edition to the original *Women and Crime*.[3] Specifically she sought to answer the following questions:

1. Have there been significant increases in female participation in criminal activities generally?
2. Have increases occurred in specific crime categories, and if they have, are the crimes more likely to be of a violent nature or in the realm of property offenses?
3. If there have been increases, have they occurred across all societies?

Table A.1 presents the total crime rates for the thirty-one nations examined in the 1991 book over the three time periods in descending order based on the crime rate in period A. The data indicate that Australia, the United States, Finland, and the Netherlands—all highly industrialized countries—produced the largest increases across the three periods.

In summary, the data presented in the 1991 publication showed that total crime rates and total arrest rates increased at about the same pace, and that the female arrest rates correlated strongly with the overall arrest rates. Examination of the data on female involvement in homicide showed a slight decline

Table A.1.   Mean Total Crime Rate: 1962–1980

Country	Mean Total Crime Rate 1962–1980	Mean Total Crime Rate 1962–1965	Mean Total Crime Rate 1969–1972	% Change	Mean Total Crime Rate 1977–1980	% Change
Sweden	7658.26	4885.58	7853.51	60.75	10235.68	30.33
New Zealand	6874.17	4696.58	6291.36	33.96	9634.57	53.14
Finland	6389.79	2899.60	6137.32	111.66	10132.46	65.10
Denmark	5240.96	3059.91	5704.32	86.42	6958.66	21.99
Canada	5189.02	3052.67	5375.08	76.08	7149.32	33.01
Israel	4531.41	3147.78	4469.45	41.99	5977.00	33.73
Australia	4295.13	1807.76	2887.35	59.72	8190.29	183.66
Germany	4282.50	3157.27	3982.67	26.14	5707.56	43.31
Austria	3739.07	3297.63	3634.55	10.22	4285.04	17.90
United States	3212.65	1269.96	3058.11	140.80	5309.87	73.63
England/ Wales	3046.99	1892.15	2617.75	38.35	4631.06	76.91
France	2961.96	1772.48	2085.01	17.63	4008.39	92.25
Netherlands	2666.49	1269.35	2390.63	88.33	4339.49	81.52
Korea	2157.26	3580.52	1404.41	−60.78	1486.84	5.87
Luxembourg	2086.16	1619.12	1990.07	22.91	2649.29	33.13
Zambia	2035.85	1283.16	2243.99	74.88	2580.39	14.99
Norway	1932.48	1241.43	1919.28	54.60	2636.73	37.38
Libya	1740.11	2372.21	1693.84	−28.60	1154.28	−31.85
Japan	1538.28	2035.25	1311.92	−35.54	1267.68	−3.37
Hong Kong	1230.13	992.75	1223.52	23.25	1474.13	20.48
Kuwait	1162.45	1772.39	1067.66	−39.76	647.30	−39.37
Malawi	793.21	635.17	745.98	17.45	998.47	33.85
Sri Lanka	485.13	266.88	483.85	81.30	704.67	45.64
Malaysia	403.54	292.89	349.45	19.31	568.27	62.62
Philippines	292.68	690.05	66.07	−90.43	121.92	84.53
Ivory Coast	245.27	300.15	251.28	−16.28	184.38	−26.62
Nigeria	189.00	146.33	173.28	18.42	247.38	42.76
Mean for Time Period	2828.89	1979.15	2644.88	30.84	3825.23	40.24
Median for Time Period	2157.26	1772.48	2085.01	26.14	2649.29	33.85

across the three time periods. Female arrests for major larceny (defined from 1981 on as robbery) remained steady at a relatively low percentage. Female arrests for minor larceny (defined from 1981 on as theft) increased, but did not attain the levels anticipated by many researchers in the 1970s.

Simon then examined the percentages of women in the labor force and in institutions of higher education in the thirty-one societies against women's crime rates. Overall, there were few significant correlations between female crime rates and either of the two socioeconomic indicators mentioned above. In addition to the two demographic indicators, she also arrayed societies by levels of economic opportunity (the private consumption of the gross domestic product divided by the population) and industrialization (the percentage of the work force engaged in industry). Computing correlations between each of those measures and female homicide, major larceny, and minor larceny, she found high positive correlations between female minor larceny and both societal indicators in all three time periods.

Simon concluded:

> over the nineteen-year time span, there were comparable levels of increase among crime, arrest, and female arrest rates from 1962 through 1980. The fears raised in the late 1960s and early 1970s that women's participation in crime would soon be commensurate with their representation in the population clearly were not realized. For homicide and major larceny, the percentages of female offenders actually decreased slightly. Thus, at least among the thirty-one countries for which longitudinal data were available, women continued to play relatively minor roles in those societies' violent criminal activities.[4]

This appendix reports crime data on twenty-seven of the original thirty-one countries from 1981 through 1995. We continued to use Interpol as our source for crime statistics, and the United Nations and the International Labor Office as our sources for societal indicators. We examined the data with an eye toward answering the following five questions:

1. Has there been an increase in the overall crime rate for women from 1962 through 1995, and has the increase been greater in the more economically developed countries?
2. If there has been an increase did it occur primarily in property and white-collar crimes (i.e., theft and fraud)?
3. Did the rates of female participation in violent crimes (i.e., homicide and robbery) decrease?
4. Is there a positive relationship between the status of and opportunity for women in the society and the amount of female participation in property and white-collar crimes in that country?
5. Is there a negative relationship between the status of and opportunity for women in the society and the amount of female participation in violent crimes in that country?

It is clear from the data in table A.2 that there has been an overall increase in crime rates across the thirty-three-year time span and that the more economically developed and industrialized countries (as measured by per capita

Table A.2. Total Crime Rates: 1962–1995

Country	Mean Total Crime Rate 1962–1995	Mean Total Crime Rate 1962–1965	Mean Total Crime Rate 1969–1972	% Change	Mean Total Crime Rate 1977–1980	% Change	Mean Total Crime Rate 1981–1985	% Change	Mean Total Crime Rate 1986–1990	% Change	Mean Total Crime Rate 1991–1995	% Change
Sweden	10,360.12	4885.58	7853.51	60.75	10235.68	30.33	11681.57	14.13	13302.73	13.88	13466.02	1.23
New Zealand	9,380.60	4696.58	6291.36	33.96	9634.57	53.14	12355.07	28.24	13246.69	7.22	14154.68	6.85
Canada	8,471.42	3052.67	5375.08	76.08	7149.32	33.01	11229.36	57.07	11607.27	3.37	10941.39	-5.74
Finland	7,863.02	2899.60	6137.32	111.66	10132.46	65.10	10755.63	6.15	8189.84	-23.86	8179.33	-.13
Denmark	7,532.54	3059.91	5704.32	86.42	6958.66	21.99	8456.85	21.53	10330.83	22.16	10453.63	1.19
Australia	6,182.56	1807.76	2887.35	59.72	8190.29	183.66	6588.00	-19.56	7629.21	15.80	9529.69	24.91
England/ Wales	5,954.03	1892.15	2617.75	38.35	4631.06	76.91	6671.70	44.06	7893.14	18.31	10274.16	30.17
Germany	5,941.10	3157.27	3982.67	26.14	5707.56	43.31	6860.90	20.21	7135.12	4.00	7807.91	9.43
Netherlands	5,191.75	1269.35	2390.63	88.33	4339.49	81.52	6737.28	55.26	7588.55	12.64	9038.02	19.10
Israel	5,132.41	3147.78	4469.45	41.99	5977.00	33.73	5882.00	-1.59	5524.72	-6.07	5508.03	-.30
Austria	4,748.10	3297.63	3634.55	10.22	4285.04	17.90	5239.84	22.28	5462.14	4.24	6267.97	14.75
France	4,544.43	1772.48	2085.01	17.63	4008.39	92.25	6590.68	64.42	5857.49	-11.12	6617.56	12.98
United States	4,070.85	1269.96	3058.11	140.80	5309.87	73.63	5137.61	-3.24	5651.08	9.99	5538.59	-1.99
Luxembourg	3,977.06	1619.12	1990.07	22.91	2649.29	33.13	4067.88	53.55	5924.31	45.64	7147.59	20.65
Norway	3,544.71	1241.43	1919.28	54.60	2636.73	37.38	3653.75	38.57	5015.38	37.27	6406.76	27.74
Korea	1,992.82	3580.52	1404.41	-60.78	1486.84	5.87	1880.15	26.45	2288.75	21.73	992.09	-56.65
Zambia	1,980.85	1283.16	2243.99	74.88	2580.39	14.99	2507.99	-2.81	x	x	596.64	x
Japan	1,480.18	2035.25	1311.92	-35.54	1267.68	-3.37	1420.18	12.03	1413.66	-.46	1467.25	3.79
Hong Kong	1,415.27	992.75	1223.52	23.25	1474.13	20.48	1779.94	20.75	1461.04	-17.92	1457.61	-.23
Philippines	1,377.07	690.05	66.07	-90.43	121.92	84.53	311.79	155.73	4831.82	1449.70	x	x
Libya	1,295.71	2372.21	1693.84	-28.60	1154.28	-31.85	794.90	-31.13	920.33	15.78	932.53	1.33
Kuwait	949.06	1772.39	1067.66	-39.76	647.30	-39.37	528.09	-18.42	684.14	29.55	1118.46	63.48
Malawi	769.13	635.17	745.98	17.45	998.47	33.85	1046.73	4.83	1006.26	-3.87	x	x
Nigeria	666.86	146.33	173.28	18.42	247.38	42.76	199.75	-19.25	x	x	x	x
Malaysia	465.80	292.89	349.45	19.31	568.27	62.62	584.62	2.88	578.28	-1.09	363.45	-37.15
Sri Lanka	461.22	266.88	483.85	81.30	704.67	45.64	461.80	-34.47	476.17	3.11	279.74	-41.25
Ivory Coast	254.65	300.15	251.28	-16.28	184.38	-26.62	331.09	79.57	280.94	-15.15	168.74	-39.94
Mean for Time Period	9410.57	1979.15	2644.88	30.84	3825.23	40.24	4583.53	22.12	5372.00	65.39	5779.49	2.36
Median for Time Period	7752.35	1772.48	2085.01	26.14	2649.29	33.85	4067.88	20.21	5524.72	7.22	6337.37	1.33

GDP) have higher crime rates than the less developed ones.[5] The most dramatic increase occurred between the time periods of 1981–1985 and 1986–1990 when the mean total crime rate increased by 65.4 percent. The smallest increase in mean crime rates was the most recent, from 1991–1995, with an increase of only 2.4 percent. A closer look at the most recent percentage change reveals that, in fact, one third of the countries experienced a decrease in their mean crime rates. The overall trend, however, is that mean crime rates have increased steadily from 1962 to 1995, particularly in the more economically advanced nations. The relationship between high crime rates and greater economic development and industrialization holds for the thirty-year time span as well as for the most recent three-year period in the mid 1990s.

Looking next at the female arrest rates in those same countries for the same time periods, we see in tables A.3A and A.3B that the same pattern prevails.

Table A.3A shows that the mean rate of female offenders increased substantially from 1962 to 1980.[6] Table A.3B shows that the percent of offenders that are female also increased from 1981 to 1995.[7] (For the years 1962–1980 Simon collected the rate of offenders per 100,000 women. From 1981 on, the data collected show the percentage of all offenders that are women. Because the two data sets are not directly comparable they are not included in the same table.) As is the case with the total crime rate, the countries with the highest percentage of offenders that are women are the most economically developed nations.

Tables A.4 through A.7 separate the percentage of women who have been arrested by the same types of offenses reported for the earlier periods: homicides, robbery, theft, and fraud.[8]

The data on the mean percent of female homicide offenders in table A.4 show that women account for no more than 12 percent of all homicide arrests.[9] Women in the more economically advanced countries have a slightly higher arrest rate than women in the less economically developed nations. The increases over time periods are small, and in the two time periods where the increase is greater than 2 percent it can be attributed to sharp increases in countries with low total female homicide offenders (e.g., Sri Lanka, Malaysia, and Malawi). For most countries, the female homicide percentages either decrease, or increase slightly.

Table A.5 shows that the overall female arrest rates for robbery, at less than 5 percent, are even lower than they are for homicide.[10]

The percentages increase substantially across time periods, with the exception of the most recent time period. From 1986 through 1990 to 1991 through 1995, the mean percent of robbery offenders who were female decreased by 19.9 percent. Even the increases, from 1962 to 1990, represent low

Table A.3A.   Rate of Female Offenders per 100,000

Country	Mean Rate of Female Offenders Per 100,000 1962–1980	Mean Rate of Female Offenders Per 100,000 1962–1969	Mean Rate of Female Offenders Per 100,000 1969–1972	% Change	Mean Rate of Female Offenders Per 100,000 1977–1980	% Change
New Zealand	223.12	75.65	202.88	168.18	390.83	92.64
Germany	207.48	134.27	197.26	46.91	290.91	47.48
United States	120.09	47.19	97.29	106.17	215.79	121.80
France	112.71	46.37	148.18	219.56	143.58	–3.10
Austria	95.72	84.91	94.37	11.14	107.89	14.33
England/ Wales	92.23	52.42	72.90	39.07	151.37	107.64
Australia	91.54	43.37	88.34	103.69	142.92	61.78
Sweden	78.74	36.11	62.01	71.73	138.11	122.72
Finland	74.39	48.02	77.81	62.04	97.34	25.10
Luxembourg	71.31	66.92	77.35	15.59	69.65	–9.95
Canada	67.49	26.70	60.16	125.32	115.60	92.15
Netherlands	61.19	48.63	67.01	37.80	67.92	1.36
Israel	56.16	63.32	53.32	–15.79	51.84	–2.78
Japan	46.08	40.15	37.82	–5.80	60.28	59.39
Korea	30.23	32.32	26.69	–17.42	31.67	18.66
Norway	17.13	13.52	20.14	48.96	17.73	–11.97
Denmark	14.71	13.54	12.66	–6.50	17.94	41.71
Hong Kong	12.13	6.55	5.43	–17.10	24.41	349.54
Sri Lanka	6.98	3.67	8.87	141.69	8.39	–5.41
Libya	6.61	10.75	4.28	–60.19	4.79	11.92
Kuwait	6.37	7.16	7.09	–.98	4.85	–31.59
Zambia	4.22	4.46	3.20	–28.25	5.01	56.56
Ivory Coast	4.06	4.28	4.12	–3.74	3.78	–8.25
Malawi	3.23	2.17	2.73	25.81	4.80	75.82
Philippines	2.48	3.78	1.69	–55.29	1.96	15.98
Nigeria	2.29	1.11	3.08	177.48	2.67	–13.31
Malaysia	.75	.77	.69	–10.39	.79	14.49
Mean for Time Period	55.91	34.00	53.24	43.69	80.47	46.10
Median for Time Period	46.08	32.32	37.82	25.81	51.84	18.66

actual percentages: the mean percentage for the most recent time period is 4.7. As in the homicide arrests, there is a higher percentage of female arrests for robbery in the more economically developed countries across the entire time span.

The mean percents for female theft offenders are higher than they are for homicide and much higher than they are for robbery.

As shown in Table A.6, between 11 and 18 percent of all theft arrestees are women.[11] In some of the more economically developed countries (e.g., Germany, the United States, Japan, and Australia) the percents range between 25 and 30 percent for the entire time period. The percentage of female theft

Table A.3B.   Percent of Offenders That Are Female

Country	Mean % Offenders That Are Female 1981–1995	Mean % Female 1981–1985	Mean % Female 1986–1990	% Change	Mean % Female 1991–1995	% Change
Germany	22.37	21.68	23.46	8.21	21.84	−6.91
Denmark	18.89	.	.	.	18.89	.
Japan	18.80	18.10	19.43	7.35	18.98	−2.32
Austria	18.38	17.08	11.48	−32.79	19.24	67.60
New Zealand	18.34	16.93	18.20	7.50	19.78	8.68
United States	18.28	16.90	17.88	5.80	19.52	9.17
Australia	17.38	17.38	.	.	.	.
France	16.79	18.78	18.16	−3.30	14.77	−18.68
England/Wales	16.25	17.00	16.00	−5.88	.	.
Sweden	15.26	.	14.90	.	15.40	3.36
Canada	13.28	11.18	13.02	16.42	16.24	24.77
Israel	12.84	12.76	13.10	2.66	12.86	−1.80
Hong Kong	12.63	9.58	13.95	45.62	15.14	8.53
Finland	12.45	10.52	13.46	27.95	13.38	−.59
Luxembourg	12.02	10.76	11.46	6.51	13.12	14.45
Zambia	11.41	14.57	9.00	−38.23	7.99	−11.22
Norway	11.31	10.56	11.20	6.06	12.67	13.13
Netherlands	11.15	9.76	12.70	30.12	12.50	−1.57
Korea	10.59	10.37	8.92	−13.98	15.10	69.28
Kuwait	10.23	7.95	10.33	30.00	13.00	25.85
Libya	7.02	6.74	10.98	62.91	4.33	−60.56
Ivory Coast	6.83	.	7.96	.	5.70	−28.39
Malawi	5.17	6.07	4.51	−25.70	3.77	−16.41
Malaysia	2.11	1.50	2.41	60.67	2.64	9.54
Nigeria	.	.	.	.	.	.
Philippines	.	7.50	.	.	.	.
Sri Lanka	.	.	.	.	.	.
Mean for Time Period	13.32	12.44	12.84	9.89	13.49	5.04
Median for Time Period	12.74	10.97	12.86	6.93	14.07	3.36

offenders has also increased steadily, with the exception of the most recent time period (as is the case for total crime rates).

Table A.7 shows the data on the percentage of female arrests for fraud that are available from 1981 through 1995.[12]

There is only a slight overall increase in the percent of female arrests for fraud, but there are sharper differences between the female arrests in the more and less developed countries for fraud than for any of the other offenses reported in tables A.4 through A.6. In the United States, over 40 percent of all arrests for fraud are of women.

Table A.8 reports the correlations between overall crime rates; percentage of female offenders for all crimes; and the percentage of female offenders for

TABLE A.4. Females as a Percent of All Homicide Offenders

Country	Mean % of Offenders that are Female: 1962–1995	Mean % Female 1962–1965	Mean % Female 1969–1972	% Change	Mean % Female 1977–1980	% Change	Mean % Female 1981–1985	% Change	Mean % Female 1986–1990	% Change	Mean % Female 1991–1995	% Change
Austria	18.90	23.20	18.80	-18.97	20.70	10.11	16.40	-20.79	18.30	11.61	16.48	-9.95
Japan	18.73	14.60	18.00	23.29	21.40	18.89	19.46	-9.07	18.60	-4.42	20.20	8.60
England/Wales	15.33	23.40	15.80	-32.48	13.70	-13.29	13.00	-5.11	9.00	-30.77	13.95	-9.98
France	14.32	14.20	14.40	1.41	13.40	-6.94	14.24	6.27	15.50	8.82	11.46	-24.62
Australia	13.78	16.60	12.80	-22.89	14.00	9.37	13.02	-6.97	15.21	16.75	9.76	-17.43
United States	13.44	18.20	15.60	-14.29	13.70	-12.18	13.00	-5.11	11.82	-9.08	10.27	-19.13
New Zealand	13.18	22.90	14.00	-38.86	10.30	-26.43	7.80	-24.27	12.70	62.82	10.45	-16.13
Germany	12.82	18.50	12.90	-30.27	11.00	-14.73	11.70	6.36	12.46	6.50	14.17	-22.64
Luxembourg	12.12	6.40	14.50	126.56	5.70	-60.69	20.13	253.16	18.32	-9.00	10.90	-20.90
Finland	11.77	13.20	16.00	21.21	8.80	-45.00	8.50	-3.41	13.78	62.12	7.05	-27.54
Norway	11.71	30.10	2.50	-91.69	11.40	356.00	9.48	-16.84	9.73	2.64	11.17	-9.67
Canada	11.05	8.70	11.70	34.48	10.50	-10.26	11.46	9.14	12.37	7.91	2.58	-49.75
Libya	9.61	18.00	15.90	-11.67	9.70	-38.99	7.44	-23.30	5.13	-30.99	13.75	14.58
Kuwait	9.50	7.00	6.40	-8.57	11.50	79.69	6.12	-46.78	12.00	96.08	9.60	9.46
Sweden	8.86	4.10	12.10	195.12	9.70	-19.83			8.77	.	9.60	9.46
Sri Lanka	8.80	4.70	5.50	17.02	6.10	10.91	6.55	7.38	7.25	10.75	35.13	384.28
Malawi	8.22	7.50	4.80	-36.00	11.90	147.92	7.12	-40.17	5.90	-17.16	25.00	323.87
Hong Kong	8.01	3.80	5.00	31.58	9.60	92.00	10.68	11.25	8.38	-21.54	9.85	17.54
Netherlands	7.41	13.20	6.00	-54.55	5.70	-5.00	5.96	4.56	5.50	-7.72	7.50	36.36
Ivory Coast	6.39	5.90	9.60	62.71	7.40	-22.92	10.12	36.76	3.71	-63.34	3.78	1.89
Nigeria	4.91	4.70	7.30	55.32	3.80	-47.95	.60	-84.21	.	.		
Israel	4.76	5.20	4.60	-11.54	3.30	-28.26	4.86	47.27	4.94	1.65	5.42	9.72
Malaysia	2.77	3.30	1.80	-45.45	3.30	83.33	1.75	-46.97	.42	-76.00	4.79	1040.48
Philippines	1.68	1.60	1.40	-12.50	2.00	42.86	1.81	-9.50				
Zambia	1.22	2.80	1.00	-64.29	.30	-70.00	.32	6.67				
Denmark	.	25.00	14.00	-44.00	12.40	-11.43						
Korea	.	.00	.00	.	.00	.	17.13	.	13.58	-20.72	11.90	-12.37
Mean for Time Period	9.97	11.73	9.72	1.18	9.31	16.05	9.55	1.93	10.58	-0.14	12.05	73.03
Median for Time Period	9.61	8.70	11.70	-12.08	9.70	-10.84	9.48	-5.11	11.82	-1.39	10.68	-9.81

Table A.5. Females as a Percent of All Robbery Offenders

Country	Mean % of Offenders that are Female: 1962–1995	Mean % Female 1962–1969	Mean % Female 1969–1972	% Change	Mean % Female 1977–1980	% Change	Mean % Female 1981–1985	% Change	Mean % Female 1986–1990	% Change	Mean % Female 1991–1995	% Change
Austria	13.32	10.30	8.50	−17.48	5.30	−37.65	20.06	278.53	15.12	−24.63	18.52	−1.98
New Zealand	9.17	2.60	5.30	103.85	11.80	122.64	13.88	17.63	13.30	−4.18	11.91	−46.29
Finland	8.79	3.60	3.50	−2.78	9.30	165.71	8.72	−6.24	15.16	73.85	10.46	−31.00
France	8.16	9.00	8.70	−3.33	7.30	−16.09	8.62	18.08	8.20	−4.90	7.42	−9.54
Norway	7.68	3.20	3.60	12.50	5.20	44.44	9.90	90.38	15.65	58.08	10.22	−47.77
Australia	7.39	3.20	3.40	6.25	5.80	70.59	10.72	84.90	8.31	−22.47	10.95	31.71
Luxembourg	7.33	4.30	7.80	81.40	12.40	58.97	5.59	−54.92	7.22	29.16	5.80	−35.76
United States	6.83	3.90	5.20	33.33	6.40	23.08	7.34	14.69	8.26	12.53	8.86	7.26
Canada	6.72	4.80	6.10	27.08	5.70	−6.56	6.62	16.14	7.40	11.72	9.53	3.06
Germany	6.26	4.00	3.60	−10.00	5.40	50.00	7.43	37.59	8.52	14.67	8.07	−24.18
Netherlands	5.53	3.70	4.40	18.92	4.80	9.09	5.48	14.17	7.60	38.69	7.75	−18.42
England/ Wales	4.79	2.50	2.90	16.00	4.40	51.72	5.20	18.18	5.60	7.69	7.20	28.57
Japan	4.03	1.10	1.70	54.55	6.80	300.00	4.44	−34.71	5.04	13.51	4.77	−24.21
Israel	3.80	3.60	2.20	−38.89	3.60	63.64	3.48	−3.33	4.47	28.51	5.04	12.70
Sweden	3.71	2.10	2.70	28.57	4.60	70.37	.		4.50		5.05	−10.22
Sri Lanka	3.50	2.00	3.40	70.00	6.40	88.24	2.00	−68.75	3.27	63.50	2.87	−64.95
Hong Kong	3.23	1.20	.80	−33.33	.60	−25.00	4.00	566.67	4.98	24.50	7.15	14.86
Korea	2.50	6.80	2.40	−64.71	1.40	−41.67	1.15	−17.86	1.20	4.35	2.00	−66.67
Ivory Coast	2.23	1.80	3.00	66.67	1.90	−36.67	4.14	117.89	1.54	−62.85	3.03	−21.33
Kuwait	2.22	1.10	1.80	63.64	2.20	22.22			2.42		5.00	23.97
Philippines	2.12	1.40	1.60	14.29	1.90	18.75					8.00	.
Nigeria	1.92	2.00	2.10	5.00	2.10	.00	.20	−90.48				
Libya	1.78	1.60	2.30	43.75	2.80	21.74	.81	−71.07	.57	−29.63	.80	−71.93
Malawi	1.25	.80	1.60	100.00	1.40	−12.50	.75	−46.43	1.61	114.67		−100.00
Zambia	0.63	.30	.50	66.67	1.10	120.00						
Malaysia	0.44	.20	.00	−100.00	.10		.20	100.00	1.13	465.00	1.33	−6.19
Denmark	.	16.00	7.90	−50.63	5.10	−35.44						
Mean for Time Period	4.82	4.82	3.60	18.20	3.59	41.91	5.94	44.59	6.57	38.66	4.71	−19.93
Median for Time Period	3.92	3.92	2.60	16.00	3.00	22.64	5.34	15.41	5.60	13.51	4.64	−18.42

Table A.6. Females as a Percent of All Theft Offenders

Country	Mean % of Offenders That Are Female 1962–1995	Mean % Female 1962–1965	Mean % Female 1969–1972	% Change	Mean % Female 1977–1980	% Change	Mean % Female 1981–1985	% Change	Mean % Female 1986–1990	% Change	Mean % Female 1991–1995	% Change
Germany	30.26	21.60	31.20	44.44	29.70	-4.81	32.17	8.32	33.92	5.44	31.68	-6.60
United States	28.17	20.30	22.40	10.34	30.60	36.61	29.84	-2.48	30.94	3.69	32.68	5.62
Japan	27.93	18.80	22.30	18.62	34.30	53.81	23.90	-30.32	29.44	23.18	28.45	-3.36
Austria	27.09	20.80	25.90	24.52	25.30	-2.32	27.42	8.38	30.78	12.25	31.33	1.79
Australia	26.13	12.10	19.20	58.68	31.90	66.15	34.28	7.46	.	.	30.15	.
New Zealand	24.01	11.70	25.80	120.51	25.30	-1.94	25.35	.20	31.70	25.05	31.95	.79
England/Wales	23.10	19.40	19.10	-1.55	28.40	48.69	22.60	-20.42	25.20	11.50	23.40	-7.14
Sweden	22.76	20.40	19.80	-2.94	21.60	9.09			24.77	.	27.73	11.95
Norway	19.57	13.60	18.50	36.03	14.30	-22.70	21.96	53.57	23.43	6.69	25.06	6.96
Canada	18.95	9.70	16.50	70.10	15.00	-9.09	18.82	25.47	23.15	23.03	9.51	-58.93
Luxembourg	18.47	18.20	24.60	35.16	17.60	-28.46	14.37	-18.35	17.47	21.60	17.82	1.98
France	18.42	14.90	17.70	18.79	18.10	2.26	20.21	11.66	20.15	-.29	19.29	-4.30
Netherlands	18.27	20.90	25.20	20.57	22.00	-12.70	15.36	-30.18	11.00	-28.39	12.25	11.36
Hong Kong	16.05	4.50	4.10	-8.89	18.20	343.90	19.12	5.05	23.80	24.48	23.88	.34
Israel	13.64	8.10	7.10	-12.35	13.20	85.92	15.16	14.85	16.35	7.82	19.42	18.81
Finland	11.12	14.40	16.30	13.19	11.50	-29.45	9.28	-19.30	9.44	1.72	7.56	-19.92
Korea	10.30	9.50	9.20	-3.16	8.10	-11.96	11.53	42.35	10.30	-10.67	21.90	112.62
Philippines	6.14	5.30	5.10	-3.77	7.60	49.02	7.85	3.29	.	.	15.33	99.87
Kuwait	5.76	1.80	4.70	161.11	5.00	6.38	4.39	-12.20	7.67	74.72	3.22	-64.14
Sri Lanka	4.95	3.90	3.60	-7.69	4.30	19.44	4.82	12.09	8.98	86.31	1.75	-31.69
Libya	4.52	3.10	1.60	-48.39	2.80	75.00	15.78	463.57	2.56	-83.76	2.21	-22.07
Malawi	2.86	2.60	2.80	7.69	3.40	21.43	2.85	-16.18	2.84	-.49	1.84	-47.37
Ivory Coast	2.84	3.20	1.90	-40.63	3.00	57.89	3.21	7.00	3.50	8.91	4.40	-60.43
Malaysia	2.62	1.70	1.60	-5.88	1.50	-6.25	1.75	16.67	11.12	535.43	1.84	
Zambia	2.39	1.90	2.70	42.11	4.50	66.67	.74	-83.56	.	.	.	
Nigeria	.	4.10	7.60	85.37	6.10	-19.74	.		.		.	
Denmark	.	4.90	4.70	-4.08	5.90	25.53	.		.		.	
Mean for Time Period	14.95	10.79	13.38	23.26	15.16	30.31	15.95	18.62	18.11	35.63	17.69	-2.45
Median for Time Period	17.16	9.70	16.30	13.19	14.30	9.09	15.57	6.03	18.81	8.91	19.35	-1.51

Table A.7.   Females as a Percent of All Fraud Offenders

Country	Mean % Offenders That Are Female 1981–1995	Mean % Female 1981–1985	Mean % Female 1986–1990	% Change	Mean % Female 1991–1995	% Change
United States	42.16	40.94	44.34	8.30	41.20	–7.08
New Zealand	34.10	29.30	34.00	16.04	38.94	14.53
Australia	28.86	28.93	28.50	–1.49	.	.
France	27.08	28.27	29.62	4.79	23.81	–19.62
Canada	25.95	23.24	26.04	12.03	29.25	12.34
Germany	23.31	22.55	24.20	7.32	23.02	–4.88
Austria	20.95	18.72	21.72	16.03	22.40	3.13
Sweden	20.73	.	22.90	.	19.42	–15.20
Norway	20.52	15.75	22.33	41.78	23.93	7.17
England/ Wales	19.00	22.00	18.40	–16.36	.	.
Finland	18.96	18.54	19.18	3.45	19.16	–.10
Korea	18.80	18.98	16.86	–11.17	23.30	38.20
Israel	18.72	19.58	19.95	1.89	16.64	–16.58
Hong Kong	14.34	10.10	14.12	39.80	18.80	33.14
Luxembourg	13.31	16.05	14.15	–11.84	10.83	–23.48
Netherlands	13.25	11.30	12.17	7.70	16.50	35.58
Kuwait	12.76	19.62	6.67	–66.00	8.75	31.18
Japan	12.41	9.18	12.54	36.60	15.50	23.60
Zambia	7.00	11.45	.	.	2.55	.
Sri Lanka	6.18	3.54	6.06	71.19	7.76	28.05
Ivory Coast	4.49	4.86	4.62	–4.94	3.99	–13.64
Libya	4.47	4.88	4.80	–1.62	3.85	–19.81
Sri Lanka	6.18	3.54	6.06	71.19	7.76	28.05
Malawi	2.14	2.29	2.03	–11.35	.	.
Malaysia	2.16	2.25	2.45	8.89	2.02	–17.55
Denmark	.	.	.	.	.	.
Nigeria	.	.	.	.	.	.
Philippines	.	.	.	.	.	.
Mean for Time Period	16.71	16.62	17.72	6.87	17.70	4.45
Median for Time Period	18.72	18.54	18.40	6.05	18.80	1.51

the violent offenses of homicide and robbery and the property offenses of theft and fraud from 1993 through 1995, by measures of the society's economic development and wealth and by women's status.[13] The specific indicators of economic development and wealth, and of women's status used, are per capita gross domestic product for 1997; expected number of years of formal schooling for women (the years included range from 1993 to 1996), the total fertility rate from 1995 to 2000, and the percent of women in the labor force.

Table A.8.   Correlations

Crime Statistic	Gross Domestic Product (Per Capita)	Years of Formal Schooling for Women	Fertility Rate	Percent of Women in Labor Force
Total crime rate (most recent data)	.45*	.47	−.53*	.63**
Females as a percent of all offenders (most recent data)	.70**	.50	−.77**	−.01
Females as a percent of all HOMICIDE offenders (most recent data)	.08	−.81**	.34	−.13
Females as a percent of all ROBBERY offenders (most recent data)	.03	.04	−.35	.21
Females as a percent of all THEFT offenders (most recent data)	.71**	.24	−.67**	.16
Females as a percent of all FRAUD offenders (most recent data)	.29	.65*	−.44	.42

* Correlation is significant at the 0.05 level.
** Correlation is significant at the 0.01 level.

On the first measure, per capita gross domestic product, the correlation with the most recent total crime rate is .45* (significant at the .05 level). The correlation with the overall percent of offenders that are female is even stronger at .70** (significant at the .01 level). The correlations between per capita GDP and violent offenses are weak (.08 for homicide and .03 for robbery), while the correlations between per capita GDP and property offenses are stronger at .29 for fraud and .71** for theft (significant at the .01 level).

The relationship between formal years of schooling for women and the most recent crime data is also interesting. The correlation between schooling and female homicide offenses is negative and significant at -.81** (significant at the .01 level) and the correlation between schooling and female fraud offenses is positive and significant at .65* (significant at the .05 level). (For the total crime rate the correlation is .47, for percent female offenders it is .50, for robbery it is .04 and for theft it is .24.)

The correlations between crime and the fertility rate also reveal significant relationships. The fertility rate is significantly and negatively correlated with the total crime rate at -.53* (significant at the .05 level), with the percent of offenders that are female at -.77** (significant at the .01 level) and with the percent of female theft offenders at -.76** (significant at the .01 level). (For homicide the correlation is .34, for robbery it is -.35 and for fraud it is -.44.)

The percent of women in the labor force is positively and significantly correlated with the total crime rate at .63** (significant at the .01 level). (The correlation with females as a percent of all offenders is -.01, with homicide it is -.13, with robbery it is .21, with theft it is .16 and with fraud it is .42.)

The correlations between the three measures of women's status and their crime rates show that in those nations where women have more years of schooling, higher representation in the labor force, and lower fertility rates they are more likely to be involved in the property offenses of theft, and especially fraud.

The answers to the questions posed above are that there has been an increase in the overall crime rates, but only a slight increase in the female crime rates. The increases that did occur were greater in the more economically developed countries. In examining the four different offense categories, we found that the increases were higher for theft and slightly higher for fraud than they were for homicide and robbery. The relationship between women's overall crime rates and the countries' economic development was positive and significant. In those countries in which women occupy higher status as measured by formal years of schooling and representation in the labor force, there were some positive and significant correlations with the arrest rates for theft and fraud. There were also some strong negative relationships between female arrests for homicide and their status in society.

Finally, returning to Simon's original observations in 1975, we see that indeed "as women become more liberated from hearth and home and become more involved in full-time jobs they are more likely to engage in the types of crimes for which their occupations provide them with the greatest opportunities."

NOTES

1. This appendix appeared originally in *Gender Issues* 18, no. 3 (Summer 2000): 1–20. Nina Chernoff is a graduate student in the Department of Justice, Law, and Society at American University, Washington, D.C.

2. Ibid.: 111.

3. Simon and Landis 1991.

4. Ibid.: 122.

5. The mean total crime rate was collected from Interpol with the following exceptions: the 1989–1994 rate for Australia was from the Australian Institute of Criminology; the 1984 and 1992–1997 rate for England/Wales was from the Government Statistical Service for the United Kingdom; and the 1995 rate for Japan was from

"Criminal Justice Systems at Work, 1998: Outline of Crime Trends, Criminal Proce-dures and Juvenile Justice System in Japan," Ministry of Justice, Japan. The mean rates for each time block were calculated by dividing the sum of the available crime rates by the number of years for which crime rates were available. So a country with no data available for four of the five years in a time period has a mean equal to the crime rate for the one year for which data was available. Countries are listed in de-scending order of the mean total crime rate.

6. Countries are listed in descending order of the mean rate of female offenders.

7. Countries are listed in descending order of the mean percentage of offenders that are female. Countries for which no mean percentage was available are listed at the bottom of the table in alphabetical order.

8. In the 1975 and 1991 volumes, the crime labeled "robbery" was described as "major larceny" and the crime labeled "theft" was described as "minor larceny."

9. The homicide data were collected from INTERPOL with the following excep-tions: the 1987–1988 and 1991–1995 data for Australia were collected from the Aus-tralian Institute of Criminology; the 1981–1982 data for the United States were col-lected from the Uniform Crime Reports.

10. The robbery data were collected from Interpol with the exception of the 1981–1982 data for the United States, which were collected from the Uniform Crime Reports.

11. The theft data are collected from Interpol with the following exceptions: the 1991–1995 data for Australia were collected from the Australian Institute of Criminol-ogy; the 1981–1984 and 1990–1995 data for England/Wales were collected from the Crime and Criminal Justice Unit of the Home Office, United Kingdom; and the 1981–1982 data for the United States were collected from the Uniform Crime Reports.

12. The fraud data were collected from Interpol with the exception of the 1981–1982 data for the United States, which were collected from the Uniform Crime Report.

13. The "most recent" data are the data available from the most recent year among 1995, 1994, and 1993. Per capita gross domestic product in U.S. dollars comes from the National Accounts database of the Statistics Division of the United Nations Sec-retariat; economic activity rates (labor force participation rates) come from Interna-tional Labour Office, *Yearbook of Labour Statistics*, table 1A (Geneva, various years up to 1998) and International Labour Organization, Caribbean Office, *Digest of Caribbean Labour Statistics 1998* (Port of Spain, International Labour Office, 1999).

The labor force participation data include the following caveats for the following countries: Australia excludes armed forces; Austria excludes conscripts; Canada ex-cludes full-time members of the armed forces and indigenous populations living on reservations; Denmark includes only persons age 15–66 years; Finland includes only persons age 15–74 years; Israel excludes conscripts and includes data related to Is-raeli residents in certain territories under occupation by Israeli military forces since June 1967; Ivory Coast excludes unemployed persons not previously employed; Ko-rea excludes resident foreigners and the armed forces; Luxembourg excludes border workers and employees of international organizations; Malawi excludes conscripts; the Netherlands includes only persons age 15–64 years and excludes persons working or seeking work for less than 12 hours per week; New Zealand includes civilians only; Nigeria excludes institutional households, armed forces, and persons doing unpaid community or social work; Norway includes only persons age 16–74 years; The Philippines includes members of the armed forces living in private households; Sri Lanka excludes northern and eastern provinces; Sweden includes only persons ages 16–64 years; England/Wales includes all persons ages 16+ years; the United States excludes conscripts; and Wales includes all persons ages 16+ years. The labor data are for 1997 with the following exceptions: Austria (1996), France (1998), Ivory Coast (1998), Kuwait (1998), Malawi (1987), Malaysia (1990), Nigeria (1986), Norway (1986), and the United States (1996).

The years of formal schooling data are from the United Nations, *Women's Indicators and Statistics database* (Wistat), version 4, CD-ROM (United Nations publication, forthcoming), based on data provided by the United Nations Educational, Scientific and Cultural Organization in January 1999. The schooling data are for 1995 with the following exceptions: Japan (1993), Korea (1996), Kuwait (1991), New Zealand (1996), and Zambia (1994). Total fertility rate estimates are for 1995–2000 and are from Population Division of the United Nations Secretariat, *World Population Prospects: The 1998 Revision, Vol. I: Comprehensive Tables* (United Nations publication, Sales No. E.99.XIII.9), supplemented by *Demographic Yearbook 1997* (United Nations publication, Sales No. E/F.99.XIII.1).

Appendix B

Women in Prison:
A Comparative Assessment[1]

Heather Ahn-Redding and Rita J. Simon

This appendix examines women prisoners as a percent of the prison populations of twenty-six countries. In this study, we hypothesize that in countries
where women have greater social, educational, and economic advancements,
women will also comprise the larger percentages of the total prison population. Findings from this study indicate that the countries where women constitute the highest percentages of the prison population are also those where
women have high literacy rates. The percent of certain crimes committed by
women correlates significantly and positively with educational and economic
indicators, as well as measures of women's advancements in the workforce.
Negative and significant correlations are seen between fertility rates and the
number of women as a percent of the prison population, as well as educational variables. Ultimately, the findings indicate that in countries where
women have advanced the greatest with regards to education, labor, and social status, the percent of women in the prison population and of all offenders for certain crime categories is also higher.

Though constituting half of the world's population, women throughout history have generally committed crimes at significantly lower rates than men.
With rapid growth in economic stimulation across the world, however, the
proportion of the world's women living in financially secure and economically developed societies is increasing, thereby altering the social and financial conditions in which they live and work. These wide-scale transformations
are also generating changes in women's roles within the criminal justice system. To understand female crime on an international level, we must examine
the larger socioeconomic framework in which these changes are occurring
and identify international trends in education, labor, and global economic development.

Today, capitalism and technology are bridging international markets, economies, and cultures, resulting in a constantly shrinking global community. We are experiencing a mass eruption of globalization where strong competitive markets are emerging in remote regions of the world, where economic growth is booming in previously underdeveloped markets, and where capitalism is thriving. This global economic expansion is stimulating financial and social growth within many countries, but it is not without costs.

Surveys conducted by the Dutch Ministry of Justice in 1988, 1991, and 1995 compared rates of victimization in industrialized countries for offenses ranging from robbery and theft to sexual crimes (Mauer 1999). With few exceptions, all of the industrialized nations experienced an "appreciable level of property and aggressive crime, particularly in more urbanized areas" (26). Mauer describes these particular offenses as the "price to be paid for living in an affluent, urbanized and democratic society, regardless of government policy on crime, or the way in which communities try to organize themselves" (26). His findings emphasize the notion that modernized nations are not immune to high crime rates.

Since her innovative theory on women, crime, and the workforce in the mid-1970s, Simon (1975) has maintained that where social and economic advancements provide men and women with equal opportunities in both education and within the labor force, women will have an "increased propensity to commit criminal acts, especially property and white-collar offenses." When women are afforded higher social status, they have more occasions to seek occupations with higher levels of responsibility. Within those roles, they assume the positions of authority and power that have traditionally been held by men. Consequently, there is increased exposure to opportunities to commit workplace and property crimes such as larceny, fraud, embezzlement, and forgery.

In addition to Simon's controversial (Lilly, Cullen, and Ball 1995) views on women and crime in the workplace, other researchers have offered alternative perspectives on female criminality, a discussion that until recently has been largely neglected by criminal justice practitioners (Culbertson and Fortune 1991). These perspectives can be classified into emancipation and social disorganization theories.

Emancipation theorists associate women's participation in crime with their refusal to accept "subordinate roles linked to the traditional sex roles" (Culbertson and Fortune 1991, 107). The social disorganization position, as described by Widom and Stewart (1977), however, attributes crime to "disruptive social conditions" (107; also see Bloom 1969 and Sutherland and Cressey 1974) that may explain recent rises in female criminality (Culbertson and Fortune 1991; also see Widom and Stewart 1977). Lilly et al.

(1995, 183) note recent patriarchal theories that recognize female crime as occurring within the context of a male-dominated society. Within this perspective, sexualized violence against women and male patriarchy influence the forms of crime that are not only directed toward women, but are also committed by women. These theories have all been used to explain and describe female crime within the United States. More recently, however, Simon's perspective on women and crime has been applied on an international level.

The summer 2000 issue of *Gender Issues* includes an article by Chernoff and Simon that examines female crime rates in twenty-seven countries over the past thirty-five years. The major findings reported were that there had been slight increases in the percent of crimes committed by women. When the data were broken down by types of crimes, they showed that the percentages of violent crimes committed by women, especially homicide and robbery, were consistently low across countries and increased only slightly over time. The percentages of property and financial crimes committed by women, especially theft and fraud, were consistently higher than the percentage for violent crimes and increased substantially over time. The article also reported a positive and significant relationship between women's overall crime rates and the countries' economic development. The most notable increase occurred where women held "higher status as measured by formal years of schooling and representation in the labor force" (Chernoff and Simon 2000: 5–20) and in crimes of theft and fraud. They also reported negative relationships between female arrest rates for homicide and their status in society. While women's total crime rates still remain highly disparate from those of men, Chernoff and Simon's findings suggest that women's global participation in criminal activity is nonetheless rising in certain regions and in specific crime categories.

Changes within the United States within the past sixty years illustrate the findings from Chernoff and Simon's analysis. For example, the percent of married women who participated in the labor force increased from 22.0 percent in 1948 to 55.8 percent in 1987 (Simon 1993). In addition, the percentage of bachelor's, master's, and doctorate degrees obtained by women increased dramatically over the past five decades, growing from 23.9 percent, 29.3 percent, and 9.1 percent respectively in 1950 (Simon 1993) to 55.0 percent, 56.0 percent, and 40.0 percent in 1997 (Simon and Landis 1991). Yet over the past forty years, the percentages of females arrested for serious, violent, and property crimes have also increased (Small 2000).

In 1963, Small (2000) reports, women accounted for 11.40 percent of total arrests for all crimes in the United States, but by 1998, they accounted for 21.8 percent of total arrests, an overall rate of change of 0.91. Examining arrests data by specific crimes, women's share of total arrests for serious crimes grew from 11.7 percent in 1963 to 25.6 percent in 1998, a rate of change amounting to 1.19. Whereas women's share of total arrests for violent crimes in the United States grew from 10.3 percent in 1963 to 16.8 percent in 1998 (a 0.63 overall rate of change), the percent of women's share of total arrests for property crime increased even more during that same period, growing from 12.0 percent to 28.9 percent (a 1.41 overall rate of change). Data also indicate that the rates of change in women's share of property crimes were greater than for other types of offenses. The changes in rates in women's share of total arrests between 1963 and 1998 was 1.04 for robbery, 0.83 for larceny, 2.79 for burglary, and 3.24 for auto theft. For Type II offenses, the rates of change in women's share of arrests for embezzlement was 1.83, 1.41 for fraud, and 1.21 for forgery and counterfeiting. The overall rate of change for criminal homicide decreased by 0.28, whereas the rate for aggravated assaults was 0.40, 0.23 for narcotic drug law violations, and -0.25 for prostitution and vice.

More recently, the number of women convicted of property felonies in state courts increased from 48,206 in 1990 to 69,536 in 1996, an increase of 44.2 percent (Bureau of Justice Statistics 1999). Not only have female crime rates increased in certain offense categories, but the number of women incarcerated in the United States has increased as well. In 1986, 41.3 percent of prison inmates convicted of property offenses were women, a 4.5 percent increase since 1979 (Simon 1993). Between 1971 and 1996, the number of women as a percentage of the sentenced federal prison population grew from 3.7 to 7.3 and the number of women as a percentage of the sentenced state prison population increased from 4.7 to 6.3 (Small 2000). By 1996, there were approximately 73,192 women in state and federal prisons, approximately 11.5 times the figure in 1971.

In 1998, there were nearly 950,000 women in the United States who were under the "care, custody, or control of correctional agencies" (BJS 1999: 1), a rate of approximately 1 out of every 109 adult women. The growing number of women's prisons in the United States is also evidence of the increasing rate of female criminal activity, as indicated by the 17 new women's prisons built in the 1970s and the twenty-four additional women's prisons built during the 1980s (Donziger 1996). Not only do these facilities accommodate the growing female inmate population, but they also house the mothers of thousands of children (152–154).

The United States remains a leading country with respect to economic security, technology, gender equality, and financial growth. Yet, it has still experienced significant growth in the number of women participating in crime and in the proportion of women comprising federal and state inmate populations (Simon 1993). While rising incarceration rates at a national level may be partially attributed to recent changes in drug laws, public demands for more punitive criminal justice policies, and harsher sentencing practices, the growing number of property crimes committed by women (Simon 1993) appears independent of these changes.

Chernoff and Simon's (2000) study indicates that economically developed countries are experiencing growths in female crime rates that are similar to the United States. Their findings suggest that those countries may experience similar increases in female incarceration rates as they undergo heightened economic development, promote gender and social equality, and provide women and men with equal opportunities within the workforce. Understanding the correctional changes that have emerged within the United States may shed light on the issues and dilemmas faced by the other developing nations that are reaching similar economic modernization and social development.

Regarding international crime rates, Lynch (2002) reports that the rate of serious property crimes reported to the police in the United States is significantly lower than in similar countries. In 1998, 862 burglaries per 100,000 population were reported to the police in the United States, whereas the rate is 2.7 times greater in Australia, 1.3 times greater in Canada, 2.1 times greater in England and Wales, 1.7 times greater in Germany, and 3.6 greater in the Netherlands. But, the United States imposes lengthier prison sentences for property crimes, such that those convicted of burglary in the Unites States receive sentences that are 2.7 times longer than sentences handed down in England and Wales, and 3.9 times longer than sentences given in Sweden.

Countries with already high rates of property offenses that are following the United State's lead by imposing lengthier sentences for property crimes may encounter a dilemma similar to that faced by our country, which is described by Lynch: ". . . the United States will have larger prison populations than other institutionally similar nations largely because of the relatively high levels of lethal violence" (2002: 40).

Similarly, if the rate of reported property offenses continues to increase in the United States, due in part to the rise in women's participation in property offenses, our country will be forced to choose between imposing even lengthier sentences for property crimes or considering alternative approaches to incarceration.

While each country is unique with respect to its social and cultural norms, legal foundation, and criminal justice policies, the ramifications of globalization may ultimately result in shared social issues and legal concerns, creating nations that are less heterogeneous. As the world's villages are being drawn closer together, Mahbubani (2002) notes: "a single mental universe and a single global society are in the process of being created" (45). Nations sharing common criminal justice concerns may be similar to the extent that they have comparable institutions of informal social control, political and legal institutions, and criminal justice practices as permitted by the legal climate (Lynch 2002).

As is occurring within the United States, the growth in the female prison population in other developing or developed countries may bear significant policy implications within each criminal justice system. The ramifications of incarcerating more women around the world may result in the review or implementation of policies that address:

1. The needs of pregnant offenders and inmates with children,
2. the financial costs of building or maintaining facilities to accommodate a growing female prison population,
3. community alternatives to corrections,
4. changes in correctional officer training,
5. a review of prison education programs, and
6. modifications in treatment/medical services to accommodate female inmates.

European nations are confronting the reality of the 100,000 women who are incarcerated in their prisons. These facilities do not provide appropriate accommodations for the numerous children who are permitted to stay with their confined mothers up to a certain age in countries such as Germany, Spain, the Netherlands, England and Wales, Iceland, Switzerland, Finland, and Russia (Vis 2000). Attachment difficulties, emotional problems, and personality disorders have been linked to early maternal separation, yet babies who remain with their mothers and are reared in confined environments, such as prisons, are highly vulnerable to long-term developmental retardation (Vis 2000). Clearly, the incarceration practices are critical not only to women and children's well-being, but also to the overall health of communities and families throughout the world.

While the international economic community will enjoy many positive trends in social and financial prosperity in the future, they will also share the challenges of handling the growing global correctional population and rising female participation in traditionally masculine criminal activity.

This paper hypothesizes that in countries where women have greater social and economic advantages, as indicated by the country's economic development, and where women have higher social status and levels of education, the rates of incarceration of women will also be greater than in developing nations. Specifically, the paper expands Simon's (1975) earlier opportunity theory and Chernoff and Simon's (2000) more recent study of international female offending, suggesting that where women are ascending in social status and are exposed to opportunities to engage in the crimes that have traditionally been committed by men, they will be incarcerated at higher rates.

METHOD

In this appendix we compare imprisonment rates for women among twenty-six countries. Eleven of the countries are the same as those included in the piece on female crime rates. They include the United States, Canada, Australia, the Western European countries of the United Kingdom, France, Sweden, Germany, the Netherlands, Finland, one Middle Eastern country, Israel, and one Asian country, Japan. The female crime data for Nigeria are available only until 1980. In addition, the countries for which we have female prison rates are two from Eastern Europe (Russia and Poland), two more from the Middle East (Lebanon and Iran), four more from Asia (India, Pakistan, Thailand, China), two more from Africa (Madagascar and South Africa), and four from Central and South America (Mexico, Belize, Brazil, Argentina). The countries for which we have female prison rates represent a more representative sample of countries worldwide.

DATA

Table B.1 describes the total prison population and the rate of prison population over a ten-year time period (data from International Centre for Prison Studies 2002).

With nearly 2 million individuals behind bars, the United States leads the other twenty-five countries with the largest total prison population, followed by China (1.4 million) and Russia (977,700). Prison population rates per 100,000 population are also compared in table B.1. At 690, the United States has the highest prison population rate among the twenty-six countries. The only country that comes close is Russia at 676. Belize and South Africa rank third and fourth at 456 and 406, respectively. India at 28 has the lowest rate followed by Japan at 48 and Pakistan at 57. The countries of Western Europe (France, Sweden, Germany, the Netherlands, Finland) have rates of less than 100.

Over the past decade, countries with the largest percent increases in prison population rates are Thailand (2.11), the Netherlands (1.89), and Madagascar (1.69). Countries with the lowest percent increase are France (1.01), Sweden (1.07), and Japan (1.29). Countries with a decrease in the percent change over

Table B.1. Trends in Total Prison Population and Prison Population Rates

Country	Total Prison Population[a]					Prison Population Rate[b]				
	1992/1993	1994/1995	1997/1998	1999/2000/ 2001/2002	% Change	1992/1993	1994/1995	1997/1998	1999/2000/ 2001/2002	% Change
United States	1,295,150	1,585,586	1,816,931	1,965,495	1.51758	505	600	669	690	1.366
Canada	30,723	33,759	32,951	31,624	1.0293	113	116	112	102	-0.9026
United Kingdom	45,817	51,047	65,298	71,233	1.5547	90	99	125	133	1.4777
Australia	14,174	15,957	18,692	22,458	1.58445	81	88	101	116	1.432
France[c]	48,113	51,623	50,744	50,714	1.05406	84	89	86	85	1.0119
Sweden	5,431	5,767	5,290	6,089	1.12115	63	65	60	68	1.079
Germany	57,448	66,146	78,584	78,707	1.3701	71	81	96	96	1.352
Netherlands	7,397	10,249	13,333	14,968	2.0235	49	66	85	93	1.898
Finland	3,295	3,018	2,569	3,040	-0.9226	65	59	50	59	-0.908
Russia	722,636	920,685	1,009,863	977,700	1.3529	487	622	688	676	1.388
Poland	58,619	62,719	57,382	81,165	1.3846	153	163	148	210	1.373
Israel	10,144	10,148	8,683	9,421	-0.929	201	189	147	153	-0.761
Lebanon	3,780	—	—	7,296	1.9301	133	—	—	221	1.662
Pakistan	72,950	72,700[d]	74,485	79,938	1.0957	54	50[d]	50	51	-0.944
Iran	101,801	—	—	158,000	1.552	157	—	—	233	1.484
India	—	—	—	281,320	—	—	—	—	28	—
Thailand	93,652	102,950[d]	197,214[e]	217,697[f]	2.3245	162	173[d]	324[e]	342	2.111
China	—	1,236,534	1,440,000	1,428,126[g]	—	—	101	115	111	—
Japan	45,802	46,622	50,897	61,242	1.3371	37	37	40	48	1.297
Brazil	126,152	148,760	170,602	233,859	1.8537	81	92	102	133	1.642
Belize	617	630	1,043	1,097	1.7779	310	293	448	459	1.481
Mexico	87,723	92,623	123,032	154,765	1.7642	102	102	108	156	1.529
Argentina	21,016	25,852	35,808	38,604	1.8368	63	75	100	107	1.698
Madagascar	18,370	21,658	19,743	20,109	1.0946	137	151	124	130	-0.949
South Africa	111,798	118,731[d]	141,441	177,701	1.5894	282	280[d]	359	406	1.44
Nigeria	—	—	44,797[e]	44,450[h]	—	—	—	41[e]	39	—

[a] Total prison population.
[b] per 100,000 nationals.
[c] Figures refer to metropolitan France.
[d] 1996 data.
[e] 1999 data.
[f] 2001 data.
[g] Sentenced prisoners only.
[h] 2000 data.

the last ten years are Canada (–0.90), Finland (–0.90), Israel (–0.76), Pakistan (–0.90), and Madagascar (–0.94).

Table B.2 describes the total prison population, the number of male and female prisoners, and the percent of female prisoners for the most recent time period (International Centre for Prison Studies 2002).

Looking at the percent of women in prison in table B.2, we see that Thailand leads all of the nations with 18.1 percent of the total prison population.

Table B.2.   Female Prisoners

Country	Prison Population[a]	Women Prisoners (% of Prison Population)	Estimated Number of Female Inmates[h]	Estimated Number of Male Inmates[i]
United States	1,965,495	8.1[d]	159,205.095	1,806,289.91
Canada	31,624	5.0	1,581.2	30,042.8
United Kingdom	71,233	6.2	4,416.446	66,816.55
Australia	22,458	6.7	1,504.686	20,953.31
France	50,714	3.7	1,876.418	48,834.58
Sweden	6,089	5.1	310.539	5,778.46
Germany	78,707	4.5	3,541.815	75,165.18
Netherlands	14,968	8.2 [e]	1,227.376	13,740.624
Finland	3,040	5.3	161.12	2,878.88
Russia	977,700	4.7	4,5951.9	931,748.1
Poland	81,165	2.7	2,191.455	78,973.54
Israel	9,421	2.0	188.42	9,232.58
Lebanon	7,296	3.1	226.176	7,069.82
Pakistan	79,938	1.7 [f]	1,358.946	78,579.05
Iran	158,000	3.0	4,740.0	153,260.0
India	281,320	3.1	8,720.92	272,599.08
Thailand	217,697	18.1	39,403.157	178,293.84
China	1,428,126 [e]	3.7	52,840.662	1,375,285.34
Japan	61,242	5.4	3,307.068	57,934.93
Brazil	233,859	4.2	9,822.078	224,036.92
Belize	1,097	6.4 [c]	70.208	1,026.79
Mexico	154,765	4.4 [g]	6,809.66	147,955.34
Argentina	38,604	8.6 [b]	3,319.944	35,284.06
Madagascar	20,109	3.1	623.379	19,485.62
South Africa	177,701	2.4	4,264.824	173,436.18
Nigeria	44,450	1.6	711.2	43,738.8

[a] Some figures include number in penal institutions and pretrial detainees or pretrial detainees/remand.
[b] 1996 data.
[c] 1998 data.
[d] 6.4 percent of state and federal inmates, 11.6 percent of local jail inmates.
[e] 6.0 percent if civil law juveniles are not included.
[f] Only adult prisoners.
[g] Of convicted prisoners.
[e] Sentenced prisoners only.
[h] Calculated by dividing women percent of prison population by 100 and multiplying by prison population.
[i] Calculated by subtracting estimated female prison population from total prison population.

Argentina, the Netherlands, and the United States rank second through fourth with 8.6 and 8.1 percent of the total prison population. The countries with the lowest percent of women in prison are Nigeria at 1.6 percent, Pakistan at 1.7 percent, Israel at 2.0 percent, and South Africa at 2.4 percent. Excluding Thailand, the range in the percentages of women in the prison population of the remaining twenty-five countries is seven, from 1.6 to 8.6. Only the United States and Belize have higher rates of male and female imprisonment. Russia at 4.7 percent and South Africa at 2.4 percent have relatively small percentages of women prisoners.

World Economic Development

The United Nation's *Human Development Report 2002* includes various indicators of economic growth and performance, as shown in table B.3 (United Nations Development Programme 2002). In 2000, countries with the largest GDP per capita (in PPP U.S. dollars) were the United States, Japan, and Australia; countries with the smallest GDP per capita (PPP in U.S. dollars) were Madagascar and Nigeria. (PPP is purchasing power parity.)

From 1975 to 2000, China and Thailand showed the greatest GDP per capita annual percentage growth rate, while Russia, Iran, Madagascar, South Africa, and Nigeria showed negative growths. More recently, from 1990 to 2000, China, Poland, and Lebanon showed the greatest GDP per capita annual percentage growth rate, whereas Russia, Madagascar, and Nigeria showed declines in annual growth rates.

Women's Status in Society

The United Nations Statistics Division's *The World's Women 2000: Trends and Statistics* reports the status of the world's women using statistical techniques. It compares women and men's social, physical, financial, and labor situations around the world. The report found that gender gaps in primary and secondary level education are closing, yet significant differences remain in some regions in Africa and South Asia. But, "women have made significant gains in higher education enrollment in most regions of the world" (United Nations Statistics Division 2002: ch. 4). Further, the report indicates that even though women constitute a growing share of the international labor force and are working more during their reproductive years, they still remain unemployed at higher rates and for longer durations than men (ch. 5). Today's women have increased opportunities to participate in the labor force through self-employment and part-time and home-based work, yet those positions are characterized as insecure, lacking in benefits, and low-income. The report also found that women still "re-

Table B.3.   Economic Growth and Progress

Country	GDP (US$ Billions) 2000	GDP Per Capita (PPP[a] US$) 2000	GDP Per Capita Annual Growth Rate (%) 1975–2000	GDP Per Capita Annual Growth Rate (%) 1990–2000
United States	9,837.4	34,142	2.0	2.2
Canada	687.9	27,840	1.5	1.9
United Kingdom	1414.6	23,509	2.0	2.2
Australia	390.1	25,693	1.9	2.9
France	1,294.2	24,223	1.7	1.3
Sweden	227.3	24,277	1.4	1.6
Germany	1,873.0	25,103	1.9	1.2
Netherlands	364.8	25,657	1.8	2.2
Finland	121.5	24,996	2.0	2.4
Russia	251.1	8,377	−1.2	−4.6
Poland	157.7	9,051	–	4.5
Israel	110.4	20,131	2.0	2.2
Lebanon	16.5	4,308	–	4.2
Pakistan	61.6	1,928	2.8	1.2
Iran	104.9	5,884	−0.7	1.9
India	457.0	2,358	3.2	4.1
Thailand	122.2	6,402	5.5	3.3
China	1,080.0	3,976	8.1	9.2
Japan	4,841.6	26,755	2.7	1.1
Brazil	595.5	7,625	0.8	1.5
Belize	0.8	5,606	2.9	1.6
Mexico	574.5	9,023	0.9	1.4
Argentina	285.0	12,377	0.4	3.0
Madagascar	3.9	840	−1.7	−0.9
South Africa	125.9	9,401	−0.7	–
Nigeria	41.1	896	−0.7	−0.4

[a] Purchasing power parity.

main at the lower end of a segregated labour market and continue to be concentrated in a few occupations, to hold positions of little or no authority and to receive less pay than men" (ch. 5).

Women's Education

Table B.4 shows each country's adult literacy rates by gender, and combined primary, secondary, and tertiary gross enrollment ratios for men and women (data from United Nations Development Programme's *Human Development Report 2002*). Literacy rate measures includes persons age 15 and above.

Appendix B

Table B.4. Literacy and Education by Gender

Countries	Female Adult Literacy[a] Rate (% Age 15 and Above), 2000	Male Adult Literacy[a] Rate (% Age 15 and Above), 2000	Gross Difference Between Adult Female and Male Literacy Rates	Female Combined Primary, Secondary and Tertiary Gross Enrollment Ratio[b] (%), 2000	Male Combined Primary, Secondary and Tertiary Gross Enrollment Ratio[b] (%), 2000	Gross Difference Between Female and Male Enrollment Ratios
United States	99.0	99.0	0.0	91	99	8
Canada	99.0	99.0	0.0	96	98	2
United Kingdom	99.0	99.0	0.0	100	112	12
Australia	99.0	99.0	0.0	114	118	4
France	99.0	99.0	0.0	93	96	3
Sweden	99.0	99.0	0.0	95	107	12
Germany	99.0	99.0	0.0	95	93	2
Netherlands	99.0	99.0	0.0	104	100	4
Finland	99.0	99.0	0.0	99	108	9
Russia	99.4	99.7	0.3	75	82	7
Poland	99.7	99.7	0.0	83	86	3
Israel	92.4	96.8	4.4	82	84	2
Lebanon	80.3	92.1	11.8	76	81	5
Pakistan	27.9	57.5	29.6	51	28	23
Iran	69.3	83.2	13.9	76	69	7
India	45.4	68.4	23.0	62	49	13
Thailand	93.9	97.1	3.2	60	61	1
China	76.3	91.7	15.4	73	73	0
Japan	99.0	99.0	0.0	83	81	2
Brazil	85.4	85.1	−0.3	79	80	1
Belize	93.2	93.3	0.1	73	72	1
Mexico	89.5	93.4	3.9	71	70	1
Argentina	96.8	96.8	0.0	80	86	6
Madagascar	59.7	73.6	13.9	46	43	3
South Africa	84.6	86.0	1.4	89	96	7
Nigeria	55.7	72.4	16.7	49	41	8

[a] Defined by the United Nations as: "The percentage of people aged 15 and above who can, with understanding, both read and write a short, simple statement on their everyday life."
[b] As defined by the United Nations: "Gross enrolment ratios are calculated by dividing the number of children enrolled in each level of schooling by the number of children in the age group corresponding to that level."

Countries with the lowest female adult literacy rates were Pakistan (27.9 percent), India (45.4 percent), and Nigeria (55.7 percent). Pakistan (57.5 percent) and India (68.4 percent) also had the lowest male adult literacy rates. Canada, France, the United States, Finland, Netherlands, Japan, Sweden, the United Kingdom, Australia, Poland, and Russia all had adult literacy rates of 99 percent or above for both men and women. The largest gaps between male and female literacy rates were in Pakistan (29.6 point difference) and India (23.0 point difference). Interestingly, Brazil had a higher adult female literacy rate than the male literacy rate.

The combined first, second, and third level gross enrollment ratios reflect "the number of students enrolled in a level of education, regardless of age, as a percentage of the population of official school age for that level" (United Nations Development Programme 2002). Countries with the highest female combined gross enrollment ratios in 1999 were Australia (118 percent), the United Kingdom (112 percent), Finland (108.0 percent), and Sweden (107.0 percent). Pakistan and Nigeria had the lowest gross enrollment ratios for females at 28.0 percent and 41.0 percent, respectively. The largest gaps in gross enrollment ratios between males and females were seen in Pakistan (23), India (13), Sweden (12), and the United Kingdom (12).

Countries with the highest percentage in 1999 for males were the United Kingdom (100 percent), the Netherlands (104 percent), and Australia (114 percent). Countries with the lowest percentage for males were Madagascar (46.0 percent), Nigeria (49.0 percent), and Pakistan (51.0 percent).

Women in the Workforce

Women make up over 45 percent of the adult labor force in the United States, Canada, Sweden, Finland, Russia, and Poland. Table B.5 shows females as a percentage of each country's total number of professional/technical workers, and legislators, senior officials, and managers (data retrieved from UNDP Human Development Reports 2002, 2001, 1999, 1998; United Nations Statistics Division's *The World's Women 2000: Trends and Statistics*).

In Sweden, for example, 49 percent of the country's professional and technical workers are women, whereas they comprise only 29 percent of the country's legislators, senior officials, and managers.

Women's Share of Earned Income

Women in industrialized western countries appear to earn a larger share of income than women in Asia, Africa, and the Middle East, as seen in table B.5. Data were unavailable in six countries. When examining women's share of earned income, those with the highest shares were in the United States (40 percent), Finland (42 percent), and Sweden (45 percent). Women with the lowest shares of earned income were in Iran (19 percent) and Belize (18 percent).

Women's Fertility

As seen below in table B.6 (United Nations Statistics Division), Madagascar and Pakistan have the highest fertility rates, with 5.4 and 5.0 births per woman, respectively.

Table B.5. Women's Participation in the Labor Force

Country	Female Professional and Technical Workers[a] (as % of Total)	Female Legislators, Senior Officials, and Managers[a] (as % of Total)	% Women Among Admin. & Managerial Workers, 1985–1997	% Women in Adult Labor Force, 1995–2000	Women's Share of Earned Income[b]	Estimated Earned Income[h] (PPP US$) Female 1999	Estimated Earned Income[h] (PPP US$) Male 1999
United States	54	45	44.0	47[c]	40	24,302[l]	39,655[l]
Canada	53	35	43.0	46	38	20,016[l]	32,607[l]
United Kingdom	45	33	33.0	44[c]	38	16,753	27,611
Australia	48	26	24.0	43	.	19,721	29,469
France	56[b]	.	10.0	45	39	17,525	28,554
Sweden	49	29	59.0	48[f]	45	18,302[l]	27,065[l]
Germany	50	27	19.0	43	35	15,846	31,994
Netherlands	46	27	17.0	42[g]	34	16,405	32,170
Finland	56	27	25.0	47[d]	42	18,402[l]	28,023[l]
Russia	64	37	.	48[e]	.	5,877[l]	9,283[l]
Poland	61	33	66.0	46	39	6,453[l]	10,561[l]
Israel	55	26	19.0	45	33	12,360[l]	24,687[l]
Lebanon	.	.	.	28	.	2,160[l]	7,364[l]
Pakistan	26	9	4.0	13	21	826[l]	2,787[l]

Iran	33[b]	·	2.0	12	19	2,331[i]	8,581[i]
India	21[b]	·	2.3[i]	31	25	1,195[i]	3,236[i]
Thailand	55	27	21.0	45	37	4,634	7,660
China	45[b]	·	12.0	45	38	2,841[i]	4,350[i]
Japan	45	9	9.0	41	34	15,187	35,018
Brazil	62	·	37.0	41	29	4,067	10,077
Belize	39	37	36.6[i]	31	18	1,858[i]	7,972[i]
Mexico	41	24	20.0	34	26	4,486	12,184
Argentina	·	·	·	37	·	6,319[i]	18,467[i]
Madagascar	·	·	·	44	·	595[i]	1,005[i]
South Africa	47[b]	·	19.0	37	31	5,473[i]	12,452[i]
Nigeria	·	·	6.0	36	·	520[i]	1,182[i]

[a] Data refer to the latest year available during the period 1991–2000.
[b] Data from the United Nations Human Development Report 1998—Gender Empowerment Measure
[c] Ages 16 or older.
[d] Age 15 to 74.
[e] Age 15 to 72.
[f] Age 16 to 64.
[g] Age 15 to 64.
[h] "Because of the lack of gender-disaggregated income data, female and male earned incomes are crudely estimated on the basis of data on the ratio of the female nonagricultural wage to the male nonagricultural wage, the male and female shares of the economically active population, and the total female and male population and GDP per capita (PPP US$).
[i] "No wage data available. For purposes of calculating the estimated female and male earned income, an estimate of 75 percent, the unweighted average for the countries with available data, was used for the ratio of the female nonagricultural wage to the male nonagricultural wage.
[j] Data based on Human Development Report 1999.

Table B.6.   Total Fertility Rate[a]: 1995–2000

Country	Total Fertility Rate (Births Per Woman) 1995–2000
USA	2.0
Canada	1.6
UK	1.7
Australia	1.8
France	1.7
Sweden	1.6
Germany	1.3
Netherlands	1.5
Finland	1.7
Russia	1.3
Poland	1.5
Israel	2.7
Lebanon	2.7
Pakistan	5.0
Iran	2.8
India	3.1
Thailand	1.7
China	1.8
Japan	1.4
Brazil	2.3
Belize	3.7
Mexico	2.8
Argentina	2.6
Madagascar	5.4
South Africa	3.3

[a] Indicates births per woman.

The countries with the lowest fertility rates of 1.3 births per woman are Germany and Russia.

Women and Crime

Table B.7 describes the mean percent of female offenders by types of offenses from 1981 through 1995 and from 1995 through 2000 (data retrieved from Interpol data as reported in Chernoff, and Simon 2000).

The country with the highest percent was Germany (22.37 percent). The Netherlands had the lowest percent of female offenders (11.5 percent). In addition, the countries are ranked by the percent of female offenders responsible for all offenses recorded in each country's National Crime Statistics between 1995 and 2000, with 1 indicating the highest percentage. Of the nineteen countries with available data, Germany (23.1 percent) had the highest percentage

Table B.7. Female Offenders, Percent of Crime by Type Committed by Females, and Ranking of Women Prisoners as Percent of Total Prison Population by Country

Country	Mean % of Offenders Who Are Female, 1981–1995	% of All Offenders[c] Who Are Female, 1995–2000[a]	Countries Ranked by % of Female Offenders Responsible For All Offenses 1995–2000[b,c]	% of All Thefts Committed by Females, 1995–2000[a]	% of Fraud Committed by Females, 1995–2000[a]	% of Counterfeit/Currency Offenses Committed by Females, 1995–2000[a]	% of Drug Offenses Committed by Females, 1995–2000[a]	Countries Ranked by Women Prisoners as % of Total Prison Population[b,c]
USA	18.28	22.20	2	28.80	44.90	39.00	17.60	4
Canada	13.28	18.40	5	22.30	30.60	19.00	14.30	11
UK	16.25	18.10	6	23.30	29.10	.	10.70	7
Australia	17.38	.	.	.	.	.	.	5
France	16.79	13.60	9	14.10	25.30	16.70	8.00	16
Sweden	15.26	19.00	4	29.00	25.00	8.00	15.00	10
Germany	22.37	23.10	1	30.20	25.50	18.10	12.20	13
Netherlands	11.15	10.00	14	12.00	19.00	16.00	12.00	3
Finland	12.45	15.20	8	14.50	27.80	.	13.30	9
Russia	.	16.30	7	9.30	37.00	17.00	14.50	12
Poland	.	9.60	15	6.80	19.50	14.00	11.60	22
Israel	12.84	13.40	10	9.44	15.60	7.80	9.60	24
Lebanon	.	10.15	13	8.10	7.06	1.01	6.45	18
Pakistan	.	1.00	19	1.00	1.00	1.00	1.00	25
Iran	.	.	.	.	.	.	.	21
India	.	4.30	17	1.90	2.90	1.80	3.80	18
Thailand	.	.	.	.	.	.	.	1
China	.	5.13	16	.	9.83	.	16.44	16
Japan	18.80	19.50	3	28.60	14.00	13.30	18.50	8

(continued)

Table B.7. Female Offenders, Percent of Crime by Type Committed by Females, and Ranking of Women Prisoners as Percent of Total Prison Population by Country (*continued*)

Country	Mean % of Offenders Who Are Female, 1981–1995	% of All Offenders[c] Who Are Female, 1995–2000[a]	Countries Ranked by % of Female Offenders Responsible For All Offenses 1995–2000[b,c]	% of All Thefts Committed by Females, 1995–2000[a]	% of Fraud Committed by Females, 1995–2000[a]	% of Counterfeit/ Currency Offenses Committed by Females, 1995–2000[a]	% of Drug Offenses Committed by Females, 1995–2000[a]	Countries Ranked by Women Prisoners as % of Total Prison Population[b,c]
Brazil	.	.	.	.	.	.	.	15
Belize	.	2.04	18	1.00	1.00	.	.	6
Mexico	.	10.94	12	8.11	12.77	10.25	14.55	14
Argentina	.	12.39	11	9.70	15.12	.	5.31	2
Madagascar	.	.	.	.	.	.	.	18
South Africa	.	.	.	.	.	.	.	23
Nigeria	.	.	.	.	.	.	.	26

[a] Interpol data.
[b] Rankings only include countries with available data, 1 = highest.
[c] Includes all offenses recorded in each country's National Crime Statistics.

of female offenders responsible for all offenses, followed by the United States (22.2), and Japan (19.5). Countries with the lowest percentage were Pakistan (1.0), Belize (2.04), and India (4.3).

The countries were also ranked by the percentage of the total prison population who are female. A ranking of 1 indicates the highest percent and a ranking of 26 the lowest. Countries with the highest percent of female inmates are Thailand (1), Argentina (2), and the Netherlands (3). The countries with the lowest percents are Nigeria (26), Pakistan (25), and Israel (24).

The crimes committed by women from 1995 through 2000 are broken down to include thefts, fraud, counterfeit/currency offenses, and drug offenses. Table B.7 shows the percent of females committing those crimes in each category for each country. Of eighteen countries with available data, Germany (30.2 percent) had the highest percent of women who committed all thefts between 1995 and 2000, followed by the United States (28.8 percent) and Japan (28.6 percent). Countries with the lowest percent of women responsible for all thefts were Pakistan (1.0 percent), Belize (1.0 percent), and India (1.9 percent).

Nineteen counties reported the percent of fraud committed by women. The United States had the highest percent (44.0 percent), followed by Russia (37.0 percent) and Canada (30.6 percent). Countries with the lowest percentages were Pakistan (1.0 percent), Belize (1.0 percent), and India (2.9 percent). Of the fourteen countries with data regarding counterfeit/currency crimes, the United States (39.0 percent) and Canada (19.0 percent) had the highest percent of women offenders. Pakistan (1.0 percent) and Lebanon (1.01 percent) had the lowest percents of women committing counterfeit/currency offenses.

Data regarding drug offenses were available for eighteen countries. Japan (18.5 percent), the United States (17.6 percent), and China (16.44 percent) had the highest number of women committing drug offenses from 1995 to 2000, whereas countries with the smallest percents were Pakistan (1.0 percent), India (3.8 percent), and Madagascar (5.31 percent). Despite the paucity of data for many countries, it is clear that the types of crimes committed by women vary per region, as do the actual number of women in each country's prison population.

RESULTS

Table B.8 shows the correlations with the variables described above.

Comparing the social status of women in the countries in which they represent the highest percent of the prison population, we find that they are also countries in which women have high literacy rates. Significant positive

Table B.8. Correlations

	Female Adult Literacy Rate, 2000	Female Combined Primary, Secondary, and Tertiary Gross Enrollment Ratio (%), 2000	Female Prof. and Tech. Workers as % of Total	Female Legislators, Senior Officials, and Managers as % of Total	% Women Among Admin. & Managerial Workers, 1985–1997	Women's Share of Earned Income %	% Women in Adult Labor Force, 1995–2000	GDP Per Capita Annual Growth Rate (%), 1975–2000	Total Fertility Rate, 1995–2000	% of All Thefts Committed by Females, 1995–2000	% of Fraud Committed by Females, 1995–2000	% of Counterfeit/Currency Offenses Committed by Females, 1995–2000	% of Drug Offenses Committed by Females, 1995–2000	% of Persons Responsible for Offenses in National Crime Statistics Who Are Female, 1995–2000
Crime														
Women prisoners as % of prison population	0.427*	0.14	0.227	0.188	0.154	0.254	0.301	0.372*	−0.388*	0.358	0.382	0.586*	0.624**	0.325
Education														
Female combined primary, secondary, and tertiary gross enrollment ratio (%), 2000	0.757**	—	0.418*	0.309	0.40*	0.626*	0.435**	0.041	−0.75**	0.628**	0.614**	0.589*	0.589*	0.615**
Female adult literacy rate, 2000	—	0.757**	0.772*	0.561*	0.571*	0.632**	0.682**	0.030	−0.798	0.552**	0.633**	0.598*	0.768**	0.652*

Correlation matrix (rotated table). Row variables are listed at the foot of the table; values read left to right across the columns.

Variable	(1)	(2)	(3)	(4)	(5)	(6)	(7)	(8)	(9)
Labor Female professional and technical workers as % of total	0.598**	0.607**	0.581*	0.744**	0.358	−0.669**			
Female legislators, senior officials, and managers as % of total	0.253	0.422	0.729**	0.623*	0.084	−0.328			
% Women among admin. & managerial workers, 1985/1997	0.323	0.425	0.377	0.476*	0.264	−0.410*			
% Women in adult labor force, 1995/2000	0.683**	0.691**	0.639**	0.748**	0.579**	−0.548**	0.123		
Women's share of earned income %	0.708**	0.739**	0.574*	0.793**	0.697**	−0.793**	0.206	0.876**	
Economy GDP (US$ billions, 2000)	0.510*	0.488*	0.771**	0.495**	0.594**	−0.257	0.138	0.235	0.274

Additional inter-correlation values shown in the lower portion of the table (lower-triangular):

0.682**	0.435*	0.632**	0.216	0.246
0.782**	0.686**	0.113		
0.553*	0.321	0.485*		
0.485*	0.534	0.876**	—	

* Significant at the 0.05 level (1-tailed).
** Significant at the 0.01 level (1-tailed).

correlations are seen between women prisoners as a percent of the prison population and the female adult literacy rate (0.427), GDP per capita annual growth rate (0.372), and the percent of women responsible for counterfeit/currency offenses (0.586) and drug offenses (0.624). A significant negative correlation exists between women prisoners as a percent of the prison population and total fertility rate (–0.388). There are no significant correlations between the females as a percent of the total prison population and any of the labor/workforce indicators.

With regards to education, the female combined primary, secondary, and tertiary gross enrollment ratio positively and significantly correlates with the percent of all thefts (0.628), fraud (0.614), counterfeit/currency offenses (0.589), and drug offenses (0.589) committed by women. There is also a positive and significant relationship with the percent of persons responsible for all recorded offenses who are female (0.615). The female adult literacy rate also correlates significantly with the percent of women responsible for all thefts (0.552), fraud (0.633), counterfeit/currency offenses (0.598), drug offenses (0.768), and all offenses (0.652).

Table B.8 also suggests that the countries' economic status varies significantly with the percent of women committing certain types of crime. The measure of GDP (US$ billions) positively and significantly correlates with the percent of women who committed all thefts (0.594), fraud (0.495), counterfeit/currency offenses (0.771), drug offenses (0.488), and total offenses (0.510).

Many positive and significant correlations are seen between the female labor variables and the percent of crimes committed by women. The percent of total professional and technical workers who are female correlates with the percent of women responsible for all fraud (0.744), counterfeit/currency offenses (0.581), drug offenses (0.607), and for total offenses (0.598). Only the percent of fraud (0.623) and counterfeit/currency (0.729) offenses committed by women correlate with the percent of female legislators, senior officials, and managers. The percent of women among administrative and managerial workers positively correlates with the percent of female fraud offenders (0.476). The percent of women in the workforce positively and significantly correlates with the percent of women responsible for all thefts (0.579), fraud (0.748), counterfeit/currency offenses (0.639), drug offenses (0.691), and total offenses (0.683). Additionally, the results indicate a positive and significant correlation between women's share of earned income and the percent of women who committed all thefts (0.697), fraud (0.793), counterfeit/currency offenses (0.574), drug offenses (0.739), and total offenses (0.708).

CONCLUSION

The strong positive and significant relationship between female crime rates and women's status in society is to some extent also depicted by the prison data, although the evidence in the latter is not as robust. Nonetheless, we find that the more economically advanced the society, and the higher the status of women regarding employment and education, the greater the likelihood of having more women in prison.

NOTE

1. This appendix originally appeared in *Gender Issues* 20, no. 1 (Winter 2002): 53–75.

References

Abbot, Sidney, and Barbara Love. 1971. "Is Women's Liberation a Lesbian Plot?" In V. Gornick, B. Moran et al. *Women in Sexist Society*. New York: Basic Books, 601–621.

Adler, Freda. 1975. *Sisters in Crime: The Rise of the New Female Criminal*. New York: McGraw-Hill.

American Correctional Association. 1988. 1989 Directory of Juvenile and Adult Correctional Departments, Institutions, Agencies and Paroling Authorities. Laurel, Maryland.

Anno, B. Jaye. 2000. "Inappropriate Prison Populations." Pp. 76–81 in *Building Violence*, ed. John B. May. Thousand Oaks, Calif.: Sage.

Anthony, Debra. 1973. "Judges Perception of Women Offenders and Their Own Actions toward Women Offenders." Unpublished master's thesis. Urbana-Champaign: University of Illinois.

Archer, D., and R. Gartner. 1984. *Violence and Crime in Cross-National Perspective*. New Haven, Conn.: Yale University Press.

Arditi, R. R., F. Goldberg, Jr., H. M. Hartle, J. H. Peters, and W. R. Phelps. 1973. "The Sexual Segregation of American Prisons: Notes." *Yale Law Journal* 82, 1229–1273.

Australian Institute of Criminology. www.aic.gov.au.

Bartel, Ann P. 1979. "Women and Crime: An Economic Analysis" *Economic Inquiry* 17 (January): 29–51.

Baunach, Phyllis Jo. 1979. "Mothering from Behind Prison Walls." Paper presented to the American Society of Criminology.

Bianchi, Suzanne M., and Daphne Spain. 1986. *American Women in Transition*. New York: Russell Sage Foundation.

Black, Donald. 1976. *The Behavior of Law*. New York: Academic Press.

Box, Steven, and Chris Hale. 1983. "Liberation/Emancipation, Economic Marginalization, or Less Chivalry: The Relevance of Three Theoretic Arguments to Female Crime Patterns in England and Wales, 1951–1983." *Criminology* 22, nos. 473–497.

Burkhart, K. 1973. *Women in Prison*. New York: Doubleday.

Cernkovich, Stephen A., and Peggy Giordano. 1979. "Delinquency, Opportunity and Gender." *Journal of Criminal Law and Criminology* 70 (Summer): 145–151.

Chafe, W. H. 1972. *The American Woman.* New York: Oxford University Press.

Chapman, Jane R. 1980. *Economic Realities and the Female Offender.* Lexington, Mass.: Lexington Books.

Chernoff, Nina, and Rita J. Simon. 2000. "Women and Crime the World Over." *Gender Issues* 18: 5–20.

Chesney-Lind, Meda. 2002. "Imprisoning Women: The Unintended Victims of Mass Incarceration." Pp. 79–94 in *Invisible Punishment: The Collateral Consequences of Mass Imprisonment*, edited by Marc Mauer and Meda Chesney-Lind. New York: New Press.

———. 1987. "Female Offenders: Paternalism Reexamined." Pp. 114–139 in *Women, the Courts, and Equality*, edited by Laura L. Crites and Winifred L. Hepperle. Newbury Park, Calif.: Sage.

———. 1986. "Women and Crime: The Female Offender." *Signs: Journal of Women in Culture and Society* 12, no. 1: 78–96.

Cressey, Donald R. 1953. *Other People's Money: A Study in the Social Psychology of Embezzlement.* Reprinted in 1973. Montclair, N.J.: Patterson Smith.

Crime and Criminal Justice Unit of the Home Office, United Kingdom.

Crites, Laura L., and Winifred L. Hepperle, eds. 1987. *Women, the Courts and Equality.* Newbury Park, Calif.: Sage.

Culbertson, Robert and Eddyth P. Fortune. 1991. "Women in Crime and Prison." Pp. 105–120 in *The Dilemmas of Corrections,* edited by Kenneth C. Haas and Geoffrey P. Alpert. Prospect Heights, IL: Waveland Press.

Daly, Kathleen. 1989a. "Neither Conflict nor Labeling nor Paternalism Will Suffice: Intersections of Race, Ethnicity, Gender and Family in Criminal Court Decisions." *Crime and Delinquency* 35, no. 1: 136–168.

———. 1989b. "Rethinking Judicial Paternalism: Gender, Work–Family Relations, and Sentencing." *Gender and Society* 3, no. 1: 9–36.

———. 1989c. "Gender and Varieties of White-Collar Crime." *Criminology* 27, no. 4: 769–793.

———. 1987. "Discrimination in Criminal Courts: Family, Gender, and the Problem of Equal Treatment." *Social Forces* 66: 152–175.

———. 1983. *Order in the Court: Gender and Justice.* Washington, D.C.: National Institute of Justice.

Daly, Kathleen, and Meda Chesney-Lind. 1988. "Feminism and Criminology." *Justice Quarterly* 5, no. 4: 101–143.

Datesman, Susan, and Frank R. Scarpetti. 1980. *Women, Crime and Justice.* New York: Oxford University Press.

Death Penalty Information Center. 2003. "Women and the Death Penalty." Washington, D.C. Retrieved August 6, 2003, www.deathpenaltyinfo.org.

———. 2003. "Death Row Facts: Size of Death Row Population from 1968 to the Present." Washington, D.C. Retrieved August 6, 2003, www.deathpenaltyinfo.org.

———. 2003. *Executions in the U.S. 1608–1987: The Espy File.* Washington, D.C. Retrieved August 6, 2003, www.deathpenaltyinfo.org.

———. 2003. "Executions in 2003." Washington, D.C. Retrieved August 6, 2003, www.deathpenaltyinfo.org.

DeFleur, Lois B. 1975. "Biasing Influences on Drug Arrest Records: Implications for Deviance Research." *American Sociological Review* 40, no. 1: 88–103.

Deming, Richard. 1977. *The New Criminals*. New York: Dell.

Dodge, Mary, and Mark R. Pogrebin. 2004. "Collateral Costs of Imprisonment for Women: Complications of Reintegration." Pp. 289–299 in *The Prisoner Prison Experience*, edited by Mary K. Stohn and Craig Hemmens. Upper Saddle River, N.J.: Pearson Education.

Donziger, Steven R. 1996. *The Real War on Crime: The Report of the National Criminal Justice Commission*. New York: HarperPerennial.

Epstein, C., and W. Goode, eds. 1973. *The Other Half*. Englewood Cliffs, N.J.: Prentice Hall.

Farley, Reynolds, and Walter R. Allen. 1987. *The Color Line and the Quality of Life in America*. New York: Russell Sage Foundation.

Farrington, D. P., and A. M. Morris. 1983. "Sex, Sentencing and Reconviction." *British Journal of Criminology* 23, no. 3: 229–248.

Federal Bureau of Investigation. 2001. Press Release 2001. U.S. Department of Justice, Washington, D.C. Retrieved August 5, 2003, www.fbi.gov/pressrel/pressrel01/cius2000.htm.

Feinman, Clarice. 1986. *Women in the Criminal Justice System*. 2nd ed. New York: Praeger.

———. 1976. "Prisoner Demographic Profile, March 1975–December 1975." P. 18 in *Women's Development Unit Project Annual Report, January 1, 1975–April 6, 1979*. New York: New York City Correctional Institution for Women.

Fenster, C. 1977. "Differential Dispositions: A Preliminary Study of Male–Female Partners in Crime." Paper presented to the Annual Meeting of the American Society of Criminology, Atlanta, Georgia.

Feris, Abbot L. 1971. *Indicators of Trends in the Status of American Women*. New York: Russell Sage Foundation.

Forst, Brian. 1995. "Prosecution and Sentencing." Pp. 363–386 (esp. 376) in *Crime*, edited by James Q. Wilson and Joan Petersilia. San Francisco: ICS Press.

Freeman, Jo. 1985. "The Women's Liberation Movement: Its Origins, Structures, Impact, and Ideas." In *Women: A Feminist Perspective*, edited by Jo Freeman. Palo Alto, Calif.: Mayfield Publishing.

———. 1973. "The Origins of the Women's Liberation Movement." *American Journal of Sociology* 78, no. 4: 798–812.

Ghali, M., and Meda Chesney-Lind. 1986. "Gender Bias and the Criminal System." *Sociology and Social Research* 70, no. 2: 164–171.

Giallombardo, R. 1966. *Society of Women: A Study of a Women's Prison*. New York: John Wiley and Sons.

Glick, Ruth M., and Virginia V. Neto. 1977. *National Study of Women's Correctional Programs*. Washington, D.C.: U.S. Government Printing Office.

Gora, Joanne G. 1982. *The New Female Criminal: Empirical Reality or Social Myth?* New York: Praeger.

Gornick, Vivian, and Barbara Moran, eds. 1971. *Woman in Sexist Society.* New York: BasicBooks.

Grasmick, Harold G., Nancy J. Finley, and Deborah L. Glaser. 1984. "Labor Force Participation, Sex-Role Attitudes and Female Crime." *Social Science Quarterly* 65, no. 3: 703–718.

Hagan, John. 1985. "Toward a Structural Theory of Crime, Race and Gender: The Canadian Case." *Crime and Delinquency* 31, no. 1: 129–146.

Hagan, John and Ronit Dinovitzer. 1999. "Collateral Consequences of Imprisonment." Pp. 121–162 in *Prisons*, edited by Michael Tonry and Joan Petersilia. Chicago: University of Chicago Press.

Hagan, John, A. R. Gillis, and J. Simpson. 1985. "The Class Structure of Gender and Delinquency: Toward a Power-Control Theory of Common Delinquent Behavior." *American Journal of Sociology* 90, no. 6: 1151–1178.

Hagan, John, J. H. Simpson, and A. R. Gillis. 1979. "The Sexual Stratification of Social Control: A Gender-Based Perspective on Crime and Delinquency." *British Journal of Sociology* 30, no. 1: 25–38.

Harris, A. R. 1977. "Sex and Theories of Deviance: Toward a Functional Theory of Deviant Type-Scripts." *American Sociological Review* 42: 3–16.

Hartnagel, T. F. 1982. "Modernization, Female Social Roles, and Female Crime: A Cross-National Investigation." *Sociological Quarterly* 23: 477–490.

Heidensohn, Frances M. 1985. *Women and Crime: The Life of the Female Offender.* London: Macmillan.

Heitfield, Heather and Rita Simon. 2002. "Women in Prison: A Comparative Assessment." *Gender Issues* 20, no. 1 (Winter).

Hill, G. D., and A. R. Harris. 1981. "Changes in the Gender Patterning of Crime, 1953–1977: Opportunity vs. Identity." *Social Science Quarterly* 62: 658–671.

Hoffman-Bustamante, Dale. 1973. "The Nature of Female Criminality." *Issues in Criminology* 8 (Fall): 117–136.

Human Rights Watch. 1996. "All Too Familiar—Sexual Abuse of Women in United States State Prisons," New York, p. 16. Retrieved August 5, 2003, http://hrw.org/reports/1996/Us1.htm.

International Criminal Police Organization. www.interpol.int.

International Centre for Prison Studies. 2002. "World Prison Brief." London: International Centre for Prison Studies. Retrieved August 2002, www.kcl.ac.uk/depsta/rel/icps/worldbrief/world_brief.html.

International Labour Office. 1998. *Yearbook of Labour Statistics*, Table 1A.

International Labour Organization, Caribbean Office. 1999. *Digest of Caribbean Labour Statistics 1998*, Port of Spain, International Labour Office.

Johnson, Robert. 2002. *Hard Time: Understanding and Reforming the Prison.* 3rd ed. New York: Wadsworth.

———. 1998. *Death Work: A Study of the Modern Execution Process.* 2nd ed. New York: Wadsworth.

Kempinen, Cynthia. 1979. "Changes in the Sentencing Patterns of Male and Female Criminal Defendants." *The Prison Journal* 63, no. 2: 3–11.

Klein, D., and J. Kress. 1976. "Any Woman's Blues: A Critical Overview of Women, Crime, and Criminal Justice." *Crime and Social Justice* 5: 34.

Krohn, Marvin D., James P. Curry, and Shirley Nelson-Kigler. 1983. "Is Chivalry Dead? An Analysis of Changes in Police Dispositions of Males and Females." *Criminology* 21, no. 3: 417–437.

Kruttschnitt, Candace. 1984. "Sex and Criminal Court Dispositions: The Unresolved Controversy." *Research in Crime and Delinquency* 21, no. 3: 213–232.

———. 1982. "Women, Crime, and Dependency: An Application of the Theory of Law." *Criminology* 19, no. 4: 495–513.

———. 1980–1981. "Social Status and Sentences of Female Offenders." *Law and Society Review* 15, no. 2: 247–265.

Leonard, Eileen. 1982. *Women, Crime and Society: A Critique of Theoretical Criminology*. New York: Longman.

Leventhal, Gloria. 1977. "Female Criminology: Is Women's 'Lib' to Blame?" *Psychological Reports* 41: 179–182.

Lewis, Diane. K. 1981. "Black Women Offenders and Criminal Justice: Some Theoretical Considerations." In *Comparing Female and Male Offenders*, edited by Marguerite Warren. Beverly Hills, Calif.: Sage.

Lilly, J. Robert, Francis T. Cullen, and Richard A. Ball. 1995. *Criminological Theory, Second Edition*. Thousand Oaks, Calif.: Sage.

Lubitz, Robin L., and Thomas W. Ross. 2001. "Sentencing Guidelines: Reflections on the Future." Washington, D.C.: U.S. Department of Justice. Retrieved October 9, 2001, www.ncjrs.org/txtfiles1/nij/186480.txt.

Lynch, James. 2002. "Crime in International Perspective." Pp. 5–41 in *Crime*, edited by James Q. Wilson and Joan Petersilia. Oakland, Calif.: ICS Press.

Mahbubani, Kishore. 2002. *Can Asians Think?* Southroyalton, Vt.: Steerforth Press.

Mann, Coramae Richey. 1984. *Female Crime and Delinquency*. Tuscaloosa: University of Alabama Press.

Mauer, Marc, and the Sentencing Project. 1999. *The Race to Incarcerate*. New York: New Press.

McGowan, Brenda, and Karen Blumenthal. 1978. *Why Punish the Children? A Study of Women Prisoners*. Hackensack, N.J.: National Commission on Crime and Delinquency.

Merton, Robert. 1968. *Social Theory and Social Structure*. Glencoe, Ill.: Free Press.

Messerschmidt, James W. 1986. *Capitalism, Patriarchy and Crime: Toward a Socialist Feminist Criminology*. Totowa, N.J.: Rowman & Littlefield.

The Michigan Daily. 1998. "Abuse behind Bars: State Must End Rights Violations in Its Prisons." Retrieved August 5, 2003, www.pub.umich.edu/daily/1998/oct/10-20-98/edit/edit2.html.

Millet, K. 1973. *Prostitution Papers*. New York: Avon.

———. 1968. *Sexual Politics*. Garden City, N.Y.: W.W. Norton.

Ministry of Japan. "Criminal Justice Systems at Work, 1998: Outline of Crime Trends, Criminal Procedures and Juvenile Justice System in Japan." Ministry of Justice, Japan.

Morris, Norval. 1993. "The Honest Politician's Guide to Sentencing Reform." Pp. 303–310 in *The Socio-Economics of Crime and Justice,* edited by Brian Forst. Armonk, N.Y.: M. E. Sharpe.

Musolino, Angela. 1988. "Judge's Attitudes toward Female Offenders." Unpublished manuscript.

National Organization for Women. www.now.org.

Naffine, Ngaire. 1987. *Female Crime: The Construction of Women in Criminology.* Boston: Allen and Unwin.

Nagel, Ilene H., John Cardascia, and Catherine Ross. 1982. "Sex Differences in the Processing of Criminal Defendants." In *Women and the Law,* edited by D. Kelly Weisberg. Cambridge, Mass.: Schenkman.

Nagel, S. S., and L. J. Weitzman. 1971. "Women as Litigants." *Hastings Law Journal* 23, no. 1: 171–198.

Norland, Stephen, and Neal Shover. 1978. "Gender Roles and Female Criminality." *Criminology* 15: 97–104.

O'Shea, Kathleen. 2000. *Women on the Row: Revelations from Both Sides of the Bars.* Ithaca, N.Y.: Firebrand Books.

Pollack-Byrne, Joycelyn. 1990. *Women, Prison & Crime.* Pacific Grove, Calif.: Brooks/Cole.

Pollack, Otto. 1950. *The Criminality of Women.* Philadelphia: University of Pennsylvania Press.

Riveland, Chase. 1999. "Prison Management Trends, 1975–2025." Pp. 163–203 in *Prisons,* edited by Michael Tonry and Joan Petersilia. Chicago: University of Chicago Press.

Ryan, T. A. 1984. *Adult Female Offenders and Institutional Programs: A State of the Art Analysis.* Washington, D.C.: National Institute of Corrections.

Small, Kevonne. 2000. "Female Crime in the United States, 1963–1998: An Update." *Gender Issues* 18: 75–94.

Simon, Rita J. 1993. "Women, Crime, and Justice." Pp. 121–154 in *The Socio-Economics of Crime and Justice,* edited by Brian Forst. Armonk, N.Y.: M. E. Sharpe.

———. 1975. *Women and Crime.* Lexington, Mass.: Lexington Books.

Simon, Rita J., and Sandra Baxter. 1989. "Gender and Violent Crime." In *Violent Crime, Violent Criminals,* edited by Neil Weiner and Marvin Wolfgang. Beverly Hills, Calif.: Sage.

Simon, Rita J., and Jean Landis. 1991. *The Crimes Women Commit: The Punishments They Receive.* Lexington, Mass.: Lexington Books.

Simon, Rita J., and Navin Sharma. 1979. *The Female Defendant in Washington, D.C.: 1974 and 1975.* Washington, D.C.: Institute for Law and Social Research.

Simpson, S. S. 1989. "Feminist Theory, Crime and Justice." *Criminology* 24, no. 4: 605–632.

Singer, L. 1973. "Women and the Correctional Process." *American Criminal Law Review* 11 (Winter): 295.

Smart, Carol. 1979. "The New Female Criminality: Reality or Myth?" *British Journal of Criminology* 19, no. 1: 50–59.

——. 1976. *Women, Crime and Criminology: A Feminist Critique.* Boston: Routledge and Kegan Paul.

Spohn, Cassia, John Gruhl, and Susan Welch. 1987. "The Impact of the Ethnicity and Gender of Defendants on the Decision to Reject or Dismiss Felony Charges." *Criminology* 25, no. 1: 175–191.

Spohn, Cassia, Susan Welch, and John Gruhl. 1985. "Women Defendants in Court: The Interaction between Sex and Race in Convicting and Sentencing." *Social Science Quarterly* 66, no. 1: 178–185.

Stallard, K., B. Ehrenreich, and H. Sklar. 1983. *Poverty and the American Dream.* Boston: South End Press.

Stanford, Rosemary, Manuel Vega, and Ira K. Silverman. 1982. "A Study of the Female Forger." *Journal of Offender Counseling, Services and Rehabilitation* 6, no. 4: 71–81.

Steffensmeier, Darrell J. 1982. "Trends in Female Crime: It's Still a Man's World." In *The Criminal Justice System and Women*, edited by B. R. Price and N. J. Sokoloff. New York: Clark Boardman.

——. 1980a. "Assessing the Impact of the Women's Movement on Sex-Based Differences in the Handling of Adult Criminal Defendants." *Crime and Delinquency* 26, no. 3: 344–357.

——. 1980b. "Sex Differences in Patterns of Adult Crime, 1965–1977: A Review and Assessment." *Social Forces* 25, no. 3: 1080–1108.

——. 1978. "Crime and the Contemporary Woman: An Analysis of Changing Levels of Female Property Crime, 1960–1975." *Social Forces* 57, no. 2: 566–584.

Steffensmeier, Darrell J., and Emilie A. Allan. 1988. "Sex Disparities in Arrests by Residence, Race, and Age: An Assessment of the Gender Convergence/Crime Hypothesis." *Justice Quarterly* 5, no. 1: 53–80.

Steffensmeier, Darrell, and John H. Kramer. 1982. "Sex-Based Differences in the Sentencing of Adult Criminal Defendants." *Sociology and Social Research* 66, no. 3: 289–304.

Steffensmeier, Darrell, and Robert M. Terry. 1986. "Institutional Sexism in the Underworld: A View from the Inside." *Sociological Inquiry* 56, no. 3: 304–322.

Stimpson, C. 1971. "'Thy Neighbor's Wife, Thy Neighbor's Servants': Women's Liberation and Black Civil Rights." Pp. 622–657 in *Woman in Sexist Society*, edited by Vivian Gornick and Barbara K. Moran. New York: BasicBooks.

Streib, Victor L. 2003. "Death Penalty for Female Offenders January 1, 1973, through June 30, 2003." Retrieved August 5, 2003, www.law.onu.edu/faculty/streib/femdeath.htm.

Temen, Linda. 1973. "Discriminatory Sentencing of Women Offenders." *Criminal Law Review* 11.

Thorton, Wm. E., and Jennifer James. 1979. "Masculinity and Delinquency Revisited." *British Journal of Criminology* 19: 225–241.

Tonry, Michael. 1999a. "Reconsidering Indeterminate and Structured Sentencing." Washington, D.C.: National Institute of Justice. Retrieved October 23, 2002, www.ncjrs.org/txtfiles1/nij/175722.txt.

———. 1999b. "The Fragmentation of Sentencing and Corrections in America." Washington, D.C.: United States Department of Justice. Retrieved October 23, 2002, www.ncjrs.org/txtfiles1/nij/175721.txt.

———. 1996. *Sentencing Matters*. New York: Oxford University Press.

United Nations. Forthcoming. *Women's Indicators and Statistics Database* (Wistat), version 4, CD-ROM (United Nations publication), based on data provided by the United Nations Educational, Scientific and Cultural Organization in January 1999.

United Nations Development Programme. 2002. "Human Development Report 2002: Deepening Democracy in a Fragmented World." United Nations. Retrieved August 2002, www.undp.org/hdr2002.

——— 2001. "Human Development Report 2001: Making New Technologies Work for Human Development." United Nations. Retrieved August 2002, http://hdr.undp .org/reports/global/2001/en/default.cfm.

——— 1999. "Human Development Report 1999: Globalization with a Human Face." United Nations. Retrieved August 2002, http://hdr.undp.org/reports/global/ 1999/en/default.cfm.

——— 1998. "Human Development Report 1998: Consumption for Human Development." United Nations. Retrieved August 2002, http://hdr.undp.org/reports/ global/1998/en/default.cfm.

United Nations Population Division of the United Nations Secretariat. *World Population Prospects: The 1998 Revision, Vol. I: Comprehensive Tables* (United Nations publication, Sales No. E.99.XIII.9), supplemented by *Demographic Yearbook 1997*.

United Nations Statistics Division. 2002. "The World's Women 2000: Trends and Statistics." New York: United Nations Statistics Division. Retrieved August 2002. http://unstats.un.org/unsd/demographic/product/indwm/.

U.S. Bureau of the Census. 2003. Current Population Survey, Women and Men in the United States, March 2002. Retrieved August 5, 2003, www.census.gov/prod/ 2003pubs/p20-544.pdf.

———. 1988. *Statistical Abstract of the U.S.* Washington, D.C.: U.S. Government Printing Office.

U.S. Comptroller General. 1980. *Women in Prison: Inequitable Treatment Requires Action.* Washington, D.C.: General Accounting Office.

U.S. Department of Justice, Bureau of Justice Statistics. 2002. "HIV in Prisons, 2000." Washington, D.C.: U.S. Department of Justice.

———. 1999. "Special Report. Women Offenders." Washington, D.C.: U.S. Department of Justice. Retrieved 2001, www.ojp.usdoj.gov/bjs/pub/pdf/wo.pdf.

———. 1998. "1996 National Survey of State Sentencing Structures." Retrieved October 23, 2002, www.ncjrs.org/pdffiles/169270.pdf.

———. 1995. Census of State and Federal Adult Correctional Facilities [Computer file]. Conducted by U.S. Dept. of Commerce, Bureau of the Census. ICPSR ed. Ann Arbor, Mich.: Interuniversity Consortium for Political and Social Research [producer and distributor], 1998.

U.S. Department of Justice, Federal Bureau of Investigation. *Uniform Crime Reports: Crime in the United States, 1987, 1982, 1981.* Washington, D.C.: U.S. Department of Justice.

Vis, Rudolf. 2000. "Mothers and Babies in Prison." London, UK.: Social, Health and Family Affairs Committee. Retrieved August 2002, http://assembly.coe.int/Documents/WorkingDocs/doc00/EDOC8762.htm.

Vishner, Christy. 1983. "Gender, Police Arrest Decisions, and Notions of Chivalry." *Criminology* 21, no. 1: 5–28.

Walker, Samuel. 1993. *Taming the System: The Control of Discretion in Criminal Justice, 1950–1990.* New York: Oxford University Press.

Ward, D., M. Jackson, and E. Ward. 1968. "Crime and Violence by Women." *Crimes of Violence* 13, appendix 17 (President's Commission on Law Enforcement and the Administration of Justice).

Ward, David, and Gene Kassebaum. 1965. *Women's Prisons.* Chicago: Aldine.

Weis, J.G. 1976. "Liberation and Crime: The Invention of the New Female Criminal." *Crime and Social Justice* 6 (Fall/Winter): 17–27.

Weisheit, Ralph, and Sue Mahan. 1988. *Women, Crime, and Criminal Justice.* Cincinnati, Ohio: Anderson.

Wellford, Charles R. 1974. "Crime and the Dimensions of Nations." *International Journal of Criminology and Penology* 2: 1–10.

Widom, Cathy S. 1979. "Female Offenders: Three Assumptions about Self-Esteem, Sex Role Identity and Feminism." *Criminal Justice and Behavior* 6: 365–382.

Widom, C. S., and A. J. Stewart. 1986. "Female Criminality and the Status of Women." *International Annals of Criminology* 24: 137–162.

Wise, N. B. 1967. "Juvenile Delinquency among Middle-Class Girls." In *Middle-Class Juvenile Delinquency,* edited by E. W. Vaz. New York: Harper and Row.

Wooten, Lady Barbara. 1963. *Crime and Criminal Law.* New York: Macmillan.

Zietz, Dorothy. 1981. *Women Who Embezzle or Defraud: A Study of Convicted Felons.* New York: Praeger.

Index

Page references followed by *t* indicate tables. Those followed by n indicate endnotes.

About the Authors

Rita J. Simon is a sociologist who earned her doctorate at the University of Chicago in 1957. Before coming to American University in 1983 to serve as Dean of the School of Justice, she was a member of the faculty at the University of Illinois, at the Hebrew University in Jerusalem, and the University of Chicago. She is currently a "University Professor" in the School of Public Affairs and the Washington College of Law at American University.

Professor Simon has authored twenty-one books and edited nineteen, including *In Their Own Voices*, with Rhonda Roorda (Columbia University Press, 2000); *Adoption Across Borders* with Howard Altstein (Rowman & Littlefield, 2000); *In the Golden Land: A Century of Russian and Soviet Jewish Immigration* (Praeger, 1997); *The Ambivalent Welcome: Media Coverage of American Immigration*, with Susan Alexander (Praeger, 1993); *New Lives: The Adjustment of Soviet Jewish Immigrant in the United States and Israel* (Lexington Books, 1985); *Women's Movements in America: Their Achievements, Disappointments, and Aspirations*, with Gloria Danzinger (Rowman and Allanheld, 1986); *Rabbis, Lawyers, Immigrants, Thieves: Women's Roles in America* (Praeger, 1993); *Continuity and Change: A Study of Two Ethnic Communities in Israel* (Cambridge University Press, 1978); *The Crimes Women Commit: The Punishments They Receive*, with Jean Landis (Lexington Books, 1991); *Adoption, Race and Identity*, with Howard Altstein (Praeger, 1992); and *The Case for Transracial Adoption*, with Howard Altstein and Marygold Melli (American University Press, 1994).

Professor Simon is currently editor of *Gender Issues*. From 1978 to 1981, she served as editor of *The American Sociological Review* and from 1983 to 1986 as editor of *Justice Quarterly*. In 1966, she received a Guggenheim

Fellowship. Since 1993, Professor Simon has served as President of the Women's Freedom Network.

Heather Ahn-Redding is a doctoral student in American University's Department of Justice, Law and Society. She received her B.A. in psychology at the University of Michigan and her M.A. in forensic psychology at John Jay College of Criminal Justice.